Edward Hartwell Savage

Police Records and Recollections or Boston by Daylight and Gaslight

For Two Hundred and Forty Years

Edward Hartwell Savage

Police Records and Recollections or Boston by Daylight and Gaslight
For Two Hundred and Forty Years

ISBN/EAN: 9783337268213

Printed in Europe, USA, Canada, Australia, Japan

Cover: Foto ©ninafisch / pixelio.de

More available books at **www.hansebooks.com**

Records and Recollections;

OR,

Boston by Daylight and Gaslight

FOR

TWO HUNDRED AND FORTY YEARS.

BY

EDWARD H. SAVAGE.

"'Tis strange but true — for truth is always strange, stranger than fiction."
— BYRON.

BOSTON:
JOHN P. DALE & COMPANY,
PILOT BUILDING,
23, 25 AND 27 BOYLSTON STREET.
1873.

TABLE OF CONTENTS.

RECORD OF THE BOSTON WATCH AND
POLICE.................................7–106

POLICE RECOLLECTIONS.

A STAMPEDE 311
A CONFIDENCE MAN.............................193
A CHARM GAME.................................244
ADVICE TO A YOUNG POLICEMAN..................341
A TRIP AMONG THE SNOW BANKS 202
A CHAPTER ON HATS............................188
A WEDDING IN THE TOMBS 280
A KID GAME...................................381
BEGGARS......................................184
COMMERCIAL STREET FIRE.......................217
CIRCUMSTANTIAL EVIDENCE 136
CHURCH ROBBERY 231
CHOLERA IN 1854..............................263
CONSCRIPTION RIOT............................347
DESTRUCTION OF THE BEEHIVE 107
DEATH OF A FIREMAN 167
DEACON PHILLIPS'S OLD STONE HOUSE............291
FIGHT WITH JOHN WELCH 130

CONTENTS.

	Page
GABRIEL AND HIS HORN	113
GUESS WORK	117
GIVING A DESCRIPTION	316
IMPERTINENT POLICEMEN	338
JAKE AND HIS BOYS	155
LIQUOR LAW DISCLOSURES	249
LITTLE RAGGED NELL	397
MY FATHER'S LIKENESS	399
MY MOTHER'S GRAVE	402
MARIA WHIPPLE	179
MECHANICAL BAKERY FIRE	223
MY OLD GRAY CAT	229
NOAH'S ARK	296
NEW CITY HALL.—A DREAM	389
OLD BUILDINGS	283
PICKPOCKETS	235
POLICE DESCENTS	254
RECOLLECTIONS OF COUNTRYMEN	124
RAT PITS	160
SMALL MATTERS	274
THE JOKING LIEUTENANT	147
THE OUTCAST	171
THIEVES WITH A BAG	198
THE LOST TREASURE	226
TOUGH CUSTOMERS	321
THE OLD ELM ON THE COMMON	334
THE DRAFT	371
THOMAS SEMMES	375
THAT LITTLE CURL	401
VALUE OF CHARACTER	277
WOMAN'S REVENGE	221
WATCHMAN'S RATTLE	143

PREFACE.

The Author of this volume has been in the service of the Government of Boston as a Police Officer a large number of years, and has very good reasons for feeling a deep interest in the history and welfare of his adopted city. Under this influence, and with opportunities offered through the courtesy of numerous friends, the writer has devoted much of his leisure time for some years past, in collecting material for a Chronological History of the Town and City of Boston; and although the collection is yet incomplete, it would now fill a large volume.

From these records have been borrowed the materials that compose the "Chronological History of the Boston Watch and Police." The work has been prepared with no little labor and care, and it is hoped will prove of interest and value.

The duties of the Police Officer afford peculiar opportunities for the study of human nature; and the *views* of city life, by him witnessed, present a wide field not only for the *pen* of the novelist or critic, but also for the *hand* of the philanthropist and Christian.

The writer has not been an idle observer in his police life; and during his long term of service, no day has passed that he has not made a note of some passing event. Many of these notes are of no value except perhaps, now and then, as matters of reference. Others, consisting mostly of incidents and casualties, may be of more or less interest, and many reflect little credit on those most intimately concerned. Of this last class, few will ever meet the public eye. For although

> "Vice is a monster of so frightful mien,
> As to be hated, needs but to be seen;
> Yet seen too oft, familiar with her face,
> We first endure, — then pity, — then embrace."

And again, there is neither profit nor honor, in exposing the secrets and follies of others, for the purpose only of holding them up for contempt and ridicule; but if any one should here recognize his own identity in an unenviable position, let him improve upon the past, and fear nothing from me unless the case demands a judicial investigation.

From this volume of memoranda the Author has selected such as are believed to be unobjectionable and of interest; and, at the earnest solicitation of friends, he now offers to the public "A Chronological History of the Boston Watch and Police," together with his own "Police Recollections."

In his work, the writer has made no attempt to draw upon the imagination, believing that *truth* is not only *stranger*, but more profitable than *fiction*. Neither does he claim for himself any of the detective tact of a *Hayes* or a *Reed*, nor for his "Recollections" the historical romance in the career of a *Vidocq* or a *Jonathan Wild*. They are only the observations of a plain man, told in a plain way, and are but every-day transactions in city life.

The Author hopes to be forgiven for the many errors not only in his book, but in his life; and if he is permitted to reap the assurance that in the one he has done his duty, and in the other he has been successful in an attempt to please and instruct, his highest aim will be accomplished, and his fondest hopes realized.

E. H. SAVAGE.

RECORD

OF THE

BOSTON WATCH AND POLICE

FOR

TWO HUNDRED AND FORTY YEARS.

A WELL-REGULATED Police is the strong right arm of all local civil governments; its presence is ever a guarantee of peace and the supremacy of law, and a safeguard to life and property.

In reviewing the history of the "Boston Watch and Police" since its first organization, covering a period of two hundred and forty-two years, the limits of this work will allow but a brief outline. In fact, its character and duties can only be gathered from the customs, opinions, and tastes of the people, — the nature of transpiring events, and the peculiar condition of things. As we pass along, "catching the manners living as they rise," an attempt will be made to give a "bird's-eye view" of the character of the times, the Internal or Police Regulations of the town, with here and there an inkling of the civil and criminal Jurisprudence.

The peninsula now called Boston, was probably first visited by Englishmen in the year 1621. A colony of English emigrants had commenced a settlement at Plymouth in 1620, and on the eighteenth day of September, the year following, ten Englishmen of the colony, accompanied by three Plymouth Indians as guides and interpreters, set sail in a " Shallop, to visit *The Massachusetts*, for the purpose of exploring the country and trading with the natives."

The party arrived " at the head of the Bay " the same evening, and early next morning they " landed under the cliff," supposed to be on the beach at the foot of Copp's Hill.

On landing, they found a pot of lobsters that had been left unguarded by the unsuspecting natives, which they without ceremony appropriated to their own use (the Harbor Police had not been established then); after which they started over the hill in search of the inhabitants.

They had not proceeded far, however, when they met an Indian woman going for her property, little dreaming it had been so unceremoniously confiscated by her civilized visitors. The party seeing that their mistake was about to be detected, concluded to "fork over a sum of *hush* money, (the Record says, " they contented the woman for them,") and the matter was settled without an *expose*.

The party, finally, had an interview with the Sachem, and formed a treaty. It was said that

"He submits to the King of England, on our promising to be a safeguard against his enemies." The agreement was undoubtedly kept by one party about as well as by the other, as it does not appear that the visit was repeated or returned for years afterwards.

In the summer of 1630, the ship Arbella, with several other emigrant vessels, having on board Governor John Winthrop and party, who were called the "Massachusetts Company," arrived at Salem and Charlestown, and commenced permanent settlements there.

At this time the peninsula, which by the Indians was called "Shawmut," but by the English "Trimountain," (because, from Charlestown, "the westerly part had the appearance of three contiguous hills,") was inhabited by only one white man, a Mr. William Blaxton (or Blackstone), who lived at the westerly part, near where is now Louisburg Square. How long he had lived here, no one seems to know; he was not here in 1621, when the Plymouth party paid their first visit; but it was said he had a house and garden, which indicated an age of seven or eight years.

Trimountain was then described as being very uneven, abounding in hills, hollows, and swamps, and was covered either with wood, or blueberry and other wild bushes, and abounded in bears, wolves, snakes, and other beasts, birds, and reptiles too numerous to mention.

The location at Charlestown being low, wet, and short of good water, in a few weeks proved quite unhealthy, and Trimountain offering much better inducements for a settlement, at the invitation of Mr. Blackstone several persons went over to dwell on his grounds, till it was finally determined to make the place the seat of Government for the colony; and on the seventh day of September, at a court holden at Charlestown, it was ordered that Trimountain be called Boston, at which time the settlement of Boston has since been reckoned, the seventh of the month *old style* answering to the seventeenth according to the present reckoning. The name was said to have been given in honor of several distinguished persons of the colony, who were emigrants from an old town called Boston in Lincolnshire, England.

The Massachusetts people in their new homes were almost surrounded with a wild, unexplored wilderness, inhabited by uncivilized men, whose numbers and strength were unknown, some of whom it was said would "tie their prisoners to trees, and gnaw the flesh from their bones while alive." This, perhaps, had its influence in making Boston the seat of Government, as it was almost surrounded by water, and could be fortified much easier than any place near it.

Although the inhabitants of Boston were at first quite numerous, yet not until 1631, (April 12), was it ordered " by **Court** " that *Watches* be set at sunset, **and if** any person fire off a piece after the watch is set, **he shall** be fined forty shillings, or be whipped." **And two** days after, it was said, " we began a **Court of** Guard upon the *Neck*, between Roxburie **and** Boston, whereupon shall always be resident an officer and six men."

This was an organization of the first *Boston Watch;* and although it partook more of the character of a military guard than otherwise, it was well adapted to the wants of the people, as all Police arrangements should be; and was probably continued, with greater or less numbers, till the organization of a watch by the selectmen.

For several years after the settlement of Boston, "The Court," consisting of the Governor, Deputy Governor, Secretary, and a certain number of assistants, constituted the Legislative, Judicial, and also the Executive power, **not only of Boston** but of the whole colony; and, judging from the number and character of their laws, and the frequency of their violations, they must have had a pretty busy time of it. Nor was there then, more than now, complete perfection in the executive, **for at one time one of** the assistants was fined five pounds **for whipping a culprit** unlawfully, no other assistant being present. However, in time, population and business had so much increased, and the duties of " The Court" had become so oppressive, that it was deemed expedient to institute a new order of things, and on the first day of September, 1634, a Town Government was organized for Boston, by choosing nine " *Townes Occasions* " (Selectmen), and various other officers, for superintending the local affairs of the town, the name of William Chesebrough first appearing on the records as *Constable*.

From the first, the people had plenty of "Court," yet a grand jury was not organized till September 1, 1635, and that was none too soon, for at its first setting it was said they found " over one hundred presentments, *and among them were some of the Magistrates.*"

Although a Watch had been established as early as 1631, it does not appear that the authorities of the town assumed the prerogatives of its appointment and control till the twenty-seventh day of February, 1636, when, at a Town Meeting, " upon pryvate warning, it was agreed y^t there shalbe a watch taken up and gone around with from the first of the second month next for ye summertime from sunne sett an houre after ye beating of ye drumbe, upon penaltie for every one wanting therein twelve pence every night."

The organization of a Town Watch here established, under various names and hundreds of different modifications (with perhaps the exception of a brief period during the Revolution), has existed to the present time. The duties of the Watch, as appears by the order, were to be performed in turn by the inhabitants; they were not " citizen soldiers," but citizen Watchmen, and having an interest in their work, no doubt did it well. What their duties were is not laid down in the record, and can only be inferred from the condition of things at the time.

The dwellings of the inhabitants had mostly been thrown up in a hurry, with such material as was at hand, and were built of wood or mud walls, thatched roof and stick chimneys, plastered with clay; this left them particularly exposed to fire, and a fire in those days was a calamity indeed. There were numerous straggling Indians, who paid their nocturnal visits from the wilderness, and they were not over scrupulous in relation to etiquette or the ownership of property. There were also among the inhabitants (if we believe the report), a set of knaves, thieves, and burglars, of their own " kith and kin." Wolves and bears were also numerous, and came into Boston even, and carried off young kids and lambs. Nor was this all; *masters* were sorely annoyed by the frequent desertions of their *slaves;* for Boston men had slaves, and not only black slaves, but white ones. (At one time a ship-load of one hundred and fifty Scotch emigrants were sold in Boston to pay their passage;) and these, especially, were prone to take French leave of their masters the first opportunity, preferring a wild life and a wigwam with liberty, to civilization and bondage.

These and attending circumstances would plainly indicate what might be the nature of the duties required of the Town Watch at that time.

1637. This year Rev. John Wheelwright was banished from Boston for entertaining heretical opinions, and the year following Dorothy Talbe, a poor insane woman, who killed her child to save it from being miserable hereafter, was hanged. It was believed that the devil prompted her to do it, and hanging her would punish him. It was said that Mr. Peters and Mr. Wilson, the ministers, went with her to the place of execution, but they "could do her no good."

1639. Edward Palmer was employed to build the stocks (a place in which to set criminals for punishment); when completed, he presented his bill of £1. 13s. 7d. This was thought to be exorbitant, and poor Palmer got placed in his own machine, and fined five pounds. The next year Hugh Bewett was banished, "for maintaining that he was free from original sin."

1645. The inhabitants were not allowed to entertain strangers, for fear they might become paupers, and a law was passed forbidding any person to swear an oath; "and if an Indian powwow, he shall pay 10s. and stop powwowing." No house shall be sold without liberty from the Selectmen.

1648. Margaret Jones was hung for witchcraft. "A little child was seen to run from her, and when followed by an officer, it vanished." This sealed her fate. Her husband, Thomas, attempted to escape on a vessel for Barbadoes, but the ship being in light ballast, and having on board eighty horses, "fell a rolling." An officer was sent for, and when he came, one said, "you can tame men, can't you tame the ship?" Said the officer, drawing a warrant, "I have here what will tame her," and arrested Jones. "At that instant she began to stop, and stayed, and when Jones was put in prison moved no more."

1650. The court passed a law forbidding the wearing of "great boots," and other extravagant articles of dress, unless the wearer was worth two hundred pounds. — Oliver Holmes was whipped for being a Baptist. Some persons who shook hands with him after the whipping, were fined, and others whipped.

1652. Fires began to do much damage, and ladders and swabs were to be prepared by the inhabitants to extinguish them, and "*Bell Men* shall goe aboute ye town in ye night, from ten to five o'clock in ye morninge."

1655. The people were very poor, and money

scarce, taxes were paid in rye, peas, and corn, and no man was allowed to carry more than twenty shillings out of town.

1657. "Christopher Holder and John Copeland, *Quakers*, were whipped through town with knotted cords, with all the strength the *hangman* could command. The prisoners were gagged with a stick in the mouth, to prevent their outcries." Horred Gardner, a Quakeress with a child at her breast, was brutally whipped; and when liberated, knelt down and prayed for her persecutors." The year following, the penalty of death was added to the law against Quakers.

1659. William Robinson and Marmaduke Stephenson, men of irreproachable character, were hanged to the limb of a tree on the Common, as Antinomians and heretics. When dead, they were rudely cut down by the hangman, Robinson falling so as to break his skull. Their friends were not allowed their bodies, but they were stripped, and cast naked into a hole, without any covering of dirt, and were soon covered with water." "A Mr. Nichols built a fence about the place to protect them." Mary Dyer was to have been hung at the same time, but was reprieved for a season. Peter Pearson, Judith Brown, and George Wilson, were whipped through the town to the wilderness, tied to a cart-tail, "the executioner having prepared a cruel instrument wherewith to tear their flesh."

These were no solitary instances, but the heart sickens at the thought, and we gladly drop the curtain over these scenes of cruelty and bloodshed.

1661. "Ordered y^t ye constables begin their rounds from May first all night."

1665. Sir Robert Carr, sent over by the king to modify the abuses of the Colonial Government, spent his time on Sunday at a noted tavern called "Noah's Ark," in Ship Street. The Governor issued a warrant against Sir Robert, for violation of the Sunday law, and Richard Bennett, the Constable, was sent to make the arrest. Sir Robert caned the officer, and sent him away. The Governor then sent a summons for Sir Robert to appear before him, but he would not come." Arthur Mason, a spirited officer, was then sent to bring Carr, when some high words arose between the officer and Carr, and ere long poor Mason found himself in prison for attempting to obey his superior, and was eventually fined for an honest effort to do his duty, the Governor being glad to find a scapegoat in the person of his subordinate, whereby to escape punishment himself in abusing the King's agent.

1670. An Indian hung in gibbets on Boston Common, for the murder of Zachary Smith in Dedham woods.

1672. Governor Bellingham imprisoned George Heathcock for neglecting to take off his hat when he came to bring a letter. — "Boston had fifteen hundred families, and there were not twenty houses that had ten rooms apiece. There were no musicians by trade. A dancing school was set up, but it was put down."

1676. A terrible fire destroyed all the buildings between what is now Richmond, Hanover, Clark streets, and the water. Soon after this, cages were set up about town to put violators of the Sabbath in, and constables were ordered to "search out and arrest Quakers." Margaret Brewster went into the South Church, and pronounced her curse. She had her face blackened, and wore sackcloth. Margaret was hurried off to jail, and brought to court next day. She had been washed, and the officer could not identify her, but she was whipped.

1679. A fire consumed eighty buildings, near the dock. A Frenchman, "who was *suspected*" of setting the fire, was sentenced to stand in the pillory, to have both ears cut off, pay charges of court, give five hundred pounds bonds with sureties, and stand committed till sentence was performed. (Query. What would have been the sentence if there had been *proof* of guilt?)

1686. It was said the affairs of the town were much neglected in consequence of trouble with the Home Government. The charter had been taken away. Town officers were officers no longer, and the people were disfranchised, and the agents of the Home Government, without having an interest, had the control of the town. Town meetings held but once a year.

1689. Governor Andros got into a quarrel with the people, who became exasperated, and the Governor, for safety, fled to the castle, and from thence to a man of war lying in the harbor; but the captain of the frigate being on shore, fell into the hands of the people, and would not let the frigate fire on the town, for fear of his own safety. Governor Andros was finally given up, put in jail, and sent home to England.

1692. Governor Phipps arrived in Boston with a new charter. — Giles Corey was pressed to death for being a wizzard. — A cage and watch-house had been built near the market.

1698. A Mr. Ward, who visited New England this year, said of Boston: "The buildings, like their women, are neat and handsome, and their streets, like the hearts of their men, are paved with pebbles. They have four churches, built with clapboards and shingles, and supplied with four ministers, — one a scholar, one a gentleman, one a dunce, and one a clown. The captain of a ship met his wife in the street after a long voyage, and kissed her, for which he was fined ten shillings. What a happiness, thought I, do we enjoy in old England, where we can not only kiss our own wives, but other men's, without a danger of penalty." So much for Mr. Ward.

1701. At town meeting, "Watchmen are enjoined to be on duty from ten o'clock till broad daylight." "They are to go about silently with *watch bills*, not using any bell, and no watchmen to smoke tobacco while walking their rounds; and when they see occasion, to call to persons to take care of their light." — "Those intending to build, must have permission of the Selectmen." — "Many ordinaries, beer-shops, and stands out of doors were licensed." — "Several persons warned out of town for fear they will become paupers." — "Three warehouses near the dock were blown up with powder, to stop the progress of a fire."

1703. John Barnard built a watch-house for the town at North End, with a sentry-box on top of it; and another near the powder-house on the Common. — *April* 24. The first newspaper in North America, issued by John Campbell, postmaster.

1707. The main street towards the South End paved. Three hundred pounds appropriated to support the Watch. Twelve watchmen were employed at forty shillings a month. James Thornby and Exercise Conant, overseers of the watch. Watch rules and regulations adopted.

1708. The various streets, over one hundred in number, named and recorded in the Town Book.—

The town petitioned the legislature for an act of incorporation as a city.

1709. Town officials fined for neglect of duty. A minister said, " The covetous office-holders are intent on gain; sometimes they are contriving to remove obstructions, sometimes to prevent discovery; sometimes in supplanting rivals, they spend many hours in imagining mischief upon their beds."—The watch increased to fifteen. They petition for leave to prosecute those who abuse them while on duty.

1710. Fortification rebuilt on the Neck, composed of brick and stone, across Washington at Dover Street, as now named, extending to the sea on the east, and south to where is now Union Park, having a parapet on which to place a cannon, with gates for teams and foot passengers at the street. — Watch-boxes set up in various parts of the town. — Male and female Indians sold at auction as servants.

1711. A terrible fire consumed the old townhouse, and about one hundred buildings about it, including the first meeting-house. Many persons were killed by blowing up houses. Several sailors perished in the flames, in trying to save the church bell. One hundred and ten families were made homeless. — Fire-wards appointed. They were " to carry a staff five feet long, colored red, with a bright brass spike at the end, six inches long, and have power to command all persons at fires." — Bounties for Indian scalps paid in Boston. — Deaths in town during the year; whites, 305; negroes and Indians, 58.

1713. George Brownell " teaches writing, ciphering, dancing, treble violin, English and French embroidering, flourishing, plain work, and marking." — Numerous colored people advertised for sale. — The half bushel of a countryman selling turnips at the dock, was found to be small. A justice ordered the measure stove to pieces, and the turnips given to the poor. — A Mr. Bacon, going with a team over the Neck one winter night, lost his way, and both he and the team perished with cold.

1714. Two men added to the watch, and " two sober, discreet men to have charge thereof." — The watchhouse near the townhouse to be removed, " and set by the schoolhouse in Queen Street, and a cage to be added." Also ordered, that " the whipping-post be removed thereto."

1715. There were four watchhouses; one in Clark Square, one near the Conduit, one near the schoolhouse, Queen Street, and one at South End, with about four watchmen at each. The watch went on duty at nine o'clock P. M. in winter, and ten o'clock P. M. summer, remaining till daylight next morning, at forty shillings per month. There were two overseers. — The town was divided into eight wards this year, three of which were north of Mill Creek.

1718. Mary Porcell, Abigail Thurston, and Esther Ray, were publicly whipped for being night-walkers, and afterward fined ten shillings each.

1720. "*Ordered*, That trucks shall be no more than eighteen feet long, tires four inches wide; two horses to one team, and one ton load."

1721. A great linen wheel-spinning exhibition on the Common, where "all classes met and vied with each other in skill. A great concourse of people from town and country."

1722. Boston contained ten thousand six hundred and seventy persons; four thousand five hundred and forty-nine lived north of Mill Creek. There were said to be one thousand brick, and two thousand wood houses, forty-two streets, thirty-six lanes, twenty-two alleys. — The watch reduced to twelve men; the south watch discontinued.

1723. Five divisions of the watch established, and called the "Old North, New North, Dock Watch, Townhouse Watch, and South Watch. The names indicated the locality. The South watch were supposed to be located in a narrow, one-story brick house in Orange Lane, which was recently to be seen at No. 518 Washington Street (another story having since been added), and which was occupied for a watchhouse over one hundred years." There were five watchmen at each house. They were ordered to " walk their rounds slowly and silently, and now and then stand still and listen."

1725. A lad aged seventeen years, for abusing some smaller children, sentenced " to be whipped thirty-nine stripes at the cart tail, twelve at the gallows, thirteen at the head of Summer Street, thirteen below the townhouse, and be committed to Bridewell six months." — Hoop petticoats were a subject of ridicule in Franklin's newspaper. He advertises, " Hoop Petticoats, just published and sold by the printer, arraigned and condemned by the light of nature and law of God — price 3d."

1726. William Fly, Samuel Cole, and Henry Grenville, hung for piracy. Two days before execution they were taken to Mr. Colman's church, to listen to a sermon, for which they cared little. Fly was hung in gibbets on an Island in the harbor. The wind whistling through his bones many months after, was a warning to sailors passing in and out of the harbor.

1727. The General Court passed laws prohibiting violations of the Sabbath, such as swimming, unnecessary walking in the highways, in fields, or on the Common; violators " to be put in jail," " set in the stocks," &c.

1728. Henry Phillips and Benjamin Woodbridge, two aristocratic youths, got in a quarrel at Royal Exchange Tavern, went to the Common, and fought a duel with swords. Woodbridge was run through the body and killed, and Phillips made his escape. Shortly after, a law was made against duelling. The offender was to be " carried in a cart, with a rope about his neck, to the gallows, to sit thereon one hour, and be imprisoned twelve months;" the person killed " to be buried with a stake driven through his body, and stones piled on his grave." — Ratable polls in Boston, about three thousand. — Governor Burnet quarrelled with the House of Representatives, and removed the general court to Salem.

1730. Boston cast 530 votes. The following Town Officers officiate: Town Clerk, 1; Selectmen, 9; Treasurer, 1; Overseers Poor, 8; Assessors, 7; Constables, 16; Sealers of leather, 5; Clerks of Market, 8; Measurers of boards and shingles, 7; Fence viewers, 7; Scavengers, 16; Hogreeves, 4; Watchmen, 25. It does not appear that the town held any centennial celebration of its settlement, but Mr. Prince preached a sermon to the legislature, in which he says, " A flood of irreligion and profaneness has come in upon us, — so much terrible cursing and swearing, lying, slandering, and backbiting, cruel injustice, oppression, rioting, and drunkenness."

1732. The town had seven fire engines, and eighty-seven firemen. It was said that " John and Thomas Hill have a newly constructed engine at their Distil House, drawn by a horse, that throws a great quantity of water twelve feet high. It is a great improvement, and the first of the kind." — The Selectmen authorized to *award* faithful watchmen, " not exceeding ten shillings a month."

1733. At town meeting, an application was made to have Mathew Young appointed watchman, " that he and his children do not become a town charge." — The whipping-post that had been blown down was " ordered to be set up near the town house Watchhouse."

1734. Three market-places established, " one in Orange Street, one in Dock Square, and one in Market Square." — A mob demolished a house of ill-fame, under the countenance of some well-meaning Magistrates." — The town voted to build a workhouse. — The weight of bread was established, bakers to put their initials on each loaf.

1735. Watchmen " Ordered to cry the time of night and state of the weather, in a moderate tone, as they walk their rounds after 12 o'clock, — One o'clock, clear, and all's well." Boston divided into twelve wards, names dropped, and numbers used instead. — Thirty shillings a winter allowed each watchhouse for coal.

1736. Porters to be licensed, and to " wear a badge with the figure of a Pine Tree." — The number of watchmen reduced to sixteen, watchhouses four, viz: " Old North, New North, Townhouse, and South End." — The badge of the overseers to be "a quarter pike;" "one watchman to attend at each watchhouse door all night, to inspect persons."

1737. A workhouse built near the Granary and a house at Rainsford Island for persons with contagious diseases. — Quarantine established.

1739. John Chambers and other gravediggers inform the Selectmen, that The Johnson and Granary burial-grounds are so full, they are ofttimes obliged to bury four deep. — The School Committee reported that "there are five schools, with 595 scholars, all satisfactory." — Dock Square Markethouse torn down by a mob.

1740. The overseer of the watch petitioned to have a coal-hole door to a watchhouse repaired. — The watch ordered "to look out for disorderly Negroes and Indians." — There were fifteen churches in Boston.

1741. William Shirley, Esq., an Episcopalian, was appointed Governor of the Province. — Fifty-five persons in the workhouse.

1742. There were said to be in Boston, 16,382 inhabitants, 1,200 widows, 1,719 dwelling-houses, 116 warehouses, 1,514 negroes, 418 horses, 141 cows.

1746. "The Justices in town agree to walk and observe the behavior of the people on Lord's day." — A law passed to prevent firing guns.

1747. A riot occurred on the wharves, by Commodore Knowles pressing laborers into service. — The Townhouse again destroyed by fire; valuable ancient books destroyed.

1748. Able-bodied watchmen allowed seven pounds, ten shillings per month, but fined twenty shillings for getting asleep on duty.

1749. Some Englishmen, for their own amusement, got up theatrical exhibitions at the Royal Exchange. Some interlopers, endeavoring to force an entrance, the matter became public, and the Exhibition was broken up. — Written rules prepared for the government of the watch.

1750. A Town meeting called, and a remonstrance formed against the duty levied on tea, coffee, chaises, coaches, and various other articles, which operated unequally and unjustly on the people.

1751. The General Court authorized a lottery to raise $26,700, for supplying the Treasury. Hon. Mr. Watts, manager. Office at Faneuil Hall. Tickets, $3.00 each.

1752. By an act of British Parliament, this year began on January 1, instead of March 25, as heretofore; and all Deeds and Public Documents, began to be dated to correspond. The old style followed the Julian method of computing the months and days in the calendar, as established by Julius Cæsar, in which every fourth year consists of 366 days, and the other years of 365 days. This is something like 11 minutes in a year too much. Pope Gregory Thirteenth reformed the calendar by omitting 10 days in October, 1552, in order to bring back the Vernal Equinox to the same day as at the Council of Nice, A. D. 325; which reformation was followed by Parliament, as above stated, by which 11 days in September, 1752, were left out, calling the 3d the 14th. This mode of reckoning is called " New Style," according to which, every year divisible by 4, unless it is divisible by 100, without being divisible by 400, has 366 days, and every other year has 365 days.

1753. A revolting spectacle in King Street. " A female, accused of lewdness, was exposed nearly naked on a scaffold near the Townhouse, for the space of an hour, facing each of the four cardinal points fifteen minutes, suffering the most disgusting and brutal treatment by a mob."

1754. It was said that Benjamin Franklin " has greatly surprised and obliged the world, by the discovery of the Electrical Substance, as one great and main instrument in lightning and thunder." — Thomas Williston appointed Captain of Watch. — Concert Hall built. — Elizabeth Creighton whipped for cohabiting with a negro.

1756. In consequence of numerous evening processions got up by the lower clases, and ending often in bloodshed, a law was passed to prevent such assemblages. — The Common burial-ground was purchased of Mr. Andrew Oliver.

1757. Although there was a law against lotteries, the Town was carrying on one, and on one occasion the inhabitants were notified that, " If they do not adventure before a given day, they will be excluded, as the Town had voted to take all unsold tickets to itself." — Another lottery was also got up to raise money to pave the highway.

1760. A terrible fire near Oliver's Dock. A subscription of $28,000 was raised for the sufferers, who were each required to bring in a schedule of their loss. Mrs. Davis presented the following. " Lost in the fire, March 20, 1760, a velvet jacit and pr close Briches, 2£. 8s. 0d.; a dark alpine Peticote, £1. 4s. 0d.; seven Shetes, £1. 6s. 0d.; Baby linings; one doz. Dipers, Clotes, £1. 14s. 8d.; one new warming Pan, £0. 10s. 0d.; one half dozen pewter Plates, £1. 0s. 0d.; one Meal Barrel, £0. 8s. 0d.; half dozen Chiny Tea-cups and Sarsers, £0. 6s. 0d.; Bosten Errus exsepted, lawful Munny, £7. 16s. 8d." At this fire it was said 350 buildings were burned, and 1,000 people left without homes.

1763. Serious difficulties arose between the Revenue officers and the people. — James Otis delivered his " remarkable speech against the *Writs of Assistance*, in the Council Chamber, old Townhouse." It was said that " then and there was Independence born." — The terms *Whig* and *Tory* begin to be used.

1765. Captain Semmes, of the South watch, reported that "Negro Dick came to the watchhouse, and reported rowdies under his window. Watchmen were sent, and met a gang of rowdies, one of which drew a sword. The watch cried murder and fled to the watchhouse, and the rowdies escaped." — The Union Club (or Sons of Liberty) formed under the great Elm, which on the 14th of August was christened, "The Tree of Liberty." — The house of Governor Hutchinson, and several other government officers mobbed.

November 5. This was the anniversary of the discovery of the Gunpowder Plot, in which Guy Fawkes figured, in 1605. Pope's day, however, originated in 1558, on the accession of Queen Elizabeth. At first, the Pope and the Devil were the only pageants, but it afterwards became somewhat changed. These anniversaries had long been celebrated in Boston, and for several years the competition between the North and South Ends, had caused two celebrations. The programme on these occasions, was to form processions at headquarters, and march through the streets, collecting contributions as they passed, to carry on the celebration; and woe to them who did not contribute. A pageant accompanied the procession, consisting of figures mounted on a platform on wheels, and drawn by horses. These figures generally represented three characters, — the Pope, Devil, and Pretender, with sometimes the addition of obnoxious political characters. (The Pretender, was James Francis Edward, and his effigy was added in 1702.)

Under the platform were placed half-grown boys, with rods extending up through the figures, to cause them to face to the right or left, and to rise up and look into people's windows. In front of the procession might be seen a fellow with a bell, who notified the people of their approach, and who would chant something like the following: —

> "Don't you remember the fifth of November,
> The Gunpowder treason and plot?
> I see no reason why gunpowder treason should ever be forgot.
> From Rome to Rome the Pope is come, amid ten thousand fears,
> With fiery serpents to be seen, at eyes, nose, mouth, and ears.
> Don't you hear my little bell, go chink, chink, chink?
> Please give me a little *money*, to buy my Pope some drink."

The two celebrating parties in Boston, after having marched about town, generally met near the Mill Creek, where a desperate fight would ensue for the possession of the effigies, and bloody noses and broken bones were often the result. If the *South* were victorious, the trophies went to the Common; if the *North,* Copp's Hill was the rendezvous, where the pageantry was burnt. This year the two parties formed a union, and union Pope was celebrated till the Revolution.

1769. In consequence of existing difficulties, the watch were ordered " to patrol two together," " to arrest all negroes found out after dark without a lantern." It was said soon after the order was given, " an *old darkie* was picked up prowling about in total darkness." Next morning, when asked by the magistrate if guilty, he replied " No, sa, I has de lantern," holding up before the astonished court, *an old one*, innocent of oil or candle. He was discharged, and the law amended, so as to require " a lantern with a candle." Old Tony was soon up again on the same complaint, and again entered a plea " not guilty," and again drawing forth the *old lantern with a candle;* but the wick had not been discolored by a flame. The defendant was discharged with a reprimand, and the law was made to read, " a lantern with a *lighted* candle." Old Tony was not caught again, having been heard to remark, " Massa got too much light on de subjec." — Sheriff Greenleaf was ordered to " cause a new gallows to be erected on the Neck, the old one having gone to decay."

1770. The Revenue troubles continued under

great excitement. The ladies formed an "Anti tea-drinking Society." — A custom-house informer shot a boy in the street near Faneuil Hall. — *March* 5. The Boston Massacre occurred in King Street, near Flag Alley, in which Samuel Gray, Crispus Attucks, and James Caldwell fell dead. Samuel Maverick died next day; Patrick Carr died in nine days; and others were badly injured by the discharge of firearms in the hands of British soldiers. The troops soon after evacuated the town, and went on board their ships lying in the harbor.

1773. *December* 16. The Boston Tea Party emptied three hundred forty-two chests of tea into the sea. The article was on board three vessels, lying at Griffin's (Liverpool) wharf, and the work was done in three hours. The Tea Party were in Indian costume, and went from the Old South Church.

1774. *June* 1. Boston Harbor was closed as a port of entry, no vessel being allowed to go in or out, and the collection of customs was removed to Salem. — Eleven military regiments were quartered in town.

1775. Every entrance into town was guarded by soldiers, and sentinels were posted in all the streets. — *April* 18. The Beacon Pole was taken down, and a small square fort built in its place. — *June* 17. The battle of Bunker Hill. — General

Howe had his head-quarters in the belfry of Christ's Church during the battle. The almshouse, manufactory house, workhouse, and many private houses, filled with wounded British soldiers. — *July* 12. The inhabitants of Boston held a town meeting at Concord. — Negroes were summoned by General Howe to meet at Faneuil Hall, to form a scavenger party. Oscar Merriam, a sharp old Whig darkie, remonstrates, and gets put in Jail. — *September* 1. A party of British soldiers, headed by Job Williams, cut down the " Tree of Liberty;" one jumped upon the trunk to strike off a limb, and fell dead. — *October* 8. Governor Howe issued a proclamation forbidding all persons to leave Boston without a pass, " on penalty of military execution." Old South Church was occupied by Burgoyne's Cavalry, as a riding school, with a liquor bar in the gallery. "The pulpit and pews were removed, and many loads of dirt carted in to make the floor. The South door was closed, and a rail was there fixed, over which the horses were taught to jump. An old lady who passed that way every day, used to stop and expostulate with the soldiers in their sacrilegious work, and at one time told them that the good Dr. Sewall would rise from his grave and appear to them. Soon after, a superstitious Scotchman was on guard, and late at night got terribly frightened at something he imagined he saw. He discharged his piece, set up a hue and cry, and fled. This raised the Governor's

Life Guard, at the old Province House, near by (General Howe's head-quarters), and a general commotion ensued throughout the town. On being questioned, the guard said he saw approaching a venerable old man, in a great wig and gown. He was only pacified by being told that Dr. Sewall never dressed that way."

1776. *January* 11. Major Montgomery, with one hundred men, attacked the British outposts at Charlestown, and burnt some old buildings. On the same evening the *Red Coats* were entertaining themselves at Faneuil Hall with a play called " The Blockade of Boston." In the midst of the play, a person came forward to the footlights, and with great earnestness proclaimed, " The Yankees are taking Bunker Hill ! " " The deluded wretches thought this to be a part of the play, and cheered the speaker heartily. But soon learning that the speaker meant to represent a *solemn reality*, the whole assembly left the house in the greatest confusion, and scampered off in great precipitation." — *March* 4. The Continental army, assisted by a large body of militia, were carrying on the siege of Boston with great vigor, having garrisons at Cobble Hill, Lechmere Point, and Lamb's Dam at Roxbury. " Shot and shell heard to make great crashing in Boston." — *March* 17. " General Washington secured positions in Roxbury and Dorchester to command Boston. General Howe evacuated the town, and retired on board ships in the Harbor, and General Putnam took possession of Boston in the name of the *Thirteen United States of America*." During the bombardment but little damage was done; one cannon ball went through the Lamb Tavern, another struck Brattle Street Church. The last was picked up by a Mr. Turell, and replaced where it struck; it was cemented in the west wall of the church. — *July* 18. " The people of Boston were fast returning to their homes, and pursuant to an order of the Honorable Council, there was read from the balcony of the Town House, " THE DECLARATION OF INDEPENDENCE, passed by the American Congress on the 4th inst, absolving the United Colonies from their allegiance to the British Crown." — In the evening a large number turned out, " and every sign, with every resemblance of it, whether the King's Arms, pestle, mortar and crown, heart and crown, and every sign that belonged to a *Tory* were taken down and burnt in King Street." — *September* 19. Beacon Pole again raised on Beacon Hill. — Several persons tried and sent out of the States as Tories.

1777. *September* 1. King Street to be called State Street, and Queen Street, Court Street. " Several persons who had audaciously made themselves obnoxious by renouncing their trades and commenced dealing in monopolies," were seized and conveyed out of Town in a cart, and passed from town to town till they reached the British Camp at Rhode Island. — Several persons were imprisoned for exchanging Continental money for gold at a great discount.

1779. *May* 1. "The great and General Court passed an Act confiscating the Estates of the enemies of Liberty for the benefit of the Government." "A convention of delegates from several towns met to regulate the price of goods, and take measures relative to trade and the currency." — *July* 21. At a town meeting at Faneuil Hall, the following list of prices were established : —

	£.	s.
Windward Rum, per gallon	6	6
New England Rum, per gallon	4	16
Molasses, "	4	7
Coffee, per pound	0	18
Brown Sugar, per pound	0	14
Bohea Tea, "	0	15
Salt, per bushel	0	9
Indian Corn, per bushel	4	10
Rye, "	6	00
Wheat, "	9	00
Beef, per pound	0	6
Mutton, "	0	4
Butter, "	0	12
Cheese, "	0	6
Milk, per quart		2
Hay, per cwt.	2	00
Labor, per day (find themselves)	5	00
Cloth for one pair leather Breeches	1	15
W. I. Rum Toddy, per mug	0	18
N. E. Rum Toddy, per mug	0	12

The schedule begins with rum, and ends with toddy. A long list of resolutions were passed, the drift of which indicate, " that any person taking more or less than the prices fixed, or who shall refuse Continental money, shall be published in the papers, considered enemies, and treated as such ; " and a committee was appointed to carry the resolution into practice.

1780. *May* 19. Darkness prevailed at noonday throughout New England, said to be caused by smoke from great fires in the woods in Maine and New Hampshire. Many people greatly frightened. A Mr. Willard went on to Boston Common to make observations; while there, a crowd collected, and presently a man came up in breathless haste, saying, " The tide has ceased to flow." " So it has for to-day," said Mr. W. pulling out his watch, " *'t is past twelve o'clock!* "— Thomas Gibbs and Eben Burbank sat on the gallows, for one hour, for counterfeiting Continental currency. — One hundred dollars in silver will buy four thousand in Continental bills. — *October* 25. Massachusetts has had no governor for about four years. John Hancock chosen Governor, and so " proclaimed from the balcony of the old Town House, amid the ringing of bells, firing of cannon, and great joy."

1781. It was said that " Boston begins to revive under the supervision of the Sons of Liberty." — *November* 14. Great display and rejoicing in

Boston on account of the surrender of Cornwallis at Yorktown, 19th of October.— Hucksters not allowed to purchase provisions brought into Town before one o'clock, if they intend to sell them again."

1783. The inhabitants notified to bring in their dirt to fill up the Town Dock. — Mr. Robert Hughes, the Boston Butcher, gave notice to drovers that he can " dress two hundred hogs or fifty beef cattle in a day, which he does for the offal."

1784. Mr. Joseph Otis, the jailer, solicited aid " for numerous poor debtors confined in Boston jail, who are suffering with hunger and from the inclemency of the weather."

The judges of the Superior Court " appeared in scarlet robes, and the barristers in gowns." — An effort made to make Boston a city, but the measure was voted down in Town Meeting. — A *third* row of trees set out near the Mall on the Common. — Numerous persons whipped at *the Post*, in State Street, for various offences.

1785. *May* 5. William Scott and Thomas Archibald hung on the Common for burglary. — *July* 4. It was said that " vast multitudes this day declared themselves *independent*. The Mall on the Common is filled with temporary dram-shops, and cake and ale and punch undergo a rapid annihilation. The whole rag-tag and bob-tail gentry, from the Birds of Paradise to Barefoot Molly, are in their glory and meet on a *common* level. Independence is the word, and the sequel will show many *independent of common sense.*" — A code of Town Laws published, among which were the following, viz: " to prevent damage by brick kilns ; " " to provide town bulls ; " " to prevent tan-pits being left open ; " " to prevent gaming in streets ; " " to prevent throwing snow-balls ; " " to provide for sweeping streets," &c. &c. — The court passed a law that " all idle persons who do not properly do their stint, shall be moderately whipped." Convicts began to be sent to the castle, to serve their sentence. — *April* 17. Captain John Ballard, William Billings, Christopher Clarke, and Mr. Webb, appointed *Inspectors of Police.* — The Selectmen employed four teams to remove dirt from the streets. Mr. Gardner appointed to try all Town law violations. — *June* 17. Charles River Bridge completed, and a procession of twenty thousand persons passed over it. Great demonstrations of joy in town.

1787. At the session of the Supreme Judicial Court, *September* 9, the following sentences passed : " One burglar to be hung ; five female thieves to be whipped ; four male thieves whipped ; two big thieves to sit on the gallows ; one counterfeiter to stand in the pillory, and have right ear cut off." — *November* 22. John Shean hung on the Common for burglary in the house of Mr. Eliot. — *December* 10. The Town purchased two and a third acres of land of William Foster, at southeast corner of the Common, in exchange for stores on a wharf. — Merchants began to number their stores in business streets.

1788. *May* 8. Archibald Taylor and Joseph Taylor hung on Boston Neck, for robbing Mr. Cunningham, near the place of execution. — *July* 4. A great torchlight procession in the evening.

1789. *January* 8. An Englishman gave gymnastic entertainments at the George Tavern, — a great novelty. — *April* 1. John Norman published the first Boston Directory, containing 1,425 names. — At State election, Boston cast 1,934 votes. — *August* 7. Several burglaries having been committed, it was said, " It is high time the watchmen were overhauled; they have been asleep since New Year's. The Captains are generally men in their prime, aged from ninety to one hundred years, and the crew only average about fourscore, and so we have the advantage of their age and experience, *at least the robbers do.*" — *October* 8. William Dannesse, William Smith, and Rachel Wall hung on Boston Common for highway robbery. — *October* 24. General George Washington visited Boston. A great day in town. — *December* 2. A dramatic exhibition in Boston. To avoid the law and obtain license, it was called " *School of Moral Lectures.*'

December 14. The highway from Roxbury to Elliot's Corner named Washington Street. General Washington came over it when he entered the Town on his visit.

1790. *September* 1. Boston contained 18,038 persons, and 2,376 buildings. — *September* 16. Fourteen persons whipped in State Street for crime. — *October* 14. Edward Vail Brown (white), and John Bailey (colored), hung on Boston Common, for burglary.

1793. *January* 1. Colonel Josiah Waters, the newly appointed Inspector of Police, gave notice that he " enters upon the duties of his office with much diffidence, and he asks the assistance of the citizens in executing the by-laws. He calls the attention of the inhabitants to the bad condition of wells and pumps ; recommends increase of fire-buckets, ladders, fire-bags," &c. He gave directions in relation to the management of teams, and says that " the present internal arrangement of the Town is very bad." — *January* 24. A civic feast was held in Boston, to commemorate the success of the French in their struggle for civil liberty. " The dawn was welcomed by a salute from the Castle, *Citizen* Bradley's Artillery, and by citizens in Liberty Square. At eleven o'clock an ox, weighing 1,000 pounds, devoted as an offering, having been roasted whole the previous night, was prepared for exhibition, and a procession was formed, moving in the following order : —

"Citizens on horseback, with civic flags.

"Citizen Waters, Marshal.

"Committee of nine, flanked with peace officers

"Music, full band, drums, and fifes.

"Citizens, eight and eight.

"Twelve citizens in white frocks, with cleavers, knives, and steels.

"The Ox,

"Elevated twenty feet on a car, drawn by fifteen horses, ornamented with ribbons. The horns of the ox were gilded, and on the right horn hung the French flag, and on the left the American. Forward, on a board at the end of the spit, in large gold letters, was the inscription —

"PEACE OFFERING TO LIBERTY AND EQUALITY.

"Citizens, eight deep.

"Eight hundred loaves of bread, drawn by six horses.

"A hogshead of punch, drawn by six horses.

"Eight hundred loaves of bread, drawn by six horses.

"A second hogshead of punch, drawn by six horses; which closed the procession.

"The procession moved from the foot of Middle Street through various streets to the Common, and from thence to State Street, by which time the punch had disappeared, and there the ox was carved, and disposed of with much good will." Another account says: "When the procession arrived at State

Street, *the punch had done its work;* but few could get a slice of the ox, and he who did, *used it to grease his neighbor's face,* and the scene that followed beggared description." At the close of the ceremonies in State Street, the horns of the ox were laid at the foot of the liberty pole in Liberty Square, and afterwards placed on the top of a flag-staff raised there. A few months after, news came that Louis XVI. was beheaded three days before the celebration, and the head and horns of the roasted ox were draped in mourning.

1794. *February* 3. Mr. Powell, opened the Boston Theatre in Federal Street. — *July* 30. A terrible fire in Green Lane (Atkinson Street). Seven ropewalks and forty-five dwellings burnt. — Three pirates, named Collins, Poleski, and Fertidi, hung on Boston Common.

1795. *June* 1. A new Amphitheatre established near the foot of the Mall. — *July* 4. Corner-stone of new State House laid. — *September* 14. Mr. Bowen raised the frame of the Columbian Museum at the head of the Mall. — *November* 9. The grounds of the Almshouse, Workhouse, and Granary, sold at auction.

1796. *May* 14. The Legislature passed a code of laws relating to Watch and Wards of Towns, under which the Boston Watch was soon after reorganized. — Under the new regulations, the Selectmen, or the Constable, were to *charge the watch,* "to see that all disorders and disturbances are suppressed, to examine all persons walking abroad after *ten* o'clock at night, who they have reason to suspect, to enter houses of ill-fame, to suppress disturbances, and to arrest all violators of law or disturbers of the peace. Watchmen are to walk their rounds once an hour, to prevent damage by fire and to preserve order." Constables, to superintend the watch were to be appointed for each house, and the Selectmen were the appointing and supervising power. Under the new organization, there were five Watchhouses: One on Ship near Lewis Street, one at Town Dock, one at Town House, one on Orange, near Eliot Street, and one near where the Revere House now stands, with one constable and about six watchmen at each house, at a salary of sixty cents per night for the constable, and fifty for the watchman, while on duty. The Watch went out at nine o'clock evenings in winter, and ten o'clock in summer, remaining on duty till sunrise, one half going out alternately every other night, carrying with them their badges of office, a *hook* with a bill, and the *rattle*, an appendage added this year. — *December* 26. Haymarket Theatre opened, on Tremont, near West Street.

1797. *February* 3. A terrible fire burnt the ropewalks at West Boston. — *April* 6. John Stewart, hung on the Common, for robbing the house of Captain Rust, in Prince Street. His plunder was taken, at several times, and hid in a tomb on Copp's Hill, where he was traced and detected one stormy night. — *October* 12. Stephen Smith, a colored man, hung on the Common for burglary. He confessed setting fire to several houses to get plunder. His body was given to physicians for dissection. — *October* 21. The Frigate Constitution launched from Hart's wharf.

1798. *January* 11. The Legislature met at the old Town House for the last time. A procession was formed, and possession taken of the new State House. — *April* 2. Boston cast 1,774 votes for Governor. A bitter feeling between parties called the Federal and Republican. The Federalists adopt the wearing of what was called "The *American Cockade*," a rosette of black ribbon with a white button in the centre. — *September* 15. Solomon Monroe, selling Jamaica Pond aqueduct water, near the fish market, for thirty cents a hogshead, eight cents a barrel, and one cent a pail full.

1799. *December* 24. "News received at Boston that General George Washington, the Father of his Country, died at his residence at Mount Vernon, on the 14th instant, age 67: minute guns were fired, bells tolled throughout the day, and the Town was draped in mourning."

1800. The Town officers for the year were: Selectmen, 9; Board of Health, 12; Overseers Poor,

12; Fire Wards, 20; Assessors, 5; Treasurer, 1; Clerk, 1; Town Advocate, 1; Municipal Judge, 1; Inspector Police, 1; Constables, 12; Constables of the Watch, 4; Watchmen, 20; Collectors of Taxes, 5; Fence-viewers, 3; Hogreeves, 3; Hay Wards, 4; Hemp Surveyors, 2; Wheat Surveyors, 2; Assay Masters, 2; Cullers of Fish, 3; Inspector Lime, 1; Cullers of Staves, 4; Surveyors of Boards, 11; Sealers of Leather, 3. — The watchhouses have been reduced to four, — one on Ship Street, one near the Market, one in Orange Street, one near the State House. — " Complaints for all violation of by-laws, to be made to the Inspector of Police, who is at his office from *twelve* to *one* o'clock each day." — The Board of Health have the supervision of all sanitary arrangements in town. — *July* 4. It was said, " The day was solemnized with acts of devotion to Almighty God, with pomps, shows, games, sports, guns, bells, flags, bonfires, and illuminations; and in the evening fireworks were given by Captain Gardner's company, at the Gunhouse on Copp's Hill." Population of the Town, 24,937. Ratable polls, 4,103. Votes cast at State Election, 2,149.

1801. *March* 12. Charles Bulfinch, Esq., chosen Chairman of the Board of Selectmen, and soon after Inspector of Police. — Constables and watchmen ordered to " Report all violations of the By-laws." — Subscriptions raised for town improvements. A brick front built to the watchhouse in

Orange Street. (The narrow brick building lately standing at No. 518 Washington Street.)

1802. *January* 23. The market-house robbed. The next day a newspaper paragraph said, "It is remarkable that the broken door of the market-house, is just forty feet from the watchhouse." — *March* 8. Town meeting; a pickpocket caught in the act, beat almost to death and then sent to jail. — *May* 18. A fire broke out at midday. It was said, "The alarm was communicated rapidly by the watchmen stationed on Beacon Hill." — A new almshouse built in Leverett, near Spring Street. On the front was the figure of a female with a child in her arms. "In one part was a workhouse, where constables commit vagabonds by orders from Overseers of the Poor." *December* 13 Middlesex canal opened for transportation.

1803. *March* 15. Robert Pierpont and Abiel R. Story convicted of destroying the brig Hannah to defraud the underwriters. They were sentenced to stand in the pillory two hours, and to serve two years in State Prison. The case was one of great interest. — Lottery ticket offices, with a horn of plenty for a sign, were *plenty* in State Street. Boarding-house keepers, tavern keepers, and carriage drivers, required to report the arrival of all strangers to the Selectmen, for fear of a malignant contagion prevailing in New York.

1804. *April* 9. Town meeting. It had been

the custom to decide questions by hand vote. To-day an attempt was made to divide the house on a question, the *yeas* being requested to *go* out of the house first, which they refused to do; the *nays* were then requested, but they refused also, and a most ludicrous scene occurred.— The *nays* had it. — *June* 23. An underground arch was discovered near the head of Lewis's Wharf, fifty feet long, twenty wide, and six high, the mason-work being perfect, with an iron gate at each end. All above was a garden, where trees were standing, over a foot through. It was probably an old wine-cellar. It was said that Lord Percy hid in one near Brattle Square, during the bombardment by Washington, in 1776. — *August* 1. Great funeral procession on the death of Alexander Hamilton, killed in a duel by Aaron Burr. The Selectmen declined to ring the bells or to detail constables, lest they implicate the Town, — " *but the constables may go if they choose.*" — *October* 10. A terrible gale blew down the steeple of Christ Church, and carried away the tower on King's Chapel.

1805. It was said, "The Mill Pond is a nuisance, full of putrid fish and dead dogs and cats." The Selectmen petitioned to fill it up. — At the April term of the Supreme Judicial Court, one John Nichols, who was convicted of counterfeiting, was sentenced to stand in the pillory one hour. It was said that the sentence was executed the twenty-sixth of April, and it is believed that he was the last *actor* who graced the boards of this ancient relic of Puritanism. Nichols had letters of favorable notice from President Thomas Jefferson, and an attempt was made to turn Nichols's crime to political account. The pillory and whipping-post stood in State Street, below the Town House, nearly opposite the Merchants' Bank. It was said that both were removed soon after the sentence of Nichols. Whipping was practised sometime afterwards, and was executed on a platform on the Common, near the corner of West Street. The platform was said to be " put up temporarily, when occasion required." It consisted of a frame work, the platform reached by stairs, with posts raised on two sides, and a cap across the top like a gallows, but no *drop*. A pole stood in the middle, to which the culprit was made fast with iron shackles, and with ankles in sockets, and arms extended like a malefactor, his naked back was ready for the lash. Criminals for small offences were sometimes exposed on this platform without the lash. — *June* 28. The powder-house on Mount Vernon Street removed, but a small brick house, belonging to the estate, was retained for the Town Watch. — *October* 24. A jury of inquest on the body of a man found floating in the water, reported that " He came to his death by *misfortune*."

1806. *July* 4. A bear, whose body had been shaved, and who had been taught to stand on his hind legs, and perform certain antics, was exhibited on the Common as a nondescript from the East Indies. The cheat being discovered, poor bruin attempted to escape, and got desperately hustled about. The scene ended in a general fight. — *December* 3. Thomas Oliver Selfridge, indicted for manslaughter, in shooting Charles Austin. The men were political partisans, of opposite creeds, and Selfridge being of the dominant party, was acquitted.

1807. *March* 10. The town was divided by State and Court streets into two Police districts, each under the supervision of an officer. — Several persons are fined for keeping disorderly houses. — *August* 16. Joshua Ladd fined thirty dollars for cheating the weight of his binding-poles in a load of hay. — *October* 17. Eppes Ellery fined five dollars for refusing to pass the bucket at a fire, by order of a Fireward.

1808. *April* 16. A soup-house established in Milk Street, " where the poor can procure soup from twelve to one o'clock each day." — *September* 3. A great horserace at Lynnfield. One Boston editor approved, another condemned. They got warm, and accused each other of patronizing cockfighting. A suit for libel, and a fight in the street, settled the question between them. — *December* 8. Joseph Underwood fined forty dollars for casting three votes at the election. — *December* 25. The

Overseers of the Poor gave notice that they had given away six hundred loads of wood, "and can give no more without further *subscriptions*."

1809. *May* 17. The Board of Health give notice that "all dirt-carts must have tail-boards." — *June* 25. Fish pedlers forbid blowing their horns in the streets. — *October* 19. Ezra Brown fined five pounds for forestalling. He was then complained of as an idler, and sent to the Almshouse. — *December* 2. The funeral of William Cooper, who was Town Clerk forty-nine successive years, was solemnized to-day. — *December* 30. A masquerade ball advertised, but " it was forbidden, as detrimental to morals."

1810. *January* 13. Notice given that " James Wilson, Town Crier, will receive all lost property at his house, No. 23 Cornhill. — *March* 21. The Town chose one Inspector Police, two Assistant Police officers, seventeen Constables, and thirty Watchmen. Watchhouses in Ship Street, at the Market, Mount Vernon Street, and corner of Elliot and Washington streets. — Boston had 33,234 inhabitants, 9,557 ratable polls, and cast 5,288 votes. — *July* 4. " The celebration was very spirited. Next day, seven hundred persons, without distinction of party, were regaled at Faneuil Hall on five barrels of punch, that remained of the stores provided by the Town for the celebration the day previous. *Query.* How many barrels were provided for the celebration? — *August* 3. The Town voted to open a new burial-ground on the Neck.

1811. *March* 11. Alexander Townsend, Thomas Welch, James Savage, William Minot, and Lemuel Shaw, were rival candidates for Town Advocate.

1812. *June* 24. The news of the declaration of war with England was received with great indignation by a majority of Boston people. — *August* 31. The Town appointed one hundred special watchmen to patrol the town. "In case of riot, they are to toll the bells, and in case of an alarm, all well-disposed citizens are requested to place lights in all their front windows, and all military companies, magistrates, and constables will hold themselves in readiness; and all boys or apprentices who do not wish to be considered rioters, will remain in doors." The permanent watch was also increased to forty-six, consisting of three divisions; the North, Centre, and South, as follows: at the North, fourteen men; Centre, eighteen men; South, fourteen men, and two constables at each house. A Captain was also appointed, whose office was at the centre house, and who had general supervision. One constable and half the watch being on duty alternately every other night, *all night*. "Watchmen are not to talk loud, or make any noise, nor suffer any one to enter a watchhouse without a certificate from a Selectman." — Constable's pay, seventy-five cents per night; watchman's, fifty cents. — *December* 10. Samuel Tully, for piracy, hung on Nook's Hill at South Boston. John Dalton, an accomplice, was reprieved on the gallows.

1813. *April* 9. Molly Pitcher, who has *turned* the head of many a Boston boy, died, aged seventy-five. She was said to be grand-daughter of John Diamond (a fortune teller of Marblehead), and the wife of Robert Pitcher, at Lynn, having several children herself. Her fame as a fortune-teller was known throughout the world. No vessel arrived on the coast, but some of the hardy crew visited Molly. Her dwelling stood on a lonely road near High Rock, at the gate of which were to be seen the bones of a great whale that the ocean had thrown on the banks. To this place repaired the weather-beaten mariner, the respectable merchant, and the timid swain, who often betrayed the secret of their expedition, by inquiring for the bones of the great whale. Molly had great tact in pretending to discover lost property. She generally saw it *in the bottom of a teacup*; but her information was generally derived from the inquirers themselves, while they were talking with her domestic, Molly being in the next room. But it may be asked what has Molly Pitcher to do with the Boston Watch and Police; let the frequenters of " The Old National," when " The Fortune-Teller of Lynn " was the play, answer that question.

1814. *March* 23. An Asylum for indigent boys established. — *April* 10. A report that a British fleet is off the coast, and Boston made great preparation for defence. — *April* 13. The Selectmen offer $100 reward for arrest of grave-robbers at South Burying-Ground. — *May* 10. A public dinner given to Commodore Perry for whipping the British on Lake Erie. — *June* 14. Western Avenue Company incorporated. — *July* 25. A Company called the " Sea Fencibles," formed. — *September* 10. Several thousand troops are quartered in Boston for the defence of the town against the British.

1815. *February* 22. A grand illumination in the evening, in celebration of the Treaty of Peace with Great Britain. — *September* 23. A terrible storm destroyed many trees on the Common, and did much damage in Town and harbor. — *October* 22. The Town's people practised going into the country on Sunday to get fresh air. Country people remonstrated. A stringent Sunday law was enforced, and Boston gentlemen got detained out of town over night. — The Supreme Court at Boston, decided, " A county Justice cannot issue warrants for violation of Sunday laws, against an offender living in another county; neither can an officer serve such a warrant on Lord's day." This gave Boston people a *breathing-hole*, and country people much annoyance.

1816. *January* 1. Boston Post-office removed

to corner Congress and Water Streets. — *December* 11. An effort having been made to build a new workhouse, it was said, — "As respects *The Hill*, it consists principally of drunkards, harlots, spendthrifts, and outcasts from the country; in truth, Beelzebub holds a court there, and almost every Town in the Commonwealth has a representative. These are great nuisances, but every large town has them, whether governed by Selectmen, or Mayor and Aldermen, in spite of jails and workhouses, and probably will till the millennium."

1817. *January* 20. Daniel D. Britton sent to Jail, for stealing hens. "He is a brawny chimney-sweep, and parades the streets in a big cap, a long stick, and a train of boys at his heels, to the great annoyance of people." — *March* 13. Henry Phillips hung on Boston Neck, for the murder of Gaspard Denegri, near Roebuck Tavern, in January last. "After the cap was drawn over his eyes, he sang a song of three verses, dropped the handkerchief, and was launched into eternity." — During the year, wonders were plenty. An egg, with some mysterious writing, was on exhibition, and attracted great curiosity. But the *Sea Serpent*, seen in a thousand different places and shapes, astonished *the natives*, and cast all other mysteries in the shade. — *December* 26. William McDonald sentenced to be hung, for killing his wife, but he died before the day of execution arrived.

1818. *May* 20. A heavy rain overflowed the Frog Pond, and when the water fell, a great number of small fish were left on dry land. Common people were astonished: scientific men attempted an explanation, not once dreaming the real cause. The case was a sequel to the Sea Serpent, and wonderful egg. — *November* 3. The Exchange Coffee House burned. — The light was seen at Amherst, New Hampshire, and Saco, Maine. The building contained 210 rooms, covered 12,753 feet of land, and cost $600,000.

1819. A committee of the Selectmen made several visits to the watchhouses in the night time, and reported as follows: " *January* 5. Visit the several watchhouses, and find them in good condition." — " *January* 12. Another visit. Find too many watchmen doing duty inside." — " *January* 20. One o'clock, night. South Watch doing good duty, but the two constables are asleep. At North Watch, constables awake. At Centre Watch, found an intoxicated man and an abandoned female in the Lockup." — *February* 3. Another visit made by the Inspector of Police. He said, " At one o'clock, visited South Watch; constable asleep. One and one-half o'clock, at Centre Watch found constable and doorman asleep. Two o'clock, at North Watch found constable and doorman asleep, and a drunken man kicking at the door to get in." The Inspector recommends *that the doorman be re-*

quired to wake the constable when necessary. Constable Reed arrested several persons for keeping gambling houses. One was fined $150, for keeping "a new French game called Quino." — *February* 18. John Williams, John P. Rog, Niles Peterson, and Francis Frederick, pirates, hung on Boston Neck. — *March* 21. William Johnson sent to State Prison for life, for robbing a countryman of squirrels on the Common, where he decoyed him, under pretence to find a purchaser. — *May* 31. At Town Meeting, the watch and their friends remained at the polls till near the close, till others had left, and then passed a vote to pay watchmen seventy-five instead of fifty cents per night. The vote was rescinded next Town Meeting. — *June* 17. Freeman Backhouse, sent to State Prison three years, for picking the pocket of Flavel Case, a watchman. — *November* 13. Ropewalks burnt in Charles Street.

1820. *March* 13. The North watchhouse, for many years in Ship Street, was removed to Fleet Street, near Moon Street. The Centre watchhouse was in the east basement of the Town House. The South was at the place long occupied on Washington, near Eliot Street. West watchhouse, corner Temple and Hancock streets. Number of watchmen 55. Constables of the watch, 8. Captain, 1. *May* 25. Michael Powers hung on Boston Neck, for the murder of Timothy Kennedy, in

South Russell Street, in March last. — Watchmen were served with a certificate of appointment.

1821. *May* 23. A new Captain of the Watch appointed, and a long list of instructions given. "Watchmen are not to walk or talk together on their beats. They are to go their rounds, and return to their box, and there wait till the time arrives to go round again. They are not to cry the time of night in a vociferous voice," &c. &c. — *July* 2. Milldam bridge opened for travel. — *September* 19. A man named Pearl, convicted of adultery with a young woman who had been working with him as a carpenter's apprentice, in male attire, for three years. — *December* 20. Michael Martin hung at Lechmere Point, for robbing Major John Bray, in Medford, in October last. His accomplice, the notorious Captain Thunderbolt, lived *incog.* many years after in Brattleboro', Vermont, and died there in 1835. — *December* 23. Several burglaries having been committed, some persons were very severe on the Watch, and said, "They care for nothing but their pay, and are sure to get that; give us a private watch." Others said, "A private watch, like the one in 1816, as soon as the stores are closed, would be found at the Exchange, sipping coffee. The only safe way is for merchants to watch themselves." Others said, "Who will work faithfully all night for the bare stipend of fifty cents."

1822. *February* 22. The Legislature passed an Act establishing "The City of Boston," subject to the acceptance or the refusal of the citizens. — *March* 4. At a meeting of the legal voters of the Town of Boston, held at Faneuil Hall, to adopt or reject the City Charter granted by the Legislature, the vote was as follows: Yeas, 2,797; nays, 1,881; and the Town of Boston to become a City the first day of May next. — *March* 7. Gilbert Close and Samuel Clisby hung on the Neck lands, near the burying-grounds, for robbing Ezra Haynes in Cambridge Street, on the tenth of August last. — *April* 25. Samuel Green hung on the Neck lands for killing Billy Williams in State Prison, in November last. — *May* 1. Boston City Government inaugurated, consisting of Hon. John Phillips, Mayor, eight Aldermen, and forty-eight Councilmen. Inauguration at Faneuil Hall, and they take up their offices at the old Court House, in Court Square, where subordinate officers are chosen. — *May* 24. Owing to the disorderly state of the Hill and Ann Street, constables were detailed there on Sundays. — *June* 20. The new Police Court held its first session. Honorables Benjamin Whitman, Henry Orne, and William Simmons, Judges; Thomas Power, Clerk; William Knapp, Assistant. They held criminal sessions each day, and civil sessions twice each week. — *August* 1. Several cases of yellow fever in Boston. — *September* 16. Howard Trask, a notorious murderer, who had escaped hanging on the plea of insanity, attempted to kill two prisoners confined with him in Boston Jail, after which he cut up several mysterious antics and escaped. — In consequence of the bad condition of the Jail in Court Square, prisoners were taken to Lechmere Point. — An effort was made to introduce the tread-mill, to punish criminals.

1823. *February* 13. New buildings completed, and an order passed, " That the new Court House in Leverett Street, be called City Court House." The buildings were to be occupied as a Jail, House of Correction, and Police Court House. — *May* 1. Josiah Quincy, Mayor. — *May* 3. The Mayor gave notice " That he would attend at his office," at the County Court House, every day (Sundays excepted), between nine and ten o'clock A. M., to receive communications of individual or public interest." — *May* 13. " All cows going at large, shall wear a *Tally* on their neck, with owner's name, and number of the license." " No citizen shall pasture more than one cow on the Common." The office of Superintendent of Police abolished, and Benjamin Pollard appointed City Marshal, James Morgan, Captain of the Watch. The North Watch was removed to Hancock Schoolhouse, in Middle Street. The Centre Watch was at the Town House, the West at Derne Street, and the South at the Old House on Washington Street. There appeared to be little alteration in watch regulations, except that they were increased to about sixty. — *June* 19. An order passed to sell the old Jail in Court Street, and lease the house of the Jailer. — " Shaking down," by the girls, becomes frequent on The Hill. Mayor Quincy inaugurated stringent measures there.

1824. *February* 14. The great Canal Lottery in full blast in State Street. John Beck fined fifty dollars for keeping a faro bank. — *May* 1. Josiah Quincy, Mayor. — Watch appropriation, $8,800. *June* 23. Type foundry in Salem Street burnt. — *July* 1. An Ordinance passed to renumber the streets, placing the even numbers on one side, and the odd on the other. Middle and North to be called Hanover Street; and the main street from " The Market to Roxbury line, shall be called Washington Street." — *July* 21. The City Clerk reported, " Fees received for cow and dog license, $3,247, 39." — *August* 24. General Lafayette visited Boston. — *September* 15. Dr. Harrington fined $150, for letting rooms to Susan Bryant for unlawful purposes. — *October* 14. An officer detailed to patrol Ann Street by day. — *November* 20. — The North wood-stand to be between Cross and Merrimac streets and Green Dragon Tavern; The South, between Granary Burying-ground and Samuel Phillips's House. South Hay Scales in Charles Street. New Lockup about being built at the South watchhouse. The Washington Gardens, a place of great attraction on Tremont Street, between West Street and Temple Place, were opened.

1825. *March* 26. The city voted to accept the act changing the time of the municipal election to the second Monday in December. — " Watchmen found asleep, to be discharged." — *April* 6. The old Friends meeting-house, Congress Street, sold. — *April* 27. Corner-stone of new Market House laid. — Thomas Melville, who had been Fireward forty-six years, resigned. — *May* 2. Josiah Quincy, Mayor. — *June* 4. The City Marshal gave notice that he should execute the laws. — *June* 17. Corner-stone of Bunker Hill Monument laid. — *July* 11. An order adopted to survey *head waters* near Boston, to introduce water. — Churches allowed to put chains across streets Sundays to prevent disturbance. — Watchhouse removed from Washington to Eliot Street. — *July* 22. The Beehive destroyed in Prince Street, by a mob. — *July* 24. A riot attempted at Tin Pot, Ann Street, which was suppressed. — *October* 10. Sign-boards ordered to be placed at corners of streets. — *October* 24. Tremont Street widened, taking Gardiner Greene's land.—*December* 12. Watchman Jonathan Houghton killed in State Street, by a ruffian named John Holland. — Boston contained 58,281 inhabitants. White males, 27,911; white females, 29,453.

Colored males, 974 ; colored females, 943. — *December* 21. A fearful riot occurred at Boston Thetre, Federal Street. Edmund Kean, who had previously given offence, was to play. A large number of men and boys, but no women, were present. At Kean's appearance on the stage, the riot commenced. Kean was driven out, the house and furniture nearly destroyed, and many persons badly injured. 5,000 people, more or less, connected with the riot.

1826. *January* 1. City Government inaugurated ; Josiah Quincy, Mayor. — *January* 9. Theatres charged $1,000 for license. — *January* 29. James Morgan, Captain of Watch, died, and Flavel Case was soon after appointed. — *February* 6. House of Juvenile Offenders established at South Boston. — *March* 3. John Holland, or Holloran, hung for the murder of Watchman Houghton. — War between the Government and Fire Department ; the Fire Department got the worst of it. — *May* 6. The Mayor of Boston fined for fast riding. — A stone curb ordered to be built about the Frog Pond.— Park Street Mall laid out.— *June* 17. Jerome V. C. Smith chosen resident physician at Hospital Island. — *July* 1. Bodies being removed from Quaker Burying-ground to Lynn. — *July* 4. Celebrated with great spirit. A liberty pole erected corner Essex and Washington Street. — Presidents Thomas Jefferson and John Adams both died this day. — *July* 14. A riot on Negro Hill; several houses pulled down. — *August* 26. The new market completed and opened, and ordered to be called "Faneuil Hall Market." — *October* 7. The first railroad in America, completed at Quincy. — *October* 13. John Tileston died at his residence, No. 65 Prince Street, aged eighty-nine. Had been a Boston schoolmaster seventy years. — *October* 16. Gaspipe being laid in the streets in Boston. — *November* 27. Boston Marine Railway completed. — *December* 18. Charles Marchant and Charles Colson, pirates, sentenced to be hung. When sentenced, Marchant replied, "What! is that what you brought me here for, to tell me I must die? No thanks to you, sir; I am ready to die to-morrow." He killed himself the day before execution arrived.

1827. Josiah Quincy, Mayor. — *February* 1. Colson, the pirate, and accomplice of Marchant, hung in the jail-yard, Leverett Street. — *February* 7. Edwin Forrest appeared at Boston Theatre. — *February* 19. The city exchanged land with Asa Richardson, front of City Hall. — *March* 15. A temperance meeting held at Julien Hall, Milk Street. — *April* 28. Constables ordered to patrol the Common by day. — Joshua Vose pastured cows on the Neck for eight dollars the season. *May* 18. No more liquor to be sold on the Common public days. — *June* 16. A new monument erected over the graves of the father and mother of Franklin, in Granary Burying-grounds. — *August* 11. Palm-leaf hats first worn in Boston. — *September* 24. Tremont Theatre first opened. — *October* 11. Old Gunhouse removed from Copp's Hill to Cooper Street. — The body of a drowned woman floated in the creek, from Creek Square, across Hanover Street. — *October* 31. The Statue of Washington placed in the State House. — *November* 24. Madam Celeste danced at Tremont Theatre. — *December* 15. No child to be admitted at school unless vaccinated. — *December* 17. Two watchmen detailed for duty at South Boston. — The Boston Directory this year contained 11,164 names. It had the name of a baker, a blacksmith, a cordwainer, a ship carpenter, a tailor, a house carpenter, a saddler, a druggist, a wine dealer, an auctioneer, two merchants, and two hair-dressers, that were in the first Boston Directory in 1789. One merchant kept the same store, and one hairdresser the same shop forty-six years. — During the year, 921 persons have been committed to Boston Jail for debt.

1828. Josiah Quincy, Mayor. — *January* 17. Ancient wooden house on the west side of Tremont Street, removed, a part of which was said to have been built by Sir Henry Vane, in 1635, and the other by Rev. John Cotton, in 1636. — *February* 26. The Ursuline Convent at Mount Benedict,

Charlestown, completed. — *April* 30. One hundred persons more or less injured by the falling of a floor, while witnessing the ceremonies of laying the corner-stone of the Methodist Church, North Bennet Street. — *June* 23. Persons contracted to remove night soil. — *July* 4. The corner-stone of City Hotel (Tremont House) laid. Mr. J. B. Booth appeared at Tremont Theatre. — *September* 15. Marginal (Commercial) Street from Market to Sargent's Wharf opened. — *September* 23. Federal Street Theatre (renamed the Old Drury). — *September* 26. Boston Millpond filled up, and the Company surrendered their right to the city. — Union Street opened from Hanover to Merrimac streets. — *November* 4. The Centre Watch petition for beds, but don't get them. — The Grand Jury complained of being annoyed by the noise at their quarters in Leverett Street, by prisoners hammering stone. — *December* 25. Warren Bridge opened for travel.

1829. Harrison Gray Otis, Mayor.— *January* 1. A Gas Street-lamp placed in Dock Square, as an experiment. — *January* 19. The pay of the Watch increased to sixty cents per night. — *April* 15. Clinton Street opened. — *April* 22. Common Street, from Court, by the Common, to Washington, to be called Tremont Street. That part of Common St. between Southac Court (Howard), and Court, to be called Pemberton Hill.

1829. *July* 4. Celebrated with little spirit. It was said, "on the Common no liquor, no booths, and no people. At the Washington Gardens, afternoon, Orator Emmons held forth in flights of passing eloquence and rhyme, which, with a nondescript fish, were all to be heard and seen for fourpence." In the evening, a man tried to whip Big Dick, and got the worst of it. Big Dick (Richard Cephas) was a big darkey and bully of the Hill. He was a dancing-master by profession, and a peacemaker by practice. He is remembered by some old men as standing head and shoulders above his fellows, weight 300 pounds, with short open blouse, red jacket, little round-top hat, and was feared by all. He long since "shuffled off this mortal coil," but his stately figure may still be seen not a mile from his former residence. — *August* 24. Siamese Twins in Boston. — *October* 19. A new wall to be built on Tremont Street, next Chapel burying-ground. — Cigar-smokers in streets, notified that they will be fined. — Market Street to be called Cornhill. — *November* 28. J. B. Booth comes near killing another actor in sword exercise at the Tremont, pretends to be crazy and leaves the city. — *December* 30. A great Anti-Masonic meeting at Faneuil Hall, resolved to put down the order.

1830. Harrison Gray Otis, Mayor. — *February* 1. Beecher's church in Hanover, opposite Portland Street, burnt. — *February* 15. The Franklin

Schoolhouse having been sold, was repurchased, and the South Watch soon removed thereto. The watch detailed as follows: North Watch, house in Hancock Schoolhouse, 2 constables, 25 men; Centre Watch, in Kilby Street, 2 constables, 25 men: South Watch, Franklin Schoolhouse, Common Street, 2 constables, 22 men; West Watch, Derne Street, 2 constables, 24 men; 2 men at South Boston. Flavel Case, Captain. — *March* 15. Cows excluded from the Common.—*April* 6. Mr. Joseph White, aged eighty-two years, murdered at Salem. — *May* 1. City Marshal's salary, $1,000; Captain of Watch, $800; Watch Appropriation, $11,400. — Boston had 61,381 inhabitants, of which 1,915 were colored. — *September* 17. A committee long having the matter under consideration, decided this day to be the anniversary of the Settlement of Boston, and the day was celebrated with great spirit, as the second centennial anniversary of the settlement of the Town. — The old Town House having been prepared, the City Government took possession, to occupy it as City Hall, with appropriate ceremonies. — *September* 29. John F. Knapp hung at Salem, for the murder of Mr. White. — *October* 14. Corner-stone of Masonic Temple, Tremont Street, laid. — *November* 8. Another peace officer placed on Ann Street. — North Island wharf, the last remains of what was called "the old wharf," was removed this year.

1831. Harrison Gray Otis, Mayor. — *March* 21. John Harrington astonishing Bostonians with ventriloquism, at Concert Hall. — *May* 5. Maynard's bakehouse in Broad Street, burnt. A man, wife, and three children, perish in the flames. — *June* 13. Chambers over the Market to be called Quincy Hall. The Municipal Court removed from Leverett Street, to County Court House, Court Square. — *July* 1. Joseph Gadett, and Thomas Colinett, hung in rear of Leverett Street jail, for piracy. — No. 60 State Street, corner Flag Alley, once the British Custom House, afterwards, United States Custom House, sold at auction for ten dollars per foot. — *July* 11. Oak, Ash, Pine, and adjacent streets, being graded. — *August* 3. John Gray Rogers appointed Judge of Police Court; Judge Orne resigned. — *August* 10. First sale of lots at Mount Auburn. — *August* 23. Funeral ceremonies on the death of President Monroe; died July 4. — *September* 10. The notorious swindler Mina, arrested by officer Pierce, for High Constable Hayes, of New York. — *November* 16. Mr. Anderson attempted to sing at Tremont Theatre, but was driven from the stage, for alleged abuse of the Yankees. — *December* 28. Calvin Edson, the living skeleton, on exhibition in Boston.

1832. Charles Wells, Mayor. — *February* 27. Centre Watch removed from Kilby Street, to basement in Joy's Buildings. — *May* 1. Among the appointments were Hezekiah Earl, Deputy Marshal; Zephaniah Sampson, Superintendent Streets; Thomas C. Amory, Chief Engineer, Fire Department; Samuel D. Parker, County Attorney. — *June* 11. The watch to be set at ten o'clock the year round. — *July* 3. William Pelby opened the Warren Theatre. — *July* 20. The Asiatic cholera appeared in Boston. $ 50,000 appropriated, and every preparation made to stay its progress. The contagion disappeared in a few weeks. — *August* 9. A constable to patrol South Boston on Sunday. — *August* 13. A Steamboat first placed on Chelsea Ferry.— *September* 12. Mrs. Vincent first appeared at Tremont Theatre. — *September* 24. Boston lying-in hospital established, at 718 Washington street.— *October* 1. Great complaint against the gas works on Copp's Hill. — *October* 16. Steamboat put on Noddle's Island Ferry. — *December* 21. Great excitement in Boston, in consequence of the alleged murder of Sarah Maria Cornell, by Rev. E. K. Avery, a Methodist preacher, at Tiverton, R. I. — *December* 31. Eleven o'clock at night, Bromfield Street watch-meeting broken up by rioters.

1833. Charles Wells, Mayor. — *February* 17. John B. Carter and Mary A. Bradley, a worthy young couple, committed suicide by hanging themselves together face to face, in her father's store. — *March* 26. Elisha Towers and other temperance men petitioned to have the eleven o'clock bell discontinued, but Boston would have its eleven o'clock. — *April* 8. Jim Crow Rice *jumping* at Tremont Theatre. — The city purchased Brown's Wharf. — *May* 1. First Boston omnibus run between Roxbury and Chelsea Ferry. — *May* 6. Old Court House, Court Street, removed. It stood sixty years. — *June* 3. A fight between constables and gamblers on the Common. — *June* 17. House of Correction, South Boston, opened. — *June* 21. Andrew Jackson visited Boston. — *June* 28. New Watch arrangement; the men to go out, one division one half the night, the other division the other half, commencing at six o'clock winter, and seven o'clock summer, remaining out till sunrise. The force increased eighteen men. Constable's pay one dollar. Watchmen seventy-five cents. — *September* 28. Corner-stone of New Court House, Court Street, laid. — *November* 11. Tremont Street to Roxbury line, also Dedham, and several other streets west of Washington nearly completed.

1834. Theodore Lyman, Jr., Mayor. — *January* 24. Judge Whitman, of the Police Court resigned. — *February* 4. Constables detailed to attend fires. — *February* 17. The name of Lynn Street discontinued, and Commercial to extend from State to Charlestown Bridge. — *April* 8. The first cargo of ice exported from Boston by Mr. Rogers. — *May* 4. Colonel David Crockett visited Boston. — *July* 3. During a terrible storm, the figure-head of the Frigate Constitution (the likeness of General Jackson), lying near Charlestown, was cut off and carried away. — *July* 4. The christening of the Whig party. 2,000 persons sit down to a feast under a tent on the Common. — *August* 11. Monday evening, the Ursuline Convent at Mount Benedict, Charlestown, burnt. — *August* 19. Theatres agreeing to sell no liquor were licensed for five dollars each. — *September* 19. Hair beds furnished for the watch. — *September* 22. Blackstone Street completed and named. — *November* 17. Dover Street completed. — *December* 2. Henry Joseph, hung in Leverett Street Jail yard for piracy. — *December* 4. The city indicted for a nuisance at South Boston. — There were seventy-one gas street-lamps in the city. — Ann Street widened so as to connect Merchants Row with Blackstone Street.

1835. Theodore Lyman, Jr., Mayor. — *January* 5. Men go from Central Wharf to the Castle on skates. — *April* 18. Old Mansion taken down, corner Salem and Charter Streets. — *May* 8. Pemberton Hill being removed, to build Lowell Street. The Gingko tree removed to the Common, near Joy Street. — *May* 27. Cars put on Lowell Railroad. — *June* 9. Pedro Gilbert, Manuel Costello, Monelle Bogga, Jose Bassello DeCosta, and Angelo Garcia, five Spanish pirates, hung in rear of Leverett Street Jail. — *June* 30. Special constables appointed for July Fourth. — *August* 13. Mr. George Robert Twelves Hewes, ninety-six years old, said to be the last surviving member of "The Boston Tea Party," visited Boston from his residence in New York. — *September* 5. Joyce Heth, pretending to be one hundred and sixty-one years old, and General Washington's nurse, was on exhibition at Concert Hall. — *September* 12. Ruiz, the pirate, hung in rear of the Jail. — *October* 7. Sixty-four building-lots sold in Pemberton Square. — *October* 22. George Thompson mobbed at the *Liberator* Office, Washington Street. — *October* 23. A circus opened at the Lion Tavern. — *December* 31. Charles Harris, Esq., submitted a plan for supplying Boston with soft water, by an Artesian well on Fort Hill, which he calculated would yield twelve million gallons of pure water per day. — Watch appropriation, $27,210. Special Constable appropriation, $3,630.

1836. Samuel Turell Armstrong, Mayor. — *March* 16. Simeon L. Crockett and Stephen Russell, for setting fire to Mr. Hammond's house in South Street Place, were hung in the jail yard. — *April* 1. "*Ordered*, That hereafter the church bells be rung at twelve, instead of eleven o'clock." — *April* 13. "THE BOSTON STONE," was set in a building in progress of erection, corner of Marshall and Creek Lanes. It was used for grinding paint by an early settler in Boston, whose arms are to be seen in the front walls of a building on Marshall Street, at the present day. The stone was said to have laid useless in the yard many years, but was afterwards placed at the corner of the streets, to keep truck wheels from injuring the building, which was at that time occupied by Mr. Howe. About the year 1737, the suggestion of a Scotchman, who lived near, induced Joe Whiting, whose father then kept the shop, to paint the name of "Boston Stone, Marshall Lane," on the old paint mill, in imitation of "The London Stone," in London, that it might be a landmark and directory, which character it did eventually acquire. The pestle or ball was since found, and "The Boston Stone" has now "become the head of the corner." — *June* 16. Pond Street to be called Endicott Street. — *July* 13. Church bells to be rung at one o'clock instead of twelve. — *July* 18. Mount Washington House, South Boston, opened. — *August* 22. The name of Pelby's Theatre altered from Warren to National. — *September* 22. William H. Snelling published a paper called the *Balance*, which he said, "Is to be the author of truth, a scourge to blacklegs, and a terror to unrighteous judges." — *December* 16. The iron fence around the Common completed; length 5,930; cost $80,000. $17,000 contributed by individuals. — *December* 20. The new Court House in Court Street, completed. — Benjamin Pollard, who had been City Marshal fourteen years, died, and Daniel Parkman was appointed in his stead.

1837. Samuel Atkins Eliot, Mayor. — *February*

8. The foundation of the United States Hotel laid. — *March* 3. Graham lectures at Amory Hall. — *May* 11. Boston Banks suspend specie payment. — Superintendent Common Sewers chosen. (A new office.) — Ezra Weston appointed City Marshal. — *June* 11. Sunday afternoon. " The Broad Street riot occurred between Irishmen and fire companies, in which it was said 15,000 people were engaged. The riot was finally suppressed by the military. — *June* 14. The National Lancers made their first public parade. — *June* 30. A flagstaff erected on the Common, near " The Old Elm." — *July* 5. The edgestones about the Frog Pond to be removed. — *August* 21. A watch of four men detailed for East Boston. — *September* 12. At the general military review on the Common, when the Montgomery Guards appeared, five companies left the line, and the review was suspended. — *October* 20. Lands granted to Horace Gray for " the Public Garden." — Ten deaths by cholera, and eleven by delirium tremens, during the year.

1838. Samuel Atkins Eliot, Mayor.— *February* 3. (Saturday night.) The City Marshal made a descent on gamblers in Milk Street, arresting twelve men. — *February* 19. Pemberton Square named. — *May* 21. The Legislature having passed a law giving the Mayor and Aldermen of Boston power to appoint " Police officers with any or all of the powers of Constables, except the power of execut-

7*

ing a civil process." The Board this day organized a Police force for day duty, to be under the direction of the City Marshal, and six officers were appointed, drawing pay when on actual duty, the new department having no connection with the Watch. There were four Watch-houses in the City proper. North Watch, Hancock Schoolhouse, 2 constables, 23 men; East Watch, Joy's Building, 2 constables, 28 men; South Watch, Common Street, 2 constables, 22 men; West Watch, Derne Street, 2 constables, 28 men. The South and East Boston Watch were combined, having 2 constables, and 9 men, with temporary accommodations at each place. Watch appropriation, $30,000. Police appropriation, $3,637. — *June* 18. Abner Kneeland sent to jail two months for blasphemy. — *July* 24. Great Webster dinner at Faneuil Hall. Jim Wilson, of New Hampshire, a guest. — A new division of wards. — *July* 31. The iron fence about Washington Square, completed. — Fanny Ellsler dancing at the Tremont Theatre. — *August* 27. Eastern Railroad opened for travel. — *September* 11. "The striped Pig" on exhibition at Dedham muster (and elsewhere). — The police force increased to thirteen during the year.

1839. Samuel Atkins Eliot, Mayor. — *February* 11. A committee reported one hundred and eighty gas street-lamps in the city. — *February*

15. Harnden's Express commences carrying letters to New York. — *March* 27. High Sheriff Sumner (in office many years), resigned.— *June* 4. City purchased Richardson's estate fronting on School Street. — *June* 17. Jacob's Great test liquor case in Police Court. — *October* 19. A tar and feathering liquor informer case occurred. — *November* 19. Iron fence around the Cemetery on the Common completed. — *November* 21. Steam communication between St. Johns and Boston opened. — Marcus Morton elected Governor by one vote this year.

1840. Jonathan Chapman, Mayor. — *February* 8. William Miller (Father of Millerism) first lectured in Boston. — *February* 10. Governor Morton signs a new Liquor Bill; great rejoicing. Counseller Gill preserves the Governor's pen *that did the deed.* — *March* 10. Daguerreotypes first taken in Boston. — *May* 1. James H. Blake appointed City Marshal, James Barry, Captain of the Watch. Police appropriation $4,500; Watch appropriation $40,000: Marshal's salary, $1,000; Captain of Watch, 1,000; 14 Police, 110 Watchmen. Police pay, 1.75 per day; Watchman's pay, 90 cents per night. — *May* 28. One hundred thirty-two building-lots sold on Lowell Street. — *June* 4. Steam Packet communication opened between Boston and Liverpool. — *July* 4. Celebrated with great spirit, partaking somewhat of a political character. " *Log*

Cabins," " *Coon Skins*," and " *Hard Cider*," were in the play, and "*Tippecanoe and Tyler too*," were the watchwords. — The Iron fence completed between the Granary burial-ground and Tremont Street. — *August* 8. Monsieur Bihin, the Belgian Giant eight feet high, on exhibition in Boston. — *December* 22. Hannah Kenney on trial for poisoning her husband.

1841. Jonathan Chapman, Mayor. *February* 15. Father Matthew, the Irish Temperance Reformer, in Boston. — *March* 18. Old County Court House fitted up, and named *City Hall*. The Government removed there from Old Town House. — *March* 28. Davis and Palmer's store, Washington Street, robbed of $20,000 in jewelry. Constable Clapp afterwards recovers the property. — Front Street to be called Harrison Avenue. — *April* 21. Funeral of President Harrison solemnized in Boston. — *June* 14. Boston Museum, Corner Tremont and Bromfield streets opened. — *August* 2. Corner stone of Merchants Exchange, State Street laid. — *September* 23. The first pillar of Merchants Exchange, weighing fifty-five tons, was raised to-day. — *October* 25. Circuses opened on both Haverhill and Friend streets. — *November* 15. Abby Folsom broke up a meeting in Marlboro' Chapel. — *November* 24. The French Prince De Joinville danced in Faneuil Hall with the Mayor's lady. — *December* 31. The Municipal court docket for the year showed five hundred and sixty-nine cases, Judge Thacher having been on the Bench one hundred and sixty-six days during the year.

1842. Jonathan Chapman, Mayor. — *January* 21. Elder Knapp, a revival preacher, who was reported to have said, " It is easier for a shad to climb a greased barber's pole tail foremost, than for a sinner to get to heaven," held forth in Boston. — *April* 25. Abby Folsom and Joseph Lamson created sensations. — *May* 16. The first watering-machine used for wetting streets in Boston. — *July* 4. It was said that 8,000 school children were on the Common in the day, and 100,000 witnessed the fireworks in the evening. — *July* 23. The Cap stone of Bunker Hill Monument laid. — September 27. Brigade muster on the Common. Boston represented by fourteen companies.

1843. Martin Brimmer, Mayor. — *January* 1. Merchants Exchange (State Street) opened. — *April* 23. The day fixed by the Prophet Miller for the end of the world. A large number of believers assembled at the Miller Tabernacle (Howard Street) in the evening, expecting to take their leave of earth that night; but nothing unusual happened *but the meeting.* — *May* 9. Trees ordered to be planted on Copp's Hill. — *May* 22. Tom Thumb first appeared in Boston. — *June* 16. Abner Rogers killed Warden Charles N. Lincoln, at Charlestown State Prison. — *June* 17. John Tyler, President of the United States, visited Boston. — Honorable William Simmons, Judge of the Police Court, died. — *July* 11. Judge Cushing first took his seat as Judge in the Police Court. — *August* 27. A riot in North Square between negroes and sailors. — *September* 4. General Winfield Scott visited Boston. — *September* 6. Judge Cummins held the Municipal Court, Judge Thacher late deceased. — *November* 30. Centre Watch removed from Joy's buildings to City building, Court Square. — The Captain of the Watch fined for smoking in the street. — John B. Gough lectured in Faneuil Hall. — *December* 28. The Tremont Theatre having been purchased by a Religious Society, was dedicated and called Tremont Temple.

1844. Martin Brimmer, Mayor. — *January* 1. Post Office removed from Old State House to Merchants Exchange, State Street. — *February* 3. Men drove teams and skated from Long Wharf to Boston Light. John Hill & Co. cut a ship channel for the British steamer to pass out. — *May* 20. Ole Bull gave his first Violin Concert at Melodeon, — and Mr. Franklin threw three somersets at the Circus. — *June* 4. The Fairchild excitement commenced. — *July* 2. The South Watch "ordered to be divided, the southern branch to be in Canton Place." — *July* 4. Fireworks on the easterly part of the Common for the last time. -- *July* 23. The old building, corner of Union and Hanover streets, a competitor for the birthplace of Franklin, is repaired and becomes a part of Diamond Block. — *September* 19. Great Whig meeting on Boston Common. — The close of the year is noted for a municipal political strife. — A Watchhouse built at South Boston during the fall.

1845. — *January* 6. The City Government organized without a Mayor. — *January* 30. Federal Street Church sold, to be removed. — *February* 21. Thomas A. Davis elected Mayor, at the eighth trial. — *March* 14. Peter York sentenced to State Prison for life, for killing James Norton, in Richmond Street. — *April* 10. Deacon Samuel H. Hewes, (Supt. of burials) died. He planted one hundred and seventy-two trees on the Common, and many in the burial-grounds. — *May* 26. Washington Theatre opened at 253 Washington Street. — *June* 23. Ira Gibbs appointed City Marshal. — *July* 9. Funeral ceremonies for President Jackson, who died June 8. — *July* 22. Henry Smith, the Razor Strop man in State Street, crying "a few more left." — *September* 4. Juba (the dancer), on exhibition. — *October* 6. Mayor Davis resigned on account of ill health. — *October* 18. Howard Theatre (built on the site of the Miller Tabernacle) opened. — *October* 27. Maria Bickford murdered in Mount Vernon Avenue. — *November* 8. Old Colony Railroad opened. — *November* 12. Mayor Davis died. — *November* 17. Winthrop House opened.

1846. Josiah Quincy, Jr., Mayor. *January* 15. Magnetic Telegraph line put up from Boston to Springfield. — The third row in the *National* becoming noted. — *March* 24. Albert J. Tirrell on trial for the murder of Maria Bickford. He was acquitted. — *May* 14. One hundred and twenty-nine vessels arrived in Boston Harbor. — *May* 16. War between the United States and Mexico — *May* 19. Mrs. Pelby exhibited one hundred wax figures at Phillips's Hall. — *June* 4. Recruiting parties patrolling the streets, for Mexican War volunteers. *June* 22. — Francis Tukey appointed City Marshal. — *July* 1. City Stables being removed from Haymarket Square. — *July* 17. The Old Eastern Stage House, Ann Street, removed. — *August* 20. Mayor Quincy broke ground at Wayland, for the " Boston Water Works." — *September* 21. Adams House opened. — *September* 29. Trucks and carriages to be licensed. — *November* 2. The New Boston Museum between Tremont Street and Court Square, opened. — During the year, under the direction of Marshal Tukey, the Police Department was reorganized. — The force numbered twenty-two day, and eight night officers. The former on duty from eight A. M. till nine P. M. Detailed throughout the city, reporting to the Marshal at eight A. M. and two P. M., at $2 per day. — The latter a night force, particularly for the detection of thieves, at pay of $1.25 per night. Police appropriation $12,000. — Under Captain Barry, the watch numbered about one hundred and fifty, going out half of each night, one half the force alternately, first and last watch at a pay of $1 per night. The North Watch was in Cross Street, the Centre under the Court House, the West in Derne Street, Boylston, in Common Street, South at Canton Street, South Boston in Broadway, and a new house building at East Boston.

1847. Josiah Quincy, Jr., Mayor. *January* 22. Terrible fire in Causeway, Medford, and Charlestown streets. A complete sheet of cinders covered the north part of the city, presenting one of the most sublime and terrific spectacles ever witnessed. — *February* 7. Currier & Trott's store, Washington Street, robbed of a large amount of jewelry. — *March* 13. The Grand Jury found one hundred and ninety-eight bills of indictment. — *March* 31. A temperance meeting (Deacon Grant, President) broken up at Faneuil Hall. — *April* 26. The new Custom House, at the head of Long Wharf, (began in 1837, and part completed,) illuminated. — *April* 27. Corner-stone of Boston Athenæum, Beacon Street, laid. — *May* 1. The Revere House, Bowdoin Square, completed and opened. — *May* 13. The Mayor and Aldermen voted to license no more liquor shops. — The Bridge Estate purchased by the city. — *June* 5. Mrs. Partington's witty sayings begin to appear in the newspapers. — Ship fever raging at Deer Island; a large Police force detailed there. — *June* 9. Mischievous boys come near destroying the Old Elm, by placing matches in a decayed place. — *June* 12. The house of Deacon Grant, the temperance reformer, disgracefully defaced. — *June* 16. The old Custom House, Custom House Street, sold. — *June* 24. Omnibus war between Mr. King and Boston, begun. — *June* 29. President Polk visited Boston. — *July* 27. Iron seats placed on the Common, to *bar whittlers*. — *August* 24. Alexandre Vattemare, Paris, *Prefect of Police*, donated books to Boston, which eventually formed a *nucleus* for a Public Library. — *September* 8. The Assessors' book shows real estates $97,764,500, and personal estate, $64,595,900, for Boston. — *October* 7. News reached Boston that the American Flag is flying over " The Halls of the Montezumas" in Mexico. — *October* 25. New Hancock Schoolhouse, Richmond Place, completed. — *November* 18. The Chinese Junk arrived in Boston Harbor. — *November* 20. Corner-stone of Beacon Hill Reservoir laid. — *December* 13. Workmen digging down Snowhill Street, tombs exposed.

1848. Josiah Quincy, Jr., Mayor. *January* 7. Marshal Tukey recovered $1,100, stolen from Hughes & Co., *by digging on the Public Garden*. — *February* 29. City Hall in mourning for Honorable John Quincy Adams, born July 11, 1767, died February 23, 1848. — *March* 10. The twenty-eight-gallon liquor law passed. — *March* 14. Sam Houston, of Texas, at Tremont Temple.—*April* 27. Watchman David Estes shot in Sister Street, while on duty. Night Policeman James S. Kimball narrowly escaped the same fate at the hands of burglars. — *May* 2. Marshal Tukey fined for fast driving. — *June* 16. General order to complain of all persons smoking in the streets. — *June* 28. Dearborn's Block, in Federal Street, fell with a terrible crash. — *July* 22. The Massachusetts Regiment, Colonel Isaac H. Wright, returned from the Mexican war. — *August* 9. Granite depot for Fitchburg Railroad, completed. — *August* 24. Dr. Collyer's Model Artist, at Melodeon. — *September* 18. Thrilling account of gold in California reaches Boston. — *October* 25. Grand celebration of the introduction of Lake Cochituate water into Boston, and a jet of water sent up from the fountain in the Frog Pond, — *an event worthy of commemoration.* — *December* 27. The ship Salstillo left Boston with twelve passengers for the California gold mines. — The Police number twenty-two day officers, twenty night officers, and nine specials for Sunday. A Police Clerk appointed. Police appropriation, $29,000; Watch appropriation, $58,000.

1849. John Prescott Bigelow, Mayor. — *January* 1. Good sleighing and great horseracing on the Neck. — *January* 9. Ship Edward Everett and two others, clear for California. — *February*

19. The City Government offer a reward of fifty cents for every dog's head. — *February* 21. People walk on the ice from Long Wharf to Spectacle Island. — Franklin and Blackstone squares laid out. — *March* 15. Flouring Mills at East Boston commence work. — *May* 21. Marshal Tukey showing up pickpockets at his office. — *May* 25. Washington Goode hung at the jail for the murder of Thomas Harding, in Richmond Street, in June last. — *June* 4. The Asiatic Cholera made its appearance in Boston. — *July* 27. Lieutenant Hunter, a notorious swindler, arrested. — *August* 18. William Waberton (Bristol Bill), a notorious burglar, arrested. — *September* 17. James Hayes, an Irishman, dies in Hamilton Street, aged one hundred and eight years. — *October* 11. Montgomery House opened for entertainment. — *November* 1. Eye and Ear Infirmary completed, in Charles Street. — *November* 7. Great meeting of the Sons of New Hampshire, at Fitchburg Hall. — *November* 16. Iron fence completed about Franklin and Blackstone squares. — *December* 1. The Statue of Aristides placed in Louisburg Square. — *December* 19. Deer Island Hospital completed.

1850. John Prescott Bigelow, Mayor; Francis Tukey, City Marshal; James Barry, Captain Watch. In his address, Mayor Bigelow said, " Boston has 197 schools, 20,000 pupils. The number of deaths exceeds any previous year, owing to cholera, being

5,068. There are 50 Police Officers, 225 Watchmen, the beat of each man averaging over a mile. The expense of Police and Watch, $113,000 per year. The Water Works are nearly completed, at a cost of $4,939,824; and the city debt, exclusive of water, is $1,623,863." — *January* 14. The clock in Faneuil Hall presented to the city by children. — *February* 8. "The Liberty Tree Block," corner of Essex and Washington streets, completed. — *May* 18. Chester Square laid out. — *June* 3. Mr. Glidden exhibited an Egyptian mummy at Tremont Temple. — *August* 15. Funeral procession of President Zachary Taylor. — *August* 30. Professor John W. Webster hung at the Jail yard for the murder of Dr. George Parkman, the 23d of November last, at the Medical College. — *September* 28. Jenny Lind sang at Tremont Temple. Ossian E. Dodge paid $625.00 for choice of seat. — *October* 26. Slave-catchers arrested in Boston; great excitement among colored people. — *October* 30. Great sale of building lots in Chester Square. — *November* 15. Free Soil meeting at Faneuil Hall broken up. — *December* 31. Number of dwelling-houses in Boston 13,173. Inhabitants 138,788.

Heretofore I have been under the necessity of leaving the reader to judge of the character of Watch and Police duties, from the nature of **transpiring** events, the manners, customs, opinions, and tastes of the people, and the peculiar rules and regulations that governed them at the time. Having now become intimately engaged in those duties myself, I shall hereafter generally speak of what has fallen under my own observation.

1851. John Prescott Bigelow, Mayor; Francis Tukey, City Marshal; James Barry, Captain of the Watch, who are detailed exclusively for night duty, the beats extending entirely over the city, and each man on his beat one half the night. The City Marshal had one deputy, one clerk, one superintendent hacks, one superintendent trucks, one of swill, and one of intelligence offices, who also had a particular eye after the day men; forty day officers on patrol on beats throughout the city, and about twenty night patrol officers to catch thieves, together with five detectives. It was the duty of the day men to report at the Marshal's Office at eight A. M., go on beats till two P. M., then report and go out again till nine in the evening. We looked out for our respective districts, the Marshal and his assistant when in sight of a corner, and our two dollars per day. The night police did about the same thing for $1.37½ per night. — On the eve of the 23d of April, this year, we made the great Police descent in Ann Street, capturing some one hundred and sixty bipeds, who were punished for piping, fiddling, dancing, drinking, and attending crimes. In the fall of this year, the Marshal seemed to think that things looked a little squally, and under his direction we very quietly dabbled a little (very little) in politics at the election. Our choice was successful, and we were in very good spirits at the close of the year, in anticipation of a longer job.

1852. Benjamin Seaver, Mayor; Francis Tukey, City Marshal, with the organization unchanged. — A new prohibitory liquor law was passed in May, which enjoined peculiar duties on City Marshals, imposing, as it was said, a little too much responsibility; and from that or some other cause, on the 24th of June following, the office of City Marshal was abolished in Boston, and Francis Tukey was appointed *Chief of Police*. I have said that the municipal election resulted in our choice; but no sooner had we got our man *in*, than he began to get us *out*, — and served us right, too, for meddling with politics. In filling the places of the *outs*, I must say I think the Mayor was sometimes unfortunate. This got the Mayor and his *Chief* by the ears, and the Mayor having the best hold, *pulled off the Chief's head*, together with the heads of his whole night force and a part of the day. His Honor was indeed after all of us with a sharp stick; but some were like Paddy's flea, — " When ye put yer finger on 'im, he aint thar! " It was the 19th day of July, that the Mayor pulled off Chief Tukey's head, and Gilbert Nurse, Esq. was appointed Chief of Police the same day. A better man never lived. Said a Frenchman to a Yankee one day, "Vat drinque ish dat ye have in dish countrie, vat is all *conthradiction?*" "What do you mean?" says Yankee. "Vy, dar ish de brandie, to make him sthronge, and de vatre, to make him veak; dar ish de lemon, to make him sour, an' de sugar to make him schweet." "*Punch,*" said Jonathan. "*Ah! oui, oui,*" says Francis, "he like *punch* me brain out last night." When Mr. Nurse came into office, he found our Department very much like the Frenchman's drink, and it came near accomplishing the same result on our worthy Chief; but notwithstanding all the difficulties, he went to work with a steady hand, and really made many important improvements.

1853. Benjamin Seaver, Mayor. Gilbert Nurse Chief of Police, with two deputies, the usual number of office men, and fifty-two day patrol men. No night police. The Chief's salary was $1,800, and the Police appropriation, $44,200. — In *June*, robberies on vessels and on the wharves having become very common, a *Harbor Police* was organized, consisting of a Captain and ten men; House at head of Sargent's wharf. They were furnished with row boats, and armed with Colt's revolvers; and plenty of work they found to do. Heretofore, for some years, the officers had worn leather badges, buckled round the hat, with the word

POLICE in large silver letters, and a number in front. This year, on June 1, we were furnished a new badge, to be worn on the left lapel of the coat. It was an oblong, six-pointed *brass* star, about as big as one's hand, with an unintelligible device in the centre, and looked more like a Sculpin's head than a Policeman's badge. — For some years past, there had been a talk of reorganizing the Watch and Police, and on May 23d of this year, the Legislature empowered Boston to make the change; but there were no steps taken in that direction by the City Government till the following year. — *December* 29. James Barry, having faithfully served the City as Captain of the Watch fourteen successive years, resigned his office, and Captain William K. Jones was appointed in his stead.

1854. Jerome Van Crowninshield Smith, Mayor. Gilbert Nurse, Chief of Police. I have said that the Legislature had empowered Boston to reorganize her Watch and Police, and there were probably some good reasons why it should be done. There were two departments, under different heads, and, although there was at this time no disunion, yet under the direction of other and different men at the head of so large forces, there might be. The Police by themselves, were still a little like the Frenchman's *punch*. The watch were paid only one dollar per night, and were obliged to work by day also, to support their families; and, good men as they were, who could expect them to work day and night without sleep or rest? Under this state of things, most of the people and a part of the Government were in favor of the change; but a majority of the Council were opposed to the measure, and claimed a voice in the matter. However, the appointing and the discharging power in both departments were, by law, vested in the Board of Mayor and Aldermen; and one day, Mayor Smith, with the countenance of the Aldermen, discharged every man on both Watch and Police, and out of their number appointed a Department of *Police*, the discharge and appointments to take effect on a subsequent day.

On the 26th day of May, 1854, at precisely six o'clock P. M., the Boston Watch and Police, which had lived two hundred and twenty-nine years, ceased to exist, and "The Boston Police Department" became an *Institution*.

The New Department was under the supervision of a Chief of Police, subject to the direction of the Mayor, and consisted of about two hundred and fifty men, with the following divisions: Chief, 2 Deputies, Clerk, Superintendent Hacks, Superintendent Teams, 5 Detectives. Office at City Hall. Station No. 1. Captain, 2 Lieutenants, 33 Patrolmen, House Hanover Street; No. 2, Captain, 2 Lieutenants, 44 Patrolmen, House Court Square; No. 3. Captain, 2 Lieutenants, 23 Patrolmen, House Joy Street;

No. 4. Captain, 2. Lieutenants, 43 Patrolmen, House rear Boylston Market; No. 5. Captain, 2 Lieutenants, 24 Patrolmen, House Canton Street Place; No 6. Captain, 2 Lieutenants, 25 Patrolmen, House Broadway, South Boston; No. 7. Captain, 2 Lieutenants, 19 Patrolmen, House Meridian Street, East Boston; No. 8. Captain, and 10 Boatmen and Patrolmen, House head Sargent's wharf. The territory of the whole city and harbor, were proportionately divided between the stations, and the Captain of each, assisted by his Lieutenants, had the supervision of his district and men, under the direction of the Chief. Each Station consisted of three divisions of patrolmen; one for day, and two for night duty. The day division go out at eight o'clock, A M. and remain till six o'clock P. M., when they were relieved by a night division, and report to their Station House, and are often detailed for extra duty at places of amusement, or elsewhere, in the evening, for which they get extra pay. The night division remain on duty from six P. M., to one next morning, when they are relieved by the other night division, who remain out till eight o'clock, when they in turn are relieved by the day men. The second night, the night division change watches, the last out the night previous, going out first, and the first, last; and so alternately through the year, for the convenience of giving both night divisions a better chance to do *day house* duty, which every night man does once in six days. This regulation gives every man his own beat every day and night, and gives him the opportunity to know his route, and the wants of those on it, better than any other, which is very important to both officer and citizen, and which he cannot know too well if a good man; *if not, he should not be there.* The badge of the old Police for the day, and the hook and rattle for the night, were continued for a time, and the Houses of the old watch were made Station Houses. The salary of the new Chief, Robert Taylor, Esq., was $1,800 per year; Captains, $3,00 per day; Patrolmen, $2.00 per day, or night and other officers in proportion. Every officer to devote his whole time, and have no other employment, although extra pay was allowed for extra work, when done for others than the city.

On the evening of the reorganization, about ten o'clock, the whole force, at a moment's notice, were called to Court Square, to suppress a fearful riot caused by the arrest of a fugitive slave, Anthony Burns, by United States officers, in which one man was killed and others dangerously wounded. The whole department were out nine days and nights, performing a most unpleasant duty under trying circumstances, and, with the solitary exception of one individual, met the highest anticipations of their friends. — *October* 23. The *brass badge* was exchanged for a silver octagon oval plate, little larger than a silver dollar, with a "*five-pointed star*," on which was engraved BOSTON POLICE, and the old watchhook, in use one hundred and fifty-four years, gave place to a fourteen-inch club, the night men retaining the rattle. Such was the condition of the Department when organized in 1854, and, with little variation, it is so in 1865. And although the name is now "The Boston Police Department," yet the night duties are virtually a *watch*, as heretofore, and I shall venture to continue my history under the head of "The Boston Watch and Police."

1855. Jerome Van Crowninshield Smith, Mayor; Robert Taylor, Chief of Police. Police appropriation, $188,000. — *April* 9. The Chief was ordered forthwith to report to the Mayor, " the name, age, *nativity*, residence, time of residence in Boston, and former occupation of each member of the Department, or applicant for office, and to keep a copy of said list in his office." In June, both branches of the City Government joined in forming an ordinance establishing the " Boston Police Department," and thus recognized an organization which, to all intents and purposes, had been in successful operation more than a year. Although at first the Mayor was under the necessity of appointing the Chief of Police Captain of the Watch also, and the captains, constables, a Police Committee, consisting of four Aldermen, was appointed during the year.

1856. Alexander Hamilton Rice, Mayor; and *April* 9, Daniel J. Coburn was appointed Chief of Police, with a salary of $2,200, and horse and chaise. Police appropriation, $198,000. The Police Committee consisted of three Aldermen. At the annual Police appointments, the council have a voice for the only time in the history of the city. An Assistant Clerk appointed this year.

1857. Alexander Hamilton Rice, Mayor. — *March* 30. "*Father*" Hezekiah Earl died, having been an officer twenty-five years, and one of the Deputy Chiefs since 1853. He had the care of the Internal Health Department, and was a good officer and worthy man. — *March* 30. As an act of courtesy, the Board appointed the members of the Common Council Police Officers. The regular force were increased to 266 men. A city prison was fitted up under the Court House for the reception of prisoners, night and morning from the Stations, and a Superintendent appointed. — *October* 18. Policeman Ezekiel W. Hodsdon murdered by two burglars at East Boston while attempting their arrest. Police appropriation, $205,500. A new Station House in East Dedham Street was built for Station No. 5, at a cost of $17,000.

1858. Frederic Walker Lincoln Jr., Mayor.

In *June*, the silver badge was altered, leaving off the star, and cutting numbers through the plate, the number of each officer being recorded at the Chief's Office. — In *August*, the Police Telegraph, connecting each Station (except Station No. 7) with the Chief office, was established. — *November* 1. The new Police uniform was put on, consisting of blue coat, Police buttons, blue pants and black vests, dress coat for Chief and Captains, and frock coat for Deputy and Patrolmen. Police appropriation, $214,000.

1859. Frederic Walker Lincoln, Jr., Mayor. — *February* 28. Sergeants of Police were appointed, two to each Station, except the Harbor Police. Police were detailed from each Station to do fire Police duty, formerly done by constables, and six fire Police suits of rubber were furnished for each Station. — A new Station House for No. 7 was built in Meridian Street, East Boston, at a cost of $16,000, and old Hancock Schoolhouse, in Hanover Street, was enlarged and improved for Station No. 1, costing some $6,000. Police appropriation, $229,700.

1860. Frederic Walker Lincoln, Jr., Mayor. Police Committee three Aldermen, as last year. — The Police were increased to two hundred and ninety-two men. A Captain of Detectives appointed, and a sailboat purchased for the use of the Harbor Police, manned by four men. In consequence of a difficulty with some unruly members of the Police, the Government got the idea that change was required, and each Station was organized into six divisions, each division going out six hours alternately, day and night, abolishing the regular day force; and the arrangement was such that a man went on his own beat but once in two days, this was the principal object aimed at, but the plan worked bad; the Police did not like it, the people did not like it, nor did the Government like it, and the next spring we went back on the old plan. Police appropriation, $228,000.

1861. Joseph Milner Wightman, Mayor. *February* 11. Josiah L. C. Amee, Chief of Police. — *April* 15. President Lincoln issued his proclamation, "That in consequence of the bombardment and capture of Fort Sumter, in the harbor of South Carolina, by a force inimical to the United States Government, *war is inaugurated* between the United States and the seceding States, South Carolina, Georgia, Alabama, Florida, Mississippi, Louisiana, and Texas." This was the opening scene in a tragedy the most fearful since the world began, and one in which Boston took a most active part, opening a new field, requiring vigilance, activity, and deep responsibilities on all her municipal officers, and the Police were at all times held in readiness for any emergency. During the remainder of the year, military processions, parades, receptions, reviews, and other gatherings continually filled the streets, and Police details from ten to one hundred and fifty officers were made on one hundred and thirty-six occasions for these alone. The Harbor Police were also in constant requisition for duty on the water. Deserters from both army and navy were arrested and returned to their places, and recruiting offices guarded. In fact, wherever aid or protection was required, there were the Police to be found. — A Police Tent was provided this year for furnishing refreshments, and also as a place for Police headquarters at large details. A rogue's picture-gallery was also commenced, and about one hundred valuable likenesses collected.

1862. Joseph Milner Wightman, Mayor; Josiah L. C. Amee, Chief of Police. Details for military escort, procession and receptions, continued as last year. The Police force increased to three hundred and seventeen men. — *March* 1. A Police Relief Association established among the members; assessments twenty-five cents per month for each member; benefits in sickness not over $5 per week. It was dissolved early the next year by an almost unanimous vote of the members. — *July* 25. Great war meetings commence to be held on the Common, which continued each day for several weeks. Tents and speakers stands raised. — The Old South Church opened as a recruiting office. — Sunday, *August* 31. News received of the terrible slaughter at second Bull Run Battle. Religious services at church closed and contributions of everything needed for wounded soldiers collected in large quantities, which were packed in cases, and, in charge of State and City Authorities and twenty Policemen, were immediately on their way to Washington. — *December* 22. Corner-stone of New City Hall laid. — A new Station House built in Joy Street for Station No. 3, at a cost of $28,000. The Station removed there from Leverett Street.

1863. Frederic Walker Lincoln, Jr., Mayor. *January* 10. The Old City Hall about to be removed and the City Government go to Mechanics Hall, Chauncy Street. The office of Chief of Police was removed to a place in the basement of the Court House. — *February* 24. General Amee retired from office, and Boston has no Chief of Police. By order of the Mayor, Deputy Chief E. H. Savage had temporary charge of the Department. — *March* 3. Colonel John Kurtz assumed the duties of Chief of Police. — *April* 6. Members of the Police sworn into office, having been appointed during good behavior and usefulness, subject only to removal by the Mayor, the annual appointment ordinance having been abolished, both of which were new features in our history. — *April* 28. The Police Department met at Faneuil Hall, under the Chief, for military drill, which was afterward continued at each Station. — *July* 14. The great

Conscription Riot at North End. — *August* 17. A club two feet long carried in a leather belt around the waist provided for the Police. — Several of the force have enlisted in the military service. — Details for military purposes continued, amounting to one hundred and eighty-seven, with from six to one hundred and eighty officers at each, during the year.

1864. Frederic Walker Lincoln, Jr., Mayor; Colonel John Kurtz, Chief of Police. — No new or important event connected with the Police occurred during the year, although the number of men and the duties have gradually increased. Military regiments were continually arriving and departing, and details, from five to one hundred and eighty men, have been made on over two hundred occasions; and the records show a greater amount of work done in the year, than ever before.

1865. Frederic Walker Lincoln, Jr., Mayor; Colonel John Kurtz, Chief of Police. — *February* 22. News that President Lincoln had signed the Emancipation Bill, was received. One hundred guns fired on the Common, flags displayed, bells rung, and great rejoicing. — *April* 10. The news of the surrender of Lee's Rebel army reaches Boston, and causes tremendous excitement. Cannon are roaring on the Common, flags are thrown out from almost every building, bells are pealing, twenty steam-engines are rushing, screaming through the streets, and people are running crazy with joy. A great portion of the buildings in the city illuminated in the evening. — *April* 15. The great joy of the people turned to the deepest sorrow at the reception of the news that President Lincoln fell by the hand of an assassin, last evening. Business was immediately suspended, and in a few hours, the entire city was draped in mourning. — *June* 1. Funeral in memory of the death of President Lincoln. A larger procession than ever appeared in Boston, passed through the streets, accompanied by the entire Police force; and an oration and other appropriate ceremonies closed the solemn scene.

1866. Frederic Walker Lincoln, Jr., Mayor; John Kurtz, Chief of Police. — *January* 1. The Police force numbers 375 men, rank and file. *January* 11. — Daniel J. Coburn, formerly Chief of Police, died, aged 63 years. — *June* 3. Ex-Mayor Charles Wells died, aged 79 years and 5 months. — *June* 13. Bath-houses established by the city, the Police in charge. — *June* 15. A new code of Police Rules and Regulations provided. — *July* 8. A delegation of Police carry a contribution to the Police of Portland, who were sufferers by the fire in that city July 4th. — *July* 13. A detail of 100 Police on foot, and 12 mounted officers, escort Gen. Sherman into the city. — *September* 4. Workmen break ground in commencing to level Fort Hill. — *September* 13. Reception of Loyal Southerners at Faneuil Hall. — *September* 24. Thirty night-walkers, from Police District No. 3, at court. — *October* 12. School-boys drill on the Common; a detail of 75 Police. — *November* 2. Work commenced on the bridge over the pond on the Public Garden. — *November* 14. Astronomers predicted a shower of meteors this morning. A large number of persons were on the Common to witness the event; the bells were to be rung ten strokes; watchmen were to spring their rattles; but the shower did not come. — *December* 4. Capt. Robert Taylor, of Police Station No. 6, formerly Chief of Police, died.

1867. Otis Norcross, Mayor; John Kurtz, Chief of Police. — *January* 1. The Police force numbers 383 men. — *February* 4. Gen. Josiah L. C. Amee, formerly Chief of Police, died. — *June* 1. Base Ball becoming an institution. Police Officers with ropes and stakes called into requisition on the Common. — *June* 24. Dedication of Masonic Temple, corner of Tremont and Boylston Streets. The procession was 1½ hours passing a given point; estimated 10,000 Masons present. President Andrew Johnson and suite, and many distinguished persons, witnessed the cermonies. A detail of 275 Police on duty. — *July* 4. Police force increased for the day by the appointment of 275 Specials; there were 55 separate Police details for the occasion. — *August* 15. James H. Blake, formerly City Marshal, died. — *September* 9. The citizens of Boston and Roxbury vote to unite the two cities under one Municipal Government. — *September* 12. The Blue Hill Bank, of Dorchester, robbed of $50,000. — *September* 15. Laying of the corner-stone of the Catholic church corner of Washington and Union Park Streets; 100 Police detailed for the occasion. — *October* 7. Grand reception of General Sheridan in Boston. — *November* 2. Funeral of Governor John A. Andrew; 100 Police detailed for the occasion. — *November* 18. Statue of Edward Everett presented to the city. — *November* 23. Francis Tukey, formerly Chief of Police, died in California.

1868. Nathaniel Bradstreet Shurtleff, Mayor; John Kurtz, Chief of Police. — *January* 1. The Police force numbers 347 men. — *February* 7. Soup made and distributed to the poor from the several Police Station Houses for the first time. *April* 2. The Police furnished with a new Silver Badge. — *April* 11. Resolve and order for widening Devonshire Street approved. — *April* 13. Roxbury having been annexed to Boston, the Roxbury Police were reorganized, forming District No. 9, Station House in Old City Hall, Dudley Street. — *April* 15. Policemen commence to canvass the city in aid of the Society for the Prevention of Cruelty to Animals. — *April* 26. Luther A. Ham, formerly Deputy Chief of Police, died. — *May* 30. Posts of the Grand Army of the Republic decorate soldiers' graves, having a Police escort. — *June* 3. Water first played from the Brewer Fountain on the Common. — *June* 6. Resolve and order for widening Tremont Street approved. — *June* 14. Religious meetings begin to be held in Faneuil Hall. — *June* 27. Dedication of the Ether Monument on the Public Garden. — *July* 4. The Police force increased for the day by the appointment of 200 Specials. Among the amusements was a submarine race in the harbor. — *July* 8. Reception of the 22d New York Regiment. — *July* 13. Workmen commence to raise the Church-street territory. — *August* 2. Young Men's Christian Association commence Sunday Services under a tent on the Common. — *August* 20. Reception of Hon. Anson Burlingame and the Chinese Embassy. — *October* 28. Republican torchlight procession. — *October* 29. Democratic torchlight procession. — *November* 20. A bear placed in the enclosure on the Common creates a sensation among the deer; the Police called. — *December* 2. Gen. Grant arrived at St. James Hotel. — *December* 8. Tolls taken off from the Milldam road. — *December* 18. Resolve and order for the laying out of Atlantic Avenue signed. — *December* 31. Resolve and order for widening Hanover Street, between Court and Blackstone, approved.

   1869. Nathaniel Bradstreet Shurtleff, Mayor; John Kurtz, Chief of Police. — *January* 1. The Police force numbers 412 men. — *February* 16.

Velocipede Rinks becoming a popular resort. — *February* 25. Water let into the Roxbury stand pipe. — *March* 1. The Old Bite Tavern closed as a public house. — *April* 7. Ceremonies in closing the Bromfield House as a public house. — *April* 26. Odd Fellows' Celebration: a large procession. — *May* 22. Old Concert Hall ceases to be a place of entertainment. — *May* 26. May training; artillery firing by electricity; 100 Police on duty for the occasion. — *May* 29. Decoration Day. — *June* 15. The National Peace Jubilee commences on Back Bay grounds; 300 Police detailed for the five days. — *June* 16. Military review of Gen. Butler's Brigade by President Grant, on Tremont Street, South End, and on the Common. — *June* 19. Peace Jubilee closed. The 300 Police who had been on that duty were reviewed and addressed by Mayor Shurtleff in School Street. — *June* 22. The citizens of Boston and Dorchester vote to annex. — *July* 3. Equestrian Statue of Washington on the Public Garden dedicated. — *July* 5. The National Anniversary celebrated with usual ceremonies, the Police force increased by 300 Specials for the day. — *August* 2. The territory of Roxbury, divided by Washington Street and Shawmut Avenue, making two Police Districts, the east part forming No. 9 and the west part No. 10. Station House No. 10, corner of Washington and Tremont Streets, first occupied. — *August* 6. A license granted for a haunted house in Springfield Street; but it was soon revoked. — *August* 21. Workmen commence moving back Hotel Pelham to widen Tremont Street, corner of Boylston Street. — *September* 8. A terrible hurricane blew down the Coliseum building and several other buildings in the city, tore up trees on the Common and elsewhere; a Mr. Clark was also killed by a plank blown from the sidewalk in St. James Avenue. — *September* 15. Commencement of the Mechanics' Fair at Faneuil Hall. — *September* 17. 100 Police detailed on the occasion of the Firemen's Parade. A detail of Police organized for duty at street corners in the central part of the city, numbering 14 men, headquarters in the basement of the Court House. — *September* 26. A Festival of Irish citizens, numbering 30,000 persons, held at the Coliseum, 300 police in attendance. — *October* 12. Italian citizens celebrate the anniversary of the landing of Columbus in America. — *October* 15. Resolve and order for widening Hanover Street, between Blackstone and Commercial Streets, approved. — *October* 22. Slight shock of an earthquake at half-past five o'clock in the morning. — *October* 23. Coliseum Lottery drawn: 100,000 tickets, 5,200 prizes. — *November* 20. Boylston Bank robbed of about $300,000. — *December* 7. Great fire on Commercial Wharf; flour mills burned.

1870. Nathaniel Bradstreet Shurtleff, Mayor; John Kurtz, Chief of Police. — *January* 1.

The Police force numbers 443 men. Mystic water introduced into East Boston. — *February* 5. His Royal Highness Patrick William Arthur arrived at the St. James Hotel. — *February* 8. Boston church bells toll, and flags are at half-staff, in consequence of the funeral of Mr Peabody. — *February* 9. The first grand ball of the Boston Police Department at Faneuil Hall, to raise funds for the benefit of disabled officers. — *February* 14. The Board of Aldermen abolish the Detective Police system. — *February* 19. Col. John Kurtz, having been Chief of Police 7 years, resigned, and retired from office. — *April* 4. Edward H. Savage appointed Chief of Police. — *April* 8. A deep sensation caused by the kidnapping of little Nellie Burns. — *April* 11. Captain James Quinn appointed Deputy Chief of Police. — *April* 21. The remains of Hon. Anson Burlingame arrive in Boston, and lie in state at Faneuil Hall. — A show up of rogues commenced at the office of the Chief of Police. The old system of dealing with this class of persons changed for a trial of the experiment — attempting to keep thieves *out* of Boston to prevent them from stealing *in* it. — *May* 7. The Police arrested 183 night-walkers, most of whom were subsequently sent to their friends out of the city. — *May* 25. A great military display on the Common; 150 Police in attendance. — *June* 1. The Dorchester Police reorganized, forming District No. 11; Station

House on Hancock Street, Ward 16. — *June* 2. The Police on street corners becomes a part of Division No. 2. Capt. Asa Morrill, of Police District No. 3, died. — *June* 10. A gallery of rogues' photographs commenced at the Central Police Office. — *June* 25. The School Regiment drilled on the Common; 150 Policemen keep the lines about the parade grounds. — *July* 4. The usual celebration; 200 Special Police appointed for the occasion. — *July* 13. Order to contract for raising the Suffolk-street District signed by the Mayor. — *July* 25. Great fire on Border Street, East Boston. — *September* 17. Firemen's Parade; 240 police detailed for the occasion. — *October* 1. Policemen put on the new *Boston Police Badge and Buttons.* — *October* 16. The corner-stone of the Catholic Children's Home on Harrison Avenue laid; 150 Police on duty for the occasion. — *October* 20. A slight shock of an earthquake occurred at half-past eleven o'clock A. M. — *October* 25. Water let into the lower basin at the Chestnut Hill Reservoir. — *November* 4. Resolve and order for the removal of Scollay's building signed. — *November* 24. The Police collected and distributed $1,109.60 among poor persons who were overlooked by others. — *December.* 26. The new Police Telegraph, connecting the several Police Stations with the central office, completed. — *December* 30. The resolve and order for erecting a soldiers' and sailors' monument on the Common approved.

1871. William Gaston, Mayor; Edward H. Savage, Chief of Police. — *January* 1. The Police force numbers 500 men. — *January* 13. Police Relief Association organized. — *January* 14. In consequence of the scarcity and unnecessary waste of water, the whole of the Police force appointed Water Inspectors. — *February* 2. Annual Police Ball at Music Hall. — *April* 16. Policemen at East Boston break up a prize-fight at Breed's Island. — *May* 1. The licensing of dogs transferred from the City Clerk to the Chief of Police. — *May* 12. Great meeting of the Grand Army of the Republic. — *May* 18. The removal of Scollay's building completed. — *May* 30. Decoration Day. — *May* 31. Training day called for a detail of 100 Police on the Common. — *June* 5. Little Raven and five other Kansas Indians visit City Hall. — *June* 13. The laying of the corner-stone of Odd Fellows' Hall, corner of Tremont and Berkeley Streets, called out a detail of 330 Police. — *June* 17. Reception of the New York 9th Regiment, commanded by Col. James Fisk, Jr.; a detail of 100 Police. — *June* 18. (Sunday.) Col. Fisk's regiment holds *Religious Services* on Boston Common. — *June* 23. The School Regiment drilled on the Common; 100 Police on duty. — *July* 4. Usual celebration. Police force increased for the day by the appointment of 250 Specials. — *July* 20. Slight shock of an earthquake at 12.55 o'clock in the morning. — *August* 26. A terrible accident occurred at Revere by a collision of steam cars; 32 persons killed, and many others injured. Police sent to the scene, and the wounded removed from the Eastern Depot to the Hospitals. — *September* 18. The corner-stone of the Soldiers' Monument laid on the Common; a great gathering, both of the military and civilians; 300 Police detailed for the duty. — *October* 4. The drought made it necessary to pump water from Lake Cochituate for the Reservoir. — *October* 14. Deputy Chief Quinn went to Chicago to carry contributions from the Boston Police to the Chicago Police, who suffered by the great fire. — *October* 16. The corner-stone of the new Post-Office on Milk, Devonshire, and Water Streets, laid in presence of President Grant, many distinguished persons, and a great concourse of people; 300 Police detailed for the occasion. — *October* 24. Deep sensation caused by the murder of Kate Leehan on Brookline Avenue. — *November* 29. — Thanksgiving Day. The Police collected and distributed to the poor about one thousand dollars. — *December* 7. The Grand Duke Alexis of Russia arrived in Boston.

1872. William Gaston, Mayor; Edward H. Savage, Chief of Police. — *January* 1. The Police force numbers 468 men. — *January* 25. The Third Annual Assembly of the Police Department at Music Hall. — *May* 30. Decoration Day. —

June 3. Detail of 100 Police for Artillery Election. — *June* 17. Commencement of the World's Musical Festival. The regular Police force had been increased to 532 men, with the addition of 250 Specials appointed for the occasion. At 8 o'clock A. M. the whole regular force was marshalled in Pemberton Square and marched to the Coliseum grounds, where 250 men were drawn out for duty for the twenty days' ceremonies, the remainder returning to their respective Stations, with the aid of the Specials to cover the beats throughout the city. The attendance at the Festival was said to be from 30,000 to 70,000 people daily, many days numbering nearly or quite 100,000 persons crowded together in the streets; yet during that exciting, protracted period there were no burglaries, no store robberies, few street larcenies, very few accidents, and no disturbance of the peace. — *June* 26. Grand Festival Ball; President Grant and 50,000 people present. — *July* 4. The combined attractions of the *Holiday* and the *Festival*, with the thermometer at 100 degrees, caused a serious test of the efficiency and power of endurance of the Boston Police. Ex-Mayor John P. Bigelow died, aged nearly 75 years.—*July* 7. The closing concert of the World's Musical Festival. — *July* 22. Vessels running quarantine taken back by the Police. — *August* 25. Irish citizens' concert at the Coliseum. — *September* 5. Colored citizens' convention at Faneuil Hall. — *September* 17.

Firemen's Parade; 100 Police detailed for the occasion. — *September* 22. "Father Burke" lectured at the Coliseum; 30,000 people; 100 Police. — *September* 25. The prevalence of the small-pox begins to create an alarm. — *October* 11. Great torchlight procession; detail of 50 Police. — *October* 13. Mr. Charles Lane, living on Hancock Street, Ward 16, was shot and killed in his own doorway by some unknown assassin. — *October* 25. Mr. Gilmore's Ball at the Coliseum. — *October* 26. The horse disease commenced in Boston, making it necessary to propel fire engines, horse cars, and other vehicles through the streets with human muscle. — *October* 30. A great torchlight procession. — *November* 6. The body of Abijah Ellis, cut up and packed in two barrels, was found floating in Charles River. — *November* 9. At 7.15 P. M. the Great Fire broke out at the corner of Summer and Kingston Streets, which swept off nearly all the buildings between Summer, Washington, Milk and Broad Streets, destroying nearly $100,-000,000 of property and many lives. Firemen were called from other cities; buildings were blown up to stop the progress of the flames; the military were called out for a Police relief; the gas was shut off, leaving the city in darkness two nights; and Boston presented a scene never to be forgotten. — *November* 10. Post-Office moved to Faneuil Hall. — *December* 26. The small-pox hospital at Pine Island destroyed by fire.

1873. Henry Lillie Pierce, Mayor; Edward H. Savage, Chief of Police. — *January* 1. The Police force numbers 520 men. — *January* 14. Mayor Pierce nominates, and the City Council confirm, a Board of Health of three men. — *January* 15. The Board of Health established a small-pox hospital at the old almshouse in Roxbury. — *February* 2. Post-Office opened in the Old South Meeting-house, the building having been obtained for two years. — *February* 9. Public Library first opened on Sunday. — *February* 20. Fourth annual Police Ball at the Music Hall. — *February* 27. Serious fire and loss of life at the corner of Blackstone and Hanover Streets. — *March* 6. Louis Wagner, charged with murder at the Isle of Shoals, arrested in North Street by the Boston Police. — *March* 17. A show up of burglars and burglars' tools at the Central Police Office. — *March* 21. James McElhanney hanged in Charles-street jail for the murder of his wife. — *April* 5. 420 passengers from the wrecked steamer Atlantic arrive at Faneuil Hall, *en route* for New York. — *May* 1. The Police force increased to 575 men. — *May* 11. Barnum's great ten days' show commenced at the Coliseum grounds. — *May* 12. An independent line of telegraph wire, connecting each Station House separately to the Central Police Office, completed. — *May* 13. The system of a mounted patrol inaugurated by placing one mounted Police Officer on the Milldam road. — *May* 30. Decoration Day. At 8.40 o'clock A. M., a fire broke out on Washington, near Essex Street, destroying nearly $200,000 worth of property, calling for the aid of firemen out of the city, and the services of 400 Police. — *June* 23. School Regiment drilled on the Common; detail of 80 Police. — *June* 29. Amended Police Rules and Regulations furnished for the Department. — *July* 4. — For the first time in many years, Boston had no fireworks, no balloon ascension, and no Special Police for the day; but with ample arrangements made for the occasion, and the city as full as usual of people to enjoy them. As the City Government had prudently and wisely designed, the national anniversary was celebrated in a quiet and rational manner.

RECOLLECTIONS

OF A

BOSTON POLICE OFFICER.

DESTRUCTION OF THE BEEHIVE.

As I was passing over my District one morning, I came up to where two old gentlemen were standing engaged in earnest conversation, their attention apparently attracted to some object over the way.

As I was about to pass them unnoticed, I said, " Good morning, gentlemen ; happy to meet you in your morning walk."

" That you, *Geevus*," said one of them, turning ; and scanning me from head to foot. " Well, sir, the likes of you, with your long blue coat and bright B. P. Big Poker buttons would have been a rare sight in those days."

" What days do you refer to ? " said I.

" Why, the days of the olden time ; days of the *Tinpot* and the *Beehive*," said he ; " days when citizens sometimes found it necessary to take the execution of the laws into their own hands, and pretty summary work they made of it too."

"Well, sir," said I, "what about the Beehive?"

(Shifting his cane from one hand to the other, and dropping a big quid of the weed into the empty hand and deliberately throwing his *old soldier* upon the pavement.)

"Do you know," said he, "that the street where we now stand was once called *Black Horse Lane?*" It was called so, from the Black Horse Tavern, that once stood down there by the corner, where you see the figure with a big nose standing over the apothecary's door. The tavern had the figure of a black horse for a sign; it was long before my remembrance, but when I was a boy an old darkie who lived over by the water-mill used to tell me much about it. He called it *Blackus Inn*, but that was old Ebony's abbreviation. This Inn was once noted as a place of refuge for soldiers who deserted from Burgoyne's army as it was about leaving Winter Hill, near the close of the Revolution. There was another tavern, with a like sign, up in Back Street afterwards, and one up at old No. 17 Union Street, not many years since, but this was the original one. In early times, the *North End* was the "*court end*" of the town, and it was proverbial for its numerous places of entertainment. Ann Street was then *Fore Street*, and Hanover was *Middle Street*, and Salem Street from the mill bridge to the corner down here was *Back Street*, and from Prince Street up by Christ's Church and the old Governor Phipps estate to Charter Street was called *Green Lane*.

"Since my remembrance, the millpond extended from North Margin to South Margin streets, and from the causeway to Haymarket Square. Canal boats passed through where Blackstone Street now lies, at high water coming out into the Bay near where the foot of Quincy Market now stands, and there were bridges across the canal at Hanover and at Ann streets, and there was a water mill a little north of Hanover and Blackstone streets, and another near the foot of Endicott Street. Black Horse Lane was afterwards widened and called Princess Street, in honor of some *female woman* of the English Royal family. Boston men were loyal men until the mother country by continued acts of oppression drove them to madness and desperation."

"That is very true," said I; "but tell us about the Beehive."

"O, yes," said he; "I had forgotten. Well, sir, do you see that narrow three-story house just over the way there? it was once painted lead color; it is now No. 60, I believe. Well, on that ground stood the *Beehive*."

"Why was that name given it?" said I.

"Well, I will tell you," said he; "you see it was then a two-story wooden dwelling with a sharp roof, the end to the street; had little windows, and externally it looked very much like a beehive, and then it was chuck full of cosey little cells, and old marm Cooper was the queen bee. She had two pretty daughters, and plenty of boarders of the female persuasion, and the popping in and out at the hive on an evening would remind you of the genuine article on a June day. Do you think the place rightly named? Well, the hive finally became so notorious and so noisy that respectable people would put up with it no longer, and so one night the truckmen, — yes, sir, the *truckmen*, them were the fellows when any game was on foot in those days. Well, they might not all have been truckmen, perhaps a sprinkling of mechanics and laborers, and now and then a *sailor boy*, just home from sea," said he, giving his companion a severe punch in the side with his elbow. ' *Humph!*' said the other giving a pull at the hip of his pantaloons.

"Well," continued the speaker, "just as we were knocking off work word came — let me see — yes, it was on the 22d day of July, 1825, about nine o'clock in the evening, there came down from Hanover Street way, about two hundred of the most comical-looking fellows that you ever laid eyes on. They had pitchforks, and poles, and bars, and axes, and conch shells, and gourd shells, and tin horns, and tin pans, and were dressed in all kinds of costume, and their faces were blacker than the bottom of a tar kettle. Well, just as they arrived at the beehive, the band struck up — such music — and the work began, and such work, — why sir, you could not hear yourself think, and in less than ten minutes there was not a piece of door or window or furniture left of the beehive so large as a *Truck Pin*, and such a stampede by the inmates of the *hive*. Don't you remember," said he, (turning to his friend and lowering his voice,) "don't you remember seeing old marm Cooper scudding through School alley under full sail at a rate that would have done credit to a privateersman?"

"*Exactly*," said his friend, (at the same time giving an unlucky cur who was passing a most ungenerous punch with his cane that sent him yelping down street.)

"Well," continued the old gentleman, turning to me again, "you see the wind was fresh northwest, and some dozen feather beds had been turned inside out from the windows, and the atmosphere was about as full of feathers as you ever see it of snow-flakes in a squall. To add to the scene, some one had got up a prodigious smoke by burning brimstone, feathers, and wool rags. I tell you, sir, it was a scene for a lifetime. Why, you would have thought all the feathered imps from the regions of darkness had shed their coats on this devoted ground, and were escaping with their dear lives to every lane, passage, and gateway in the neighborhood (after a pause); and so the swarm was taken up," said he.

"But where were the police all this time?" said I.

"Police," said he, "did n't I just tell you that the likes of you would have been a rarity in those days, and did n't I tell you that the citizens sometimes were obliged to take the laws into their own hands? Pity the practice has gone quite out of use. Don't you think, sir, that JUSTICE, who is seated in the big County House up town, sometimes gets a little dirt in his eye?"

"But where were the city authorities?" said I.

"City authorities," said he; "why, Boston had been a city but a short time then, and if they knew anything at all about the matter, they took good care not to come there till the trouble was all over; and beside, them truckmen done up that job about as quick as you could say Jack Robinson, and then they were off."

"Well," said I, "it must have been quick work and a comical sight indeed. But (and looking at him a little slyly), who do you suppose were the truckmen engaged in this *riot?*"

"*Riot — none of your business, you young saucebox,*" said he; and taking a fresh quid the two walked leisurely up the street, leaving me to resume my duties.

GABRIEL AND HIS HORN.

Among the many exciting events that marked the progress of the year 1854 in Boston, was the advent of Gabriel and his horn. I do not mean him of olden time, spoken of on the sacred page, but a poor, illiterate, half-breed Scotchman, with more impudence than brains, who with a three-cornered hat and cockade on his head, and an old brass horn in his bosom, took advantage of the political excitement then existing, and travelled about the city and suburbs from place to place tooting his horn, collecting crowds in the streets, delivering what he called Political Lectures, and passing round the hat for contributions.

His lectures generally consisted of a repetition of a few ill-chosen words, interspersed with some unmeaning slang, relative to some European institutions that no one ever read of, and the abuse of some sport-loving youngster who had pelted him with rotten eggs at a former lecture.

But the horn — Gabriel's horn was the great centre of attraction, and appeared to occupy as prominent a place in the hearts of his admirers, as did that which adorned the altar in King Solomon's Temple. Without that horn Gabriel would have been powerless, but with it he seemed to possess the power of a Socrates, and indeed the notes from that horn were the best arguments I ever heard him advance.

So potent was its fame, that even a sound from a conch shell made by some roguish boy, was often mistaken for the genuine article, and would fill the streets with a gaping multitude in a few moments.

Gabriel usually closed his harangue by notifying his audience of the time and place of his next lecture, which saved advertising, and when the time arrived another stampede would occur. Wherever these lectures were holden, it became necessary to detail a large force of police to preserve the peace, and rough times we often had of it. Indeed, it really seemed that everybody was bent on a row, and perfectly infatuated with humbug.

I well recollect one of these Gabriel incidents that occurred on Sunday afternoon, December 17, of this year.

Gabriel was to lecture at Chelsea, and for once he had gone down Hanover Street quietly and unnoticed; but on arriving at the ferry, as he stepped on board the boat, he must blow his horn. This was a signal for a crowd, and it was soon there, but Gabriel had gone, and no one seemed to know whither. Many of the boys collected, were deeply impressed *with the spirit* of the times, and a disturbance commencing, the police were under the necessity of making several arrests, and took one man to the Station House. They succeeded in reaching the house with the man, but the crowd supposing Gabriel had been arrested, were very indignant, and followed up, surrounded the house, and began to threaten, and call for Gabriel, in no very pacific or flattering terms.

After the prisoner had been locked up, I went out upon the steps and waved my hand to be heard, which was granted.

I then told the crowd that only an intoxicated man had been arrested, he would be kindly treated and probably discharged when sober. That Gabriel had gone to Chelsea to deliver a lecture agreeably to appointment made by him in Union Street, last Sunday, as many who now heard me would well recollect; that they would now find him speaking in his winning strains on Hospital Hill — God bless him!

This turned the tide of affairs, and the crowd began to cry out, "That's so!" "All right, old boy!" "Give us a speech yourself, Cápt'n!" Hurrah for Station One!" "Hurrah for Gabriel!" "Hurrah for the horn!" "All hands to Hospital Hill!" and a general stampede for Chelsea Ferry closed the exhibition.

I wished, from the bottom of my heart, that Gabriel, his horn, and all his followers were with the host of Pharaoh in the bottom of the Red Sea; but recollecting that the truth is not to be spoken at all times, I held my peace.

Gabriel finally became such a travelling nuisance, that the more sober portion of the people (if there were any at that time,) began to be ashamed to be seen following in his wake, and the sport for others becoming stale, his collections would not pay his lodging bills, and he left his field of labor, in disgust, for the more sunny clime of Saint Domingo.

He was not there long, however, before he was arrested as a general disturber of the peace, and sentenced to the penitentiary for three years, and died in prison soon after.

GUESSWORK.

A PORTLY, intelligent-looking man came into the Office one morning and inquired for the Captain. I said I was that celebrated individual, and inquired what could be done for him. He leaned over the railing that separated us, and stood twirling a business card between his thumb and finger for some time, apparently in a brown study. "Well," said he, finally, straightening up, "I came in to see you on a little matter of business, but on reflection, I *recon* I wont trouble you with it now," and he turned to go away. I had been watching him closely in his revery, which I saw he noticed, and it seemed to strengthen his resolution in not doing his errand. He seemed to feel that his appearance indicated a recent debauch, which he did not care to have noticed. As he was about leaving I said, "Look here, stranger, are you a *Western* man? He turned and looked me square in the face a moment, and replied, "Well, I *recon* I am. But why do you ask that?"

"Nothing in particular," said I, "only your appearance indicates that. And not only so, there is something on your mind that perplexes you somewhat; and if so, I should be most happy to render you some service."

After looking at me a moment, he walked back, came inside the railing, and took a seat by my side.

"Well, sir," said he, quite frankly, "I take you to be a *Yankee*, and I am told the Yankees are some on guessing. Now what have you to say in my case?"

"Sir," said I, we are no fortune-tellers here, only policemen; but as to the matter of Yankee guessing, as you call it, I am willing to try in your case, if you desire it, on one condition, — that you tell me when I guess *wrong*."

"Very well," said he, "go ahead."

I reached and took his hand and looked it over carefully, — and a "huge paw" it was.

"Well," said I, after considering a while, "*I guess* you have done some hard work in your day, — some farming, — lumbering some. That is an honest-looking hand, and I doubt not it is a true representative of the heart. And you have not been confined to farming and lumbering altogether; you could make a good stump speech, or draft a set of resolutions, if necessity required."

I stole a glance at his face and saw that he was quite satisfied thus far, and ready for more.

"Well, I guess you have a very pretty, blue-eyed wife, far away in a new country, near a wide, smooth stream, with four, perhaps five, little responsibilities."

"Stop," said he, with some earnestness, and pulling away his hand, "do you know me, sir?"

"Never heard of you in my life," said I; "you was to tell me if I guessed wrong."

"Well, go ahead," said he, settling back in his chair.

After quizzing him in the face awhile, "I *guess*," said I, " that you are little acquainted in Boston, are here on business, have been a little incautious, fell in with some jolly companions, took a drop, perhaps, that altogether, quite overcame you. I think, also you may have lost money, perhaps gold, large pieces I think, and I think you have lost some kind of a bundle."

At this, he sprang from his chair like a wild man.

"Good God, sir!" said he, "I will stand this no longer. Do you know me, sir, — do you know my name and business? How came you by all this knowledge, sir?"

"Knowledge," said I, quite innocently, "I have no knowledge of you, certainly. You set me to *guessing*, and I have only done according to the best of my ability. You have only to tell me when I *guess wrong*. Don't be offended; just come back and sit down, and see if you can *tell it* any better yourself; and if your case comes in my line, I shall be most happy to aid you."

"Well," said he, "I don't know who the deuce you are, nor exactly what is in *your line*, whether policeman or fortune-teller; but your proceedings with me seem very much like the latter, and pretty well posted at that. Now, sir, please just tell me how you came in possession of all these facts."

"*Facts*," said I; "then you say I have been telling you *facts*, do you? Well, I only called it guesswork. But you know better than I, and we wont dispute the point. But you come and sit down here and tell me your case, — I want something more tangible than guesswork, — and let us see what can be done."

"I might as well," said he, "although you appear to know nearly as much about it now as I do. At any rate, you guess well; and if you can guess me out of this scrape as well as you have guessed me into it, I shall be forever obliged to you."

He then told me his story.

He was a resident of Minnesota; owned a large tract of timber land on one of the rivers where the country was too level for mill privileges by water power, and he had set up several steam mills, which were a source of great profit. He came to Boston to purchase machinery for another mill; had closed his business, and was to leave by the half past five o'clock train for the West. He had an hour to spare, — took a stroll about town, — brought up in North Street, — went into a place to take a drink, — a young chap asked him to treat, — he drank once, again; after which he forgot what happened. This morning he found himself alone in a strange garret. He examined the room carefully, and found no one. His clothes were left, but the pockets were empty. He made his way out as best he could, and found his way to the Station House. He had lost all his money, consisting of seven twenty-dollar gold-pieces, and a bundle containing a valuable steam gauge. He had seen the elephant, (rather too close a view, he thought,) was many hundred miles from home, among strangers, and without a dollar in his pocket.

After getting all the information he could give me, I sent him into a saloon to get some breakfast, and set *the boys* to work. The officers soon learned that the chap who had done the *shake* had left for New Bedford. A telegraph dispatch got there first: the chap was arrested on his arrival at New Bedford, and an officer followed in the next train and brought him back with one hundred and twenty dollars of the money. He was taken before the court, and sentenced to two years' service in the House of Correction; and with what money was recovered and the steam gauge, the stranger took his leave for his home in the West, a wiser, if not a better man.

After arriving home, he wrote me a polite note, thanking me for what was done for him, and took occasion to say that if my guessing propensities were as accurate in relation to how he felt as they were on what he *lost*, I would surely sympathize with him in his folly; but he was all right now, and he had seen enough of Yankeedom to *guess* that he would be in no hurry to again look up the Boston elephant.

Should any curiosity arise relative to the *guess-work*, let me frankly say that I make no pretence to supernatural knowledge myself, nor believe it in the possession of others, and shall not attempt to throw any mystery about the affair.

My guessing was very simple when explained, as most mysteries are.

Early that morning an officer had brought in the steam gauge from a rum hole in North Street, which the keeper said was left by a countryman who came into his place the previous evening. He had any quantity of twenty-dollar gold-pieces, treated generously, and finally went off with a chap of the town well known to the officers. The steam gauge had the maker's name on it, — a well-known firm in the city. We knew, of course, that the man would lose his money in such hands, and as soon as the store of the firm was open, I repaired there to learn what I could of the owner of the gauge; and from one of the firm I learned the man's name, residence, business, and much more that I did not put into the guesswork. While he was leaning over the rail twirling the card between his thumb and finger, I saw it was the card of that same steam-gauge company, and with the description I had from one of the firm, I was sure of my man.

That man learned the science of *shaking*, but in all probability, *Yankee guessing* to him is still a mystery.

RECOLLECTIONS OF COUNTRYMEN.

As a general rule, the administration of justice is best accomplished when each branch of the Executive confines itself to its own legitimate duties. The Boston Police are appointed for the special purpose of preserving the peace of the city, executing its ordinances, and also the *criminal laws* of the Commonwealth within their jurisdiction; and to guard against their interference in civil matters, and keep them in their proper sphere, it became necessary to prescribe their duties by the Statutes, giving them "*the power, of constables in criminal cases only,*" and also by the ordinance, "*They shall not render assistance in civil cases.*" Yet, notwithstanding these special provisions in both the *statute* and the *ordinance*, but very few of even our own citizens seem to be aware of the fact. The consequence is, demands are made daily for the members of the Police to do all kinds of work, much of which they are not permitted to do by the rules of the Department, and not unfrequently that which no man can do lawfully.

The fact that the services of the Police are paid for by the city, no doubt adds to the number of demands.

An officer is fortunate enough to catch a burglar, and carries him before the Police Court. He is bound over for trial. For the sum of twenty-five dollars paid by the burglar's friends, Mr. *Brown* bails the rogue in the sum of five hundred dollars, takes him out of the hands of the officers of the law, and turns him loose to again prey upon the community. When the case comes up for trial, the rogue is not in court, and he and his bail are defaulted. If justice is done, Mr. Brown gets sued for the amount of bail. This sometimes happens. And Mr. Brown, if his bail happens not to be straw, immediately hunts up the officer who was smart enough to catch the rogue at first, and orders him to New York or Nova Scotia, after his *protégé;* and if told by the officer that he has no power in the matter, he flies in a passion and uses his influence to get the officer discharged. Another has a tenant who don't pay rent. The landlord forthwith repairs to the Station House and demands an officer to proceed without *precept* or *judgment* to put the family out at once. If told that it would be a gross violation of law for any officer, and that the police were not qualified to serve a *precept* in such cases if he had

11*

one, the officer is strongly reminded that an appointing day is soon coming that will fill the ranks of the police with men that will do their duty.

Instances of the like nature are of very frequent occurrence; but they are quite bearable in comparison with some others that sometimes occur with our own citizens. The first are excusable, because those making such demands, perhaps, have not the opportunity of knowing all the rules of law; but when members of the legal profession, and those officers whose duties are not restricted to criminal matters, make demands even more at variance with law and common sense, an excuse is not so easily found. I have been ordered by a constable to go into a store and remove a large amount of groceries on which he had made an attachment; and I once underwent a most searching examination by a "*limb of the law*" before the Police Committee because I refused to remove a constable's keeper from a store of the lawyer's client.

Yet those cases, too, are sufferable when we recollect that we are well paid for being abused, and partly by the very men who abuse us.

But the most annoying and provoking demands made on the Police, are from persons who do not belong to the city, often requiring the most unreasonable duties, and in a manner that would indicate the belief that the Police were a horde of slaves, kept for their own particular benefit. I do not mean to say that this is the general rule of all countrymen, but I do say that such cases often happen.

Officers are sometimes sent for to go many miles out of town to perform some service which no man can lawfully do, with the apparent expectation that he will go and "*find himself.*" I have been called from my bed at the dead hour of night by a countryman, *apparently sober*, to go and hunt up his worthless dog, who perhaps, disgusted with his master's peregrinations and company, had either left for home or followed off some other night wanderer by mistake. And I have known a countryman hang round the Police Office for hours, importuning for an officer to go to a bar-room, and demand for him a return of three cents, the bar-keeper having taken six cents for a drink of raw gin, the countryman declaring it should be but three. "Not that he cared for the three cents,—no, not he; but it was the *principle* of the thing, and it was the duty of the Police to see him righted."

The meanest man I ever did a job for was him for whom I recovered a stolen team. The team consisted of a fine horse, buggy, harness, robe, whip, halter, and foot-mat, all worth at least five hundred dollars, which was stolen in a country town and brought to the city. Before hearing of the theft, I had secured the buggy as it was being put aboard the Bangor steamer, believing it to be stolen; afterwards the horse, harness, and other property was all recovered,—all but the mat, valued probably at fifty cents, which I was not lucky enough to get. I had laid out upon the wharf two whole nights, after doing duty on the day, and before I could reach all the property was obliged to pay something over seven dollars from my own pocket for assistance. The thief was convicted and sentenced to State's Prison, and the property safely delivered to the owner,—all but the mat. I thought he would refund me the money I had paid out to recover his property,—I expected nothing more; but *this* he would not do, and finally told me, in so many words, that "if you had done your duty, I should have my mat also."

My recollections of that countryman are quite fresh, although it is now twelve years since the circumstance occurred. He keeps a livery stable yet, not many miles from Boston. I will not call his name, for I do not write to gratify personal feeling; but I do think if that soul ever gets into heaven, it will be because it is so small it can creep in unobserved.

As a slight illustration of country opinion of police duties in Boston, and of the progress of the schoolmaster, I give the following true copy of a letter which was received at the office of Chief of Police, except the name of the party and his place of residence.

BUNKUMVILLE, JUNE 9, 1862.

"*To the Cheafe of Polease*" : —

"Ie sende this dispache toe you toe Areste A yunge man bye the name of Nathan Stokes of this place. hea is A yunge man aboute 20 yers old an had a blacke frocke Cote an Cloth cap. hea is a Sayler bye perfesion ande George Stokes is his unkle an you ken in quier of him. an if you doe ketch im cape im til Ie ken get a permit toe tack im her for tryal your in hast. please Sende as Sone as you ken an Cape im til you her from mea."

JONATHAN JENKINS

FIGHT WITH JOHN WELCH.

WHILE on patrol duty in the summer of 1854, I was passing down Hanover Street early one evening, and when near Hanover Avenue I was met by some apparently living thing, for my life I could hardly tell what; but on removing a piece of old bedquilt, I there found the head of a Mrs. Welch among the tattered remnants of her clothing, what little she had, all of which was completely saturated with blood. A more pitiful object my eyes never saw, and the poor creature was more dead than alive. Knowing the habits of the family, I comprehended the state of affairs at once. She had again been most cruelly beaten by her brute of a husband *John*, who had already served two terms in the House of Correction for the same offence.

She said she had barely escaped with her life, and begged me to run to the house just down the avenue, for John was beating the children, two interesting little girls, who had often suffered at

JOHN WELCH.

the hands of a cruel father while begging of him not to kill their mother.

The house being but a few steps off, I was soon at the door; but all was still there. Welch lived on the second floor, over a colored family, and I immediately groped my way, in the dark, up the winding stairway to Welch's room. I had been there before under similar circumstances, thus far. On entering the room, which was dimly lighted by an old oil lamp, I cast my eyes over the apartment. The only furniture consisted of an apology for a bed, an old table, and two or three broken chairs, and some old torn garments scattered about the floor; but no one seemed to be present. On approaching the bed, however, I there discovered the veritable John himself, but apparently sound asleep. On speaking to him he roused up, and wanted to know what I wanted. I said, to see him, and asked him to get up. He got out and sat upon the side of the bed, having on his usual clothing except his shoes, but pretended to be entirely unaware that any difficulty had occurred. I asked him what caused the appearance of the room, and where his wife was. He said it was none of my d—nd business; that he was in his own house, and if I valued my life much, I had better leave soon.

Welch was a powerful man, in the prime of life, and weighing nearly two hundred pounds, and not so drunk as I had expected to find him. I had measured strength with him before, and although he was much stronger than myself, I could move much quicker than he, and I did not fear him, although I had been told that he had said he would never be again arrested by me alive. I did not doubt but a calm, decided course would subdue him.

I finally told him calmly that I was sorry he had been having trouble again; that his wife was out in the street badly hurt, and I wanted him to put on his shoes and go out with me and see to her. He finally said he supposed he might as well go, and asked me to reach him his shoes, just under the foot of the bed, near where I was standing. I stooped down for the shoes, not taking my eye off him, when, as quick as thought, he drew from beneath the head of the bed a round stick of wood about four feet long and perhaps an inch and a half in diameter, and sprang at me with the fury of a madman. I straightened up, and jumped backwards just in time to be beyond the reach of a blow that would have split my head from crown to shoulder, the sharp end of his club coming down in front of me, and near enough to tear open my vest. The second blow, with a " G—d d—mn you," quickly followed, my back now being so near the side of the room that I was obliged to jump sideways; but he was too near, and I caught the blow slantingly on my left arm. It took clothing, hide and all. Before he had time to recover for the third blow, my club, which I drew from a pocket under my left arm with my right hand, *met his head*, and he fell senseless to the floor. For a moment I was relieved; but the next came the fearful thought, "*I have killed him!*" I had struck him with a heavy lignum-vitæ billy, with all my power. I had hit him on the head; the blow must have broken his skull. I had only acted in self-defence; his next blow would have laid me lifeless at his feet. He had missed his aim, and I, to save myself, had killed him. But I had killed a man in that ill-lighted chamber, and no mortal eye was there to witness my extremity. My God! I would have given worlds to have exchanged places with him that moment. My club dropped from my hands, and I stood aghast.

But it was too late: the deed was done. I knelt down over my victim, and laid my trembling hand first on his temple and then on his heart. Gracious Heaven! he was not dead; the pulsations of his heart were as firm and as regular as my own. Was it so, — was he not dead? I felt again and again, and then with some of the rags that he had torn from the person of his wife, I wiped the volume of blood which had saturated his thick curly hair, and vainly searched for the hole in his skull which I supposed my club had made;

but it was not there. I then wiped the blood from his face, and soon found where my blow had taken effect; it was on the point of the left cheek bone; the flesh was mangled, but the blow being a downward one no bone was broken. He was still alive, and to my unspeakable joy not fatally injured.

The reaction of feeling was almost too much for me. I could have hugged the dirty rascal, so overjoyed was I to think I had not killed him. I washed the blood from his face as well as I could with some dirty water I found in a pail in one corner, and laid him on the bed, where he soon began to revive. I picked up a part of my club, which, although a very solid one, was now in two pieces, and put it in my pocket.

Welch finally recovered, so as to sit up, and said it was no use; he would go with me peaceably now, and would never attempt to fight me again. We got ready and started to go down stairs; he pretended to be weak, and leaned on me for support. We passed through the entry to the head of the stairs, and as I stepped down on the first stair, leaving him somewhat over me, he sprang for my throat with both hands, with a power I little thought he possessed. I knocked up his hand a little as he grabbed for me, so that he only got hold of my collar and a part of my throat, and we both went tumbling to the bottom of the stairs together. As we reached the bottom he broke his hold, and springing for my life, I cleared myself from him and leaped through the open outside door into the yard, well knowing that he was an overmatch for me, and would certainly kill me in close quarters, but still feeling that I was his equal while I could keep him at arms' length. But I had no time to lose, for he was upon me in a moment. As he neared me with an uplifted arm, I drew what I had left of my club, and again wielded it with all the power I possessed. The sharp edge of the broken club hit his arm, and it fell useless by his side. This time no head or cheek-bone was injured, but both bones of his arm just above the wrist were broken.

My fight with John Welch was ended. I took him to jail, where the bones were set and proper care taken of him; and when he was sufficiently recovered, the court awarded him two years in the House of Correction for cruelty to his wife.

That portion of the club that did me such faithful service may now be seen in my cabinet of Police relics at my house. I have no doubt it saved my life in the fight with John Welch; but never shall I forget the awful sensation I experienced when I thought I had killed him.

CIRCUMSTANTIAL EVIDENCE.

During the fall of 1856, a train of circumstances came under my notice that were calculated not only to reach the deepest sympathies of the heart, but they most strikingly illustrate the fact that circumstances apparently trivial in themselves, are often of the most vital importance as they are interwoven in the great web of human events, and that circumstantial evidence, in some cases, may be even more reliable and decisive than direct testimony.

In October of this year, the habitation of a highly respectable family at the north part of Boston was made desolate by the death of two beautiful children, the only surviving offspring of the heart-stricken parents, and their bodies were borne far away to be buried in a little green spot on the south shore of "the deep blue sea," the place of nativity of the father.

A few weeks after these sad ceremonies, the father, having prepared some little tombstones, again took passage on the steamboat for the purpose of placing them to mark the spot where these loved ones lay. He had already nearly reached his point of destination, and leaving the steamer with his burden in a skiff, made for the shore ; but before reaching land the frail bark upset, and the husband and father there found a watery grave.

The body was soon recovered, and the sad intelligence conveyed to the childless, heart-broken widow at home ; and she immediately repaired to this scene of renewed anguish, leaving her home in charge of several friends, most of whom had long been inmates of the family.

After paying the last sad tribute of respect to those so near and dear, the widow returned to her desolate home to find that, during her absence, her house had been robbed of some five hundred dollars in money, the savings of her late husband's many hard days' toil, and all the available funds left her in her lonely and forlorn condition.

Information of the robbery was immediately communicated to me at the Station House, and with a deep sympathy and all the energy I possessed, I at once entered on an investigation.

On visiting the house with one of my officers, I learned that the money had been taken from an inside drawer of a desk or secretary standing in the sitting-room, and consisted of bankbills, silver, and several pieces of gold of different value.

The lid of the desk on the outside had been unlocked by the robber, probably with the key belonging to the desk, but the inside drawer had been forced. On inquiry, I found the key to the outside had been kept on a shelf in the upper part of the secretary, and another key was lying by the side of it. I proceeded carefully, so as to give the persons around me no idea of my thoughts; but I soon learned that the other key wound the clock, and the clock required winding every twenty-four hours. Any one using that clock key would naturally notice the desk key; no stranger would find either.

Who wound the clock? The widow always when at home, the servant-girl in her absence. But the servant-girl was low of stature; she could not reach the clock, and had used a chair. She wound it the last thing before going to bed, and on one occasion, when her mistress was last absent, she had stepped into the chair without the key, and asked one of the gentlemen boarders to hand her the key from the secretary. The girl herself seemed to dislike to be questioned, but I could detect no mark of guilt on her.

Who were the boarders in the house? I asked many questions about each, and finally drew out, unnoticed, that the young man who handed the clock key to the servant-girl was a painter, that had been a boarder some time; that he worked by the week, very steadily, as was supposed; that he was in arrears for board, but had paid up since the widow returned from the funeral of her husband. In passing through the rooms of the boarders, I learned that this young man was not at work to-day, for I saw his working-clothes in his chamber, although they told me he was at work. I then left the house for the purpose of making outside inquiries about the young painter. On visiting his employer, I found the young man received but seven dollars a week when he worked, which was but part of the time ; that he had neither worked nor received pay for the last three weeks; that he frequented billiard rooms, and was sometimes seen in bad company. The next object was to see the young man himself, and in a few hours he came to the Station House in custody of one of our officers. He was dressed in a new suit of clothes throughout, had some seventy dollars about his person, and was highly indignant at being invited to the Station House.

On being told that he was suspected of the robbery, he denied all knowledge of the affair; told a plausible story of his circumstances; expressed great sympathy for the widow ; and hinted at my own responsibility in the course I had taken. The money he had was unlike any that was taken. I did not know his story to be false. I had no direct evidence of his guilt, but I believed I should yet find it, and I locked him up.

We again visited the house where the robbery was committed, and asked permission to look at the room where our painter slept. We searched every inch of the room, furniture, and bedding, but found nothing. The last article for examination was an old checked vest, that hung behind a door. This was the painter's vest, as it plainly showed the marks of his trade, (his room-mate being a carpenter,) and besides it was known to be the one usually worn by the painter when at work. In one corner of a pocket in this vest was a small wad of paper, a little larger than a good-sized pea. On unfolding it carefully, it was apparently a torn-off corner of an old letter, and on it appeared the letters "*Pro*," evidently part of a word written before the corner was torn off. Nor was this all; on further inspection, it appeared to have been wrapped about some round, hard substance, about the size of a five-cent piece. It seemed to be worth preserving; and as nothing else that gave any light on the subject was to be found, we again repaired to the sitting-room to further examine the secretary, and the widow showed me how the money was placed in the drawer. The bills, she said, were laid lengthwise in a long pocket-book; the pocket-book was left, and nothing missing from it but the money. The silver was in a steel purse; the silver had been emptied from the purse and taken, but the purse was left. The gold was wrapped up in an old letter written on a half sheet of note paper; the gold was gone, but the letter still remained in the drawer. I took up the letter, which was much wabbled up, and on straightening it out, found the upper left-hand corner torn off, and asked the widow if she recollected about it. On reflecting a moment she said, yes; when her husband was putting away this money she was present, and counted the gold, and did it up in this old letter; among the gold was a dollar gold-piece, and she tore off a corner of the letter, folded it about the gold dollar, and wrapped it up in the rest of the letter with the other gold. I drew out my bit of paper found in the painter's pocket, and it fitted the corner of the torn letter exactly, and the letters "Pro" on the small piece, were followed by the letters "vincetown" on the large one, which made the word complete when the two parts were joined. The evidence was circumstantial, but, with what facts were before known, rather conclusive. All were satisfied that we had discovered the thief; and to me this was not the only gratification. The discovery would not only place the guilt where it properly belonged, but it served to remove a most cruel suspicion on the character of an innocent and unprotected servant-girl, that might have thrown her out of employment, and marked her with disgrace for life.

We returned to the Station House, and our success was frankly explained to the prisoner. He was not an old criminal, and when he saw the weight of evidence against him he could hold out no longer, but frankly confessed his guilt. The money was nearly all recovered, and restored to the widow; the prisoner was remanded to court, but there admitted to bail. When the day of trial came, he forfeited his bonds by not appearing, and I have never seen him since.

WATCHMAN'S RATTLE.

The Watchman's Rattle was first provided for the use of the guardians of the night long before Boston was incorporated a city, and has been in constant use ever since. I am informed by old watchmen that the original was quite similar to that now in use, although much larger. From what cause its peculiar form was conceived, or who was its ingenious inventor, the record saith not; but it is believed to be the only police appendage that has not undergone a variety of changes, and is an article seldom if ever found in other cities.

If there is any one thing that will infuse life or anxiety, or energy, into the heart or heels of a policeman, it is the sound of the watchman's rattle in the night time. I can hardly tell how or where I acquired this feeling, but I have never heard a sound beating the air, so fraught with a spirit of trouble .and need of assistance, as the sharp crack of the watchman's rattle reverberating in the street at the dead hour of night. Its peculiar tone is different from anything I ever heard, and the sensation is as peculiarly novel and exciting.

On the morning of the 17th of October, 1854, a circumstance occurred which served to strengthen the impressions already somewhat acquired by the exciting echoes of the rattle. I was walking alone down Hanover Street, on the way from the Station House to my home, about half past one o'clock on the morning in question, and when near Richmond Street I heard the sharp crack of the rattle, which seemed to be cut short before it was fairly through. That denoted hand-to-hand work, and I well knew that some of my boys were in trouble. The air that morning was thick and heavy, and the sound seemed to fill the entire space around me; in fact it seemed to come from directly overhead. I cast a hasty glance up and around, but discovering nothing, ran immediately to the corner of Richmond Street. On reaching that point my ear again caught the sound; but still, I could not fix the direction, and thinking it most likely to come from North Street, I made hasty tracks in that direction. As I neared North Street there came a third alarm, evidently in the direction of Brick Alley. I hastened on, and, arriving at that point, by the aid of the lamp-light on the corner, I caught sight of the object of my search. It was in a man's hand, which was thrust through a pane of glass up one flight, and was twirling out its notes of distress in quick succession.

I was not a stranger in that locality, and soon

found my way up an outside stairway in the direction of the room; but the door was fastened. I stepped back a pace, and then sprang forward with my shoulder against the door with all the force I could command, and the next moment found myself at full length on the broken door in the entry. I was not long in reaching the farther end of the entry, where I found another door fastened also, and which was as soon opened the same way.

On entering the room, I there found one of my boys — and as good a fellow as ever broke bread — in what seemed to me to be rather a tight place, although in physical power and courage he was a match for two common men. He had hardly a rag of clothing left on his person, was all covered with blood, and had a man nearly his own size by the throat with one hand, and his bloody arm thrust through the window springing his rattle with the other, while three others were lying about the floor in the same room, under the influence of the muscle in his powerful arm. He had had a hard fight against fearful odds, but he was master of the field when I arrived. He had followed a burglar with his plunder into this den, where he was set upon by these four ruffians, who, after fastening the door, probably intended to make an end of him; but his strong arm and indomitable courage saved his life, and he was only calling for help to carry off his game.

The four men (three of them brothers) were taken to the Station House, and each subsequently took a lesson of Captain Robbins; but the incidents of that night to me added a new sensation to the echoes of the Watchman's Rattle.

THE JOKING LIEUTENANT.

Fun-loving policemen (for there are some jolly fellows among the craft) have some rare opportunities for gratifying that passion among the numerous specimens of human oddities that fall in their way while in discharge of their official duties, and, like the ingenious sculptor who sees symmetry and beauty in the rough block, these fellows are often successful in drawing out a comical figure to suit their taste, even from the most uncouth specimens that fall in their way.

I had a little Lieutenant with me many years, who was one of those clever, innocent jokers above alluded to; and although he was one of the most kind-hearted and humane men I ever knew, yet whatever case came up he was bound to have his fun out of it, if there was any in it; and many were the side-aching jokes I have witnessed of his getting up at the expense of some unlucky wight, and now and then have I witnessed one at his own expense, — for he sometimes found his match.

One evening two intoxicated men were brought into the Station House by different officers at about the same time. One was dead drunk, and on searching his person, as was the rule, a pint flask about half full of " Medford " was found in his pocket. The other inebriate, whose Christian name was Morrill, who was well known at the house, and whose legs were much more drunk than his head, (which was usually the case with him when he got tight,) stood hanging on to the rail, silently witnessing the searching operation. When the ullage bottle of " Medford " made its appearance, the eye of Morrill rested thereon with wistful glances. No remark, however, escaped his lips, and both he and the stranger were assisted to the Lockup, to remain till sober next morning.

On the next morning it came the little Lieutenant's turn to let out the prisoners, and Morrill was let out with the rest. But there seemed to be some weighty matter on his mind, and he hung about the house after all others had left.

As soon as Morrill had an opportunity, he took the Lieutenant one side, and the following colloquy ensued. By the way, Morrill had an unfortunate impediment in his speech, but his earnest manner made up the deficiency on that point.

" Nu-nu-now, Lieutenant," said Morrill, " yu-yu you know that I'm a real good fell-l-feller, and o-only been on a little s-p-r-e-e — and I-I'm going to have the ho-horrors, sure, nu-now. The h-a-i-r of the same dog, you know, Lieutenant. Yo-you just let me have the bottle that lo-lo-loafer left last night, and I-I 'm all right, sir. I-I-I wont tell, p-p-p-pon honor."

"Upon your honor?" said the Lieutenant, looking seriously.

"'Pon the honor of a gentleman," said Morrill, without stuttering a syllable.

"You just stop outside, so as not to be seen by any of the officers," said the Lieutenant, "and I'll meet you in the entry in a moment."

Morrill readily went out. The Lieutenant took the bottle, emptied the contents into the sink, and replaced about the same quantity from a pail of dirty water; then stepped into the entry, where Morrill was anxiously waiting, and slipped the bottle into his hand, saying —

"Just step over into the alley-way yonder and take a snifter, and bring me back the bottle; the owner may call for it."

"All r-r-r-right," said Morrill, and he made for the alley-way.

He had no sooner reached his retreat than the bottle was wrong end up, over his mouth, where it remained till completely empty, the simple liquid not penetrating the thick coating in his mouth to impart the taste till it was too late; but the contents of the bottle seemingly was as much disgusted

13*

with its new quarters as was Morrill at the joke, for it came rushing back out of his mouth with as much dispatch as it had entered. As soon as Morrill could get breath he looked up, and there, just across the street, stood the rascally Lieutenant, laughing as if to split his sides. Morrill hurled the empty bottle at his tormentor, but luckily it passed by and landed in fragments on the sidewalk. The last seen of Morrill, he was wending his way down street with both hands on his stomach, and it was confidently asserted by his friends that he was not drunk again for three weeks.

One summer day when the Lieutenant was at the desk, there came in, arm-in-arm, a couple of young sprouts apparently from upper-tendom, perfectly oblivious to all surrounding circumstances and subjects save the one idea of a *gin cock-tail*. They staggered up to the rail, and with much sang froid one of them peremptorily demanded the aforesaid luxury.

"Sh!" said the Lieutenant: "don't talk so loud. I see you are posted, gents; you know where to come for a good thing. But we have to be a little careful, you know; police are on the watch. We keep nothing at this bar, you see; but just step into the basement, where 't is cool, take a private box, and I will accommodate you with the genuine article. This way, gents. Sh! don't talk so loud. This way, — this way, gents."

And down stairs they went, taking a seat in the first box (cell), with much apparent satisfaction and high anticipation. The Lieutenant quietly locked the cell door, and stood a little one side to await the result. They sat silent some time. At length says one —

"Bill, — I say, Bill, aint that waiter — *hic* — gone — *hic* — a darned long while?"

"So I 'm thinking," said the other. "Why don't you pull the bell?"

The first speaker, with some difficulty, rose to his feet and began searching for the bell-rope, and on coming to the iron-grated door he found it fast. This seemed to impart a new idea, and he began looking about the cell, till all at once the truth seemed to burst on his benighted mind, and he sang out —

"Bill, — Bill; I say, Bill, we are in the watch-house, sure as hic!"

Bill had careened over on the bench, and was fast forgetting his troubles, and his companion finding his egress essentially impeded, soon availed himself of the same accommodation.

The pair were discharged when sober; but on leaving the house one of them *dryly* remarked, that he be darned if he ever again called at a watch-house for *refreshments*.

At some seasons of the year we had more applicants for lodging than we could accommodate, and were often obliged to send some to other stations. On these occasions the Lieutenant used sometimes to amuse himself in testing his customers a little, and selecting those most in need for his own house. When an applicant came in, the Lieutenant would take his name and description, and propound a few questions : —

"Can you work, Mr. Smith?"

"Yes, sir, if I could get it to do."

"Can you saw wood?"

"Yes, sir."

"Well, sir, it is the rule at this house for all male lodgers to saw wood one hour, in payment for bread and cheese and lodging."

This would touch some loafers in a tender spot, and I have seen them leave the Station House in high dudgeon. Others would gladly accept the opportunity, and start off for the basement with a beam of satisfaction resting on their countenance, in anticipation of honestly rendering an equivalent for what they were so much in need. However, none of them ever sawed any wood, for the very good reason that there was none to saw; but such always got the best place we had, and the bread and cheese to boot.

But I have said that the Lieutenant sometimes found his match, and among others I will note one case.

As he was letting out the prisoners one morning,

(by the way, a favorite job with him,) among the rest he espied a young scapegrace of a boot-black, who had taken up his quarters there. Now the Lieutenant was a perfect gentleman, and withal very neat in person and dress. Above all, he admired to see an elegant, genteel boot, and the thought instantly occurred to him that *Shiner* should be required to pay for his lodging.

"Hallo, Shiner," said the Lieutenant, what, you here? Why, you don't expect to come here and lodge without pay, do you? You earn too much money for that now, my lad. You just unshoulder that machine of yours, and give my boots a tip-top shine, and we will be even. That lodging-house over in Union Street charges ninepence; 'tis but half-price here, and better doings at that. Come, come, Shiner; no loafers about here. Come, *out* with your tools."

"I have got no brush, sir," said Shiner.

"What!" said the Lieutenant, no brush?"

"No, sir. I lost it in a row last night."

"Never mind," said the Lieutenant; I have a nice one up stairs, so come right up."

And up they went. The Lieutenant went to his desk and drew out a nice clothes-brush, that cost him one dollar and a half.

"There," said he, "that is none too good to brush my boots with. Now polish 'em up, my lad, while I go down and finish up below."

"All right," said Shiner; and at it he went.

When the Lieutenant came up he found one boot partly blacked; but Shiner or the new brush were never seen afterwards.

JAKE AND HIS BOYS.

On the 3d day of April, 1857, there came an order from the Central Police Office, to repair thither at five o'clock precisely. The order was promptly obeyed; and when there, appearances indicated something up, as the captains of several other stations made their appearance at the same time and place. Very little was said, however, on our arrival, but certain suspicious-looking slips of paper were placed in the hands of each captain, with an order to *execute, simultaneously,* at precisely ten o'clock that evening. The document placed in my hand said something about No— —— Street, and although it was not within the limits of my district, I asked no questions; for as bad a reputation as we enjoyed at the North End, *up town* could beat us on *faro, roulette,* and *dead props,* and give us many points the start.

Well, as if nothing had transpired, the arrangements were all completed at eight o'clock, and fourteen bunkum boys, with brave hearts and strong arms, were ready for the fray at our station.

During the evening the captain had deployed himself as a skirmisher, and made a very valuable reconnoissance; he learned where the main force of the enemy were encamped, and the exact locality of his head-quarters and his supply trains. We also obtained information of the exact position of his outposts, and, very fortunately, the password for the night.

The most important move on the onset, seemed to be to secure the outside picket, who was patrolling up and down the sidewalk, ready to give the alarm to the garrison at the very approach of danger.

However, the plan of attack was matured, and a few moments before *ten*, the storming party were at their posts, at several points, in near proximity to the enemy's camp. As the clock was chiming ten, two stalwart fellows passed down the sidewalk, and as they were seemingly about to pass the enemy's picket, from some unexplained cause the said picket passed down with them, as quietly as if nothing had happened, and all three were out of sight round a corner, quicker than it takes to tell this part of the story. The guard was disposed of, and now was the time for action. Our whole storming party were in line, ready to mount the enemy's breast-works at the word. "Rap-rap," came a sound on the outside of the outer door. "Rap," was the answer inside.

"*Jake* and the boys," said a voice outside. (Jake was the pass.)

Open came the door. "Up one flight," said the waiter; and up went Jake and the boys, without exciting the least suspicion.

On arriving at the *second room*, up one flight, Jake beheld the coveted prize, consisting of about twenty personages, seated about a long table, on which appeared certain curious little boxes, with square pieces of pasteboard, numberless little pieces of ivory, about the size of a half dollar, of various colors, snail-shells, money, and various other articles too numerous to mention, which engaged the attention of those seated at the table so closely, that the presence of any new visitors was not noticed. Jake gave a circular motion of his arm, which seemed to be well understood by his boys, who immediately commenced forming a circle about the board, and Jake, with one spring, landed with both feet on the very centre of the table at the same time taking at one grasp most of the stakes; and before one of the party had time to rise from his chair, Jake proclaimed —

"Hold on, — hold on, gentlemen; I take this trick in the name of the Commonwealth. Keep perfectly quiet, gentlemen. You shall all be well treated, but you will be under the necessity of accompanying me to the office of the Chief of Police, where, I presume, all things will be made satisfactory."

The crowd seemed thunderstruck, and most of them were shackled *by the boys*, two together, before they rose from the table, so complete was the surprise. In a short time the spoils were gathered up, and the whole party and property were on the way to the Tombs.

On arriving at our head-quarters, the names of the captured party were taken, and, strange to say, judging from the names, they seemed to belong to the same family, or to two families, at most, as they were nearly all *Smiths* and *Jones*. Jake, however, took them at their word, without asking any further questions, only remarking as he took the last, "*Gentlemen will please recollect the names they gave when they appear in Court to-morrow morning, to save mistakes.*" One among the number, who was said to hold some office in a neighboring town, wrote his name in the lining of his hat, for fear of an error.

However, it was soon apparent that if we had the whole family of Smiths and Jones in custody, there were kindred and friends outside, for several gentlemen soon appeared and offered to go bail for the whole party, some of them holding real estate in Boston valued at least at fifty thousand dollars. This course seemed to have an *indication* in the premises; at any rate, the commissioner soon made his appearance, and the whole party were bailed The next day all appeared at court, plead guilty, and were fined, except the keeper of the house, whose case was sent up to a higher court; but that party probably have not forgotten *Jake* and his boys to the present day.

RAT PITS.

A RAT PIT is one of those under-ground novelties occasionally seen in Boston by gaslight. The whereabouts, however, is not always exactly known to the uninitiated, the proprietors generally not choosing to either advertise or hang out a shingle to indicate the locality where the elephant is to be seen; nor when found is the establishment such as would be likely to impress the mind with an idea of grandeur or sublimity; at least, such has been the condition of those that I have seen.

For many years one of these subterranean establishments was kept at "North End," which I have sometimes been called on to visit in my official capacity. The establishment consisted of a bar-room on the first floor from the street, not wide but deep, the counter running the whole length on one side. Behind this counter stood females, with *vermilion* cheeks and low-necked dresses, ready to deal out New York gin and cabbage-leaf cigars to all who had the *dosh*. At the lower end of the counter, or bar, stood a low-sized, haggard-looking cockney,

RAT PIT.

anxiously waiting for an order to serve up a *raw* from a heap of rough shells before him, — the only way of dressing the bivalves known here. A bench, a few stools, and a half dozen dirty, uncouth pictures about the walls, completed the furniture of that room.

In passing through this room, (which was generally filled with pickpockets, petty knucks, fumes of tobacco, smoke and bad gin,) at the further end you find a trap-door leading down a flight of stairs to the *rat pit* below.

The pit consists of a board crib of octagon form in the centre of the cellar, about eight feet in diameter and three and one half feet high, tightly secured at the sides. On three sides of the cellar are rows of board seats, rising one above the other, for the accommodation of spectators. On the other side, stands the proprietor and his assistant and an empty flour barrel, only it is half full of live rats, which are kept in their prison-house by a wire netting over the top of the cask. The amphitheatre is lighted with oil lamps or candles, with a potatoe, a turnip, or an empty bottle for a candlestick. Spectators are admitted at twenty-five cents a head, and take their seats, when preparations for the evening's entertainment commence. The proprietor carefully lifts the edge of the wire netting over the rat barrel, and with an instrument looking much like a pair of curling tongs, he begins fishing out

14*

his game, rat by rat, depositing each carefully inside the pit until the requisite number are pitted. The assistant has brought in the dog, *Flora*, a favorite ratter, which he is obliged to hold fast by the nape of the neck, so eager is she for the fray. Then commences the betting, which runs high or low according to the amount of funds in the hands of the sports.

"A dollar. She kills twenty rats in twelve seconds!" "I take that!" "Half a dollar on the rats!" "Don't put in them small rats!" "Two dollars on Flora in fifteen seconds!" "Done, at fourteen!" "No, you don't!" "Don't put in all your big rats at once!" "Five dollars on the rats in ten seconds!" (no takers.)

The betting all seems to be well understood, but it would puzzle an outsider to tell whether there were really any genuine bets or not.

The bets having been arranged, time is called, and Flora is dropped into the ring. Flora evidently understands that her credit is at stake; but the growling, and champing, and squealing, and scratching is soon over, and the twenty rats lie lifeless at the feet of the bloodthirsty Flora, when time is again called, and the bets decided, and all hands go up and liquor. This exhibition is repeated several times, with different dogs, and lasts as long as the live rats hold out.

After the rat game is up, the proprietor generally

gets up the *Chuck game*, or something similar, for an afterpiece. The Chuck game is on this wise: a box some three or four feet long and one foot square, closed at one end, is placed in the pit, and a woodchuck or a coon is put in, who immediately burroughs in the box. *Bose* then enters the ring, and being a dog of *good blood*, he immediately sets about pulling Chuck out of his house; and when Bose crawls in, Chuck gives him battle, and being well armed, Bose generally gets a black eye and a bloody nose before his task is accomplished; and sometimes he backs out altogether, and loses his reputation, when some other misguided cur, greedy for the prize, renews the attack on poor Chuck to lose or win, as the case may be. During the fight bets run high, and the spectators are excited almost to frenzy. One who never witnessed one of these exhibitions can have no conception of the scene.

The hooting, cheering, groaning, shouting, screeching, swearing, and stamping, accompanied with ten thousand grotesque gestures of the crowd, as seen and heard by the dim light in that subterranean dungeon, beggars description, and would put to blush a pandemonium of the first water.

After the entertainment of the evening is over, which is generally at a late hour, — unless the exhibition is wound up with a fight, which is not unfrequent, — all hands adjourn to the bar to take a parting drink. Those too leg-weary to walk, lounge down in a corner, some go to a lodging-room, and others, who have no place or money, go out *prospecting* to obtain means to purchase their grub and rum for the next day.

The rat pit of which I have been speaking is now closed, the proprietor having been stabbed through the heart with a knife in the hand of one of his own pupils, in a drunken fight at a North Street bar-room.

I never objected to the matter of destroying any quantity of rats, but the ceremonies attending these rat-pit exhibitions most surely tend to cultivate and nurse the evils, vices, and crime to which the proprietors of this pit fell a victim.

While this rat-hole was in its glory, I was walking down Salem Street quite late one evening, and just before reaching Richmond Street I saw a man dodge round the corner with a bag on his back. Supposing it some thief with his booty, I put after him in *double-quick;* but on coming up I recognized in the supposed burglar a clever old darkie, familiarly known as *Jum*. Thinking I would give honest old Jum a little surprise as he was quietly trudging along, I suddenly laid my hand on his shoulder and sang out, "*Now, old covey, I have got you!*"

The poor fellow jumped more than twice his length, and as he came to a stand he was facing me, one hand still hold of the mouth of the bag as it lay on the sidewalk.

"O-o-o-a-a-a-r-r-r-umph!" cried Jum, as he brought up, — "O-o-wha-wha-wha O, golla massa, what ye want o' me?" gazing at me in perfect horror, each eye having the appearance of the surface of a tub of lard with a boy's marble in the centre.

"Ah, Jum," said I, "what have you got in that bag?"

"Wha-wha-a-o-o-u-u-o-o-a, — oh, dat you, Massa Capen?" O, Lordy, Lordy, Capen, Ize tot Ize a goner!"

"Well, well," said I, "but what's in the bag, Jum?"

"In de bag, — in de bag! why, wh-why, Massa Capen, dem's rats, — rats, dey is, — rats, noffin else, noffin else. Golly, — golly, Capen, t'out Ize a goner dat time, sure. Look out, — look out dare, Capen; dem fellers bite rite frough de bag." And sure enough poor Jum had a bag half full of live rats.

After Jum had got a little over his scare, he explained to me how and where he caught the rats. His custom was to go down to the stables in Medford Street, where horses were fed with oats or meal, after dark, and with a lantern in one hand, a bag under his arm, and a pair of curling tongs in the other hand, Jum quietly *bags his game*, and relieves the poor donkeys of a very troublesome intruder.

"An' I picks dem out pretty fast," said he. "De teamsters all like to see dis rat-catcher come; de hosses gets more meal."

"Pretty good, Jum," said I, "and you are all right. But what are you going to do with those rats; do you drown them?"

"Drown em! Lord bress you, Capen, guess not, — guess not! Dis darkey get shillin' apiece, — shillin' apiece for dem rats; Massa *Barney* give shillin' apiece. Rats scarce now, — get shillin' piece, sure."

"How many have you, Jum?"

"Well, spose dare am t'irty, — full t'irty rats in dat bag, sure, and big ones, too."

"Thirty rats at a shilling apiece, amount to five dollars," said I. "A pretty good evening's work. Well, Jum, you're a good fellow; good-night, and good luck."

"Tank ye, t'ank ye, Capen," said Jum, as he swung the bag over his shoulder and walked off, muttering to himself, "scare colored man to deff. Tink dis chile tief, I spose!"

DEATH OF A FIREMAN.

During my service for the city I have usually been in the habit of being present at any considerable fire that might occur, especially in the night time.

On the evening of July 11, 1862, having had a hard day's work, I was about to retire to my bed at an early hour, when the bells sounded the alarm of fire, in District No. 1. On throwing open the window-blinds of my house, which was in Charter Street, I saw that the heavens were lighted up by a fire apparently somewhere near Haymarket Square. I immediately threw on an old fire suit, and started out. On reaching Haymarket, I found the Square and adjoining streets filled with people; but the fire was further on up Sudbury Street, and consuming several wood buildings on the north side of Sudbury, between Adams and Hawkins Streets.

I elbowed my way through the crowd till I reached the fire, where I found the people so densely huddled together that it was necessary to shut off the streets.

An additional force of police, with ropes, were soon on the ground, and the spectators were forced back sufficiently far to give the firemen room to work.

The police had hardly accomplished their task, when a chimney near the corner of Adams and Sudbury Street, losing the support of surrounding timbers, fell upon the front wood walls, which were still standing, and the whole burning mass came tumbling into Sudbury Street, burying several firemen under the rubbish on the very place where a large number of spectators had so lately stood, and where I stood myself but a moment before.

A number of men rushed to the spot to remove the rubbish and extricate the poor fellows that lay buried beneath. There were seven in all, more or less injured, some being carried to one place and some to another, to have their wounds dressed; all but one escaped without fatal injury, and he was struck on the temple with a heavy stick of timber, that broke his skull, and he died in a few moments after, we had carried him into a shop on the opposite side of the street. He was a member of Engine Company No. 7, about thirty-five years of age, a worthy man and a good fireman, and had a wife and three small children dependent on his labors for support.

We procured a litter, and his body was conveyed

to the Station House in Court Square by his sorrowing comrades.

Then the melancholy tidings must be conveyed to his family, — to his poor wife, who, with her little ones, were patiently waiting the father's return after the fire. But the stout hearts of those brave men, who could meet death in any form without a tremor, shrank from the task of conveying the sad news to the wife. No one felt that he could go. Finally, at the earnest solicitation of the engineers and some of the members of his company, — with his employer and one other gentleman, I started off on the melancholy errand.

We reached the house about 11 o'clock at night, and on entering found the widowed mother with her children drawn closely around her, as if expecting some fearful visitation. We told our sad tale as best we could; but the scene there presented I cannot describe, neither can I recall it to memory without a most painful emotion. Her neighbors and friends gathered about her, and there was no dry eye in that sad group. The wife was calm, but a picture of despair, and spoke of her husband and her children with a depth of feeling most touching.

She had a little son about three years old, a bright, flaxen-haired child. She said when the father left the house at seven o'clock in the morning, (he had not been home since,) the child followed him out the door, hanging on to his coat, and crying, " Pa pa, don't go ; pa pa, don't go ! " as if his little heart would break. The circumstance was unusual, and produced a foreboding on the mind of the mother throughout the day. " Poor child," said she, " he will never again meet the smile nor enjoy the parting kiss of that fond father, who now sleeps in death."

We left the poor heart-broken widow in care of a few kind friends, and after rendering what further assistance I could, in caring for the body of the deceased fireman, long after midnight I found myself, almost exhausted, wending my way alone through the deserted streets to my own home, with a heart deeply depressed at the melancholy scenes I had so lately witnessed, yet grateful to Him who holdeth the lives of men in the hollow of his hand that I was spared to yet be the guardian of my own dear wife and child.

THE OUTCAST.

THE OUTCAST.

When I had charge of Station One, on a certain New Year's Eve I had taken a stroll over the district, and on coming to the Station House two of the officers were helping a poor creature into the house apparently some intoxicated, and almost perished with cold.

The person was a female, about twenty years old, tall and slim, with deep black eyes, pale, haggard countenance, and black, dishevelled hair. She was thinly but decently dressed, and had unquestionably seen better days, not a long time since. She was taken in by the fire, wrapped in blankets, hot drinks administered, and with a little attention soon revived.

During my Police life I have had many hundreds of these poor outcasts in my custody, and few, very few have I seen that had no claim for sympathy. Many an hour have I sat at the cell door and listened to their tales of woe, and often have I been led to believe that these poor creatures are frequently more "sinned against than sinning."

A false step, perhaps, at the beginning, and the tide of adversity has borne them onward and downward. Former friends forsake them, strangers ridicule and despise them, no helping hand is outstretched to save, and the victim, writhing under a sense of its wrongs, seeks refuge in the haunts of dissipation and licentiousness, and perishes in misery and degradation, uncared for and unknown.

I never could turn a deaf ear to these tales of woe; for well do I remember how near the brink of ruin I myself have been, when borne down by the weight of poverty and misfortune.

Good treatment, and a few kind words, seemed to give assurance to our new guest that she was in the care of those who would do her no harm, and little by little I drew out her history.

She was of highly respectable family, in moderate circumstances, residing in a neighboring State; had left her home and come to the city but a short time since, and her brief history is told in the following lines. They are supposed to be addressed to her mother, the night she spent at the Station House: —

"And is this New Year's Eve, mother? Oh, mother, can it be!
Oh what a sad, sad change, mother, this year hath wrought in me!

Last year there was no lighter step, there was no brighter
    eye,
There was no merrier heart than mine, — now mother,
    what am I ?

" A theme for every idle jest, sunk lower than the slave,
With blighted name and broken heart, and very near my
    grave ;
For I feel my days are numbered, my life is waning
    fast,
And the thought is strong within me, that this night will
    be my last.

" 'Tis just two years ago to-day, since Mary Ann was
    laid,
Amid the tears of young and old, within the church-
    yard shade ;
How sad we thought the fate was, for one so young and
    gay,
To die thus in the morn of life, upon her marriage day.

" But now I envy her the doom ; what joy for you and me
If I had died then, mother, when innocent and free,
Ere I became what I am now, the saddest thing in life,
Fallen, — deserted, — and betrayed, — *A mother, not a
    wife!* "

" Of a group of lads and lasses, methinks I caught a
    glance ;
My old companions are they all, just hieing to the dance :
And they will pass the night away in noisy mirth and glee,
While the shelter of a prison-house alone remains for me.

15*

"I remember last year's sleighride over the frozen snow,
 And how we danced till daylight, and the skies were in
  a glow;
 I was the lightest-hearted one of all the merry throng,
 And *he* was by my side that night whom I had loved so
  long.

"Yes I was very fond of him, he seemed so far above
 The other youths, and all the girls were envious of his
  love;
 And I was young and guileless, and how could I believe
 That when he spoke of *love* to me, he meant but to
  deceive?

"I think I was bewitched, mother, by the light of those
  dark eyes,—
 By the murmured vows of tenderness, and all those flattering lies;
 I had scorn enough for others, who sought to win my love,
 But he seemed to my unpractised eye as guileless as a
  dove.

"And even now I cannot think so ill of him as you;
 I cannot think his heart so bad as many others do:
 I know he's done me cruel wrong, and bowed my
  head with shame,
 And yet the fault was not all his; I might have been to
  blame.

"I know how oft you warned me, mother; you told me
  oft the truth,
 That village girls were seldom wed by high and wealthy
  youth;

But I thought of many tales I'd read, and of the songs
    I'd sung,
  How noble men loved lowly maids, if beautiful and
    young.

" But judge him not too harshly, mother, though I so sad
      beguiled,
    Though now he strives to blight my name; and will not
      own *his child;*
    But time may come when he will feel his need to be
      forgiven,
    And you'll forgive him for my sake, when I am gone to
      heaven.

" Some there may be who'll not regret that I am brought
        so low,
    As I was proud and haughty then; but I am humbled
        now :
    I prized too much my beauty, which so fully proved my
        bane,
    As I scorned the honest and the true that offered me
        their name.

" And now they will not speak to me, they think I am so
      vile,
    But pass me with a scornful look or with a meaning
      smile ;
    'T is very hard, perhaps 't is right, but still I think I
      know
    If they had borne what I have borne, I could not treat
      them so.

"But you have been so kind, mother, though I've dis-
    graced your name;
  You soothed me in my sorrow, nor spoke a word of
    blame :
  I should have been a solace, mother, in your declining
    years;
  I should have brought you comfort,—I have only
    brought you tears.

"I never can repay you, mother, for your patience and
    your love,
  But your kindness and your tenderness are registered
    above;
  And He will sure reward you, who said to one of yore,
  'Neither do I condemn thee, daughter; go and sin no
    more.'

"Oh, how we mourned when father died; but now tis well
    tis so;
  He never could have borne with me — as you have done,
    I know :
  He was so just, so good himself, he could not understand
  The temptations that beset the weak; the snares on every
    hand.

"But now he sees more clearly, in that blest home above,
  And he will judge more mildly, and welcome me with
    love,
  When I leave this weary world to find a heavenly home,
  Where sinful souls are purified, and sorrows cannot
    come.

"But you will keep my babe, mother, and rear her as
            your own;
    May she repay you better, mother, than ever I have
            done:
    Poor babe, she has her father's smile, his bright and
            beaming eye;
    Had she a right to bear his name, how peaceful could I
            die.

"If she is mild and gentle, and easily controlled, —
    Unlike her hapless mother, — Oh, let her not be told, —
    Oh, never let her hear her wretched mother's name,
    To sadden her young spirit, and flush her cheek with
            shame.

"But if she's like her mother, as wayward and as wild,
    Though 't is a painful legacy to leave a guiltless child,
    Then tell her all my story, though she thinks of me with
            hate;
    Better to scorn her mother's name, than share her mother's
            fate.

"And now good night, dear mother; I hope that ere the
            sun
    Sheds its first ray to-morrow morn, my troubles will be
            done:
    And do not weep for me, mother; when I have left you
            here,
    Within a peaceful dwelling-place, will dawn my next
            New Year."

I sat long that evening listening to the tale of
this poor maniac, for I soon saw that reason, if not

bereft, was trembling on its throne. The next morning the necessary means were taken to send her to her mother, and we had the satisfaction of knowing that she reached her home in safety. But I learned that her story was but too true, and a few weeks after I read an account of her death in a newspaper.

The seducer now moves in the higher circles of society in this city. I know him well, and have often watched him when he little thought that the eye of one who knew the secret of his guilt rested on him. He is wealthy, proud, and haughty; but I believe the dregs of remorse and bitterness are in his cup; and, if I am not mistaken, that ever-restless eye and nervous demeanor indicate a worm at the heart.

MARIA WHIPPLE

MARIA WHIPPLE.

In the fall of 1857, numerous reports of house robberies were made to the Police, perpetrated in various parts of the city. These robberies were mostly committed at noonday, and generally consisted of ladies' clothing. At length these complaints became so numerous, it was thought there must be an organized gang perambulating the city, and the whole police force were on the alert. Descriptions were given, by the various sufferers, of a girl that applied for board, on whom suspicions rested. Some said she was tall, slim, and good-looking; others, that she was rather short and ordinary. One thought her thick-set and ruddy; another, that she was medium size. Now, she had a full, round face and pug nose; then thin-favored, with nose aquiline. In fact, no two described the supposed thief alike at all, with the exception of one feature, — all agreed that she had red hair. The police finally arrived at the conclusion that there were either a *whole family* of red-headed thieves, or else *one* very busy individual, who had miraculous powers of ubiquity. Accordingly, red-headed ladies were objects of much interest to our department, and many and laughable were the jokes cracked at their expense, and almost any officer would readily affirm that at least every other head seen in the street had at least an *auburn* hair. Perhaps those who are unpractised in our line might think it a little odd, but, to solve the problem, let him take a walk up Hanover or Washington Street some fine afternoon, and undertake to look up some individual in a particular dress; for instance, he wants to find a boy about seventeen, dressed in short jacket, and a close-fitting, gray, round-top cap, or a lady in a black dress, with auburn curls and pink bonnet; and if he don't come in within an hour ready to swear that there are a thousand on the street of either kind, I am mistaken.

At last one of our officers got a little additional description, on which he thought he could rely, and a part of his beat being on Hanover Street, where many ladies pass, he resolved to capture one of the *red-heads*, at any rate. It was not many days before he encountered a young lady on the street who had the required description, and, in addition, a nice bundle in her arms. He followed her along till opposite the Station House, and politely tapping her on the shoulder invited her in. She appeared very modest, said her name was Maria Whipple, was a vestmaker, and the bundle contained her work, which she was taking to the shop. On examination, however, the bundle contained one silk dress, one fur victorine, one lady's mantilla, one child's apron and hood, and one checked shawl. This was rather uncommon work for a vestmaker's establishment to put out, and as none of the clothing seemed to be a fit for herself, it was thought prudent to investigate further; and on several persons who had suffered by the red-headed girl being sent for, she was identified, beyond dispute.

When the girl became satisfied that she was detected, she said if we would not be hard with her *she would tell all*, and do all she could to recover the property she had taken; but the effort proved a heavy tax on her memory, for she alone comprised the whole red-headed family we had been seeking for. The next day, her arrest having been made known, some forty victims called to see her, the estimate of their losses in the aggregate amounting to over one thousand dollars. Of this amount the officers recovered in value some eight hundred dollars. Maria was taken before the court, and although her offences might have sent her to prison a lifetime, she was sentenced but two years.

Maria's story (although that was an assumed name) was soon told. She was about twenty years old, and having no friends to care for her, she came to Boston from a neighboring State to seek employment as a vestmaker, having learned that trade at home. She engaged board with a respectable widow lady at the South End, and went out in search of work; but being a stranger, with no one to recommend her, she travelled about day after day without meeting with any success. In a short time her board-bill exceeded the small amount of funds she possessed, and one morning the landlady demanded payment. She paid all she had, and again put on her things and went out, to renew her efforts for work; but in vain. She felt she could not go back without any prospect of paying her board to ask for another meal, and the thought struck her that she must get a new boarding-place at once. She wandered about, she hardly knew where, and coming to a house where "*Boarding*" was on the door, she summoned courage to make an application. The people in the house turned her coldly away. As she passed out through the entry, an opportunity offered, and in a fit of desperation she took a lady's cloak and made her escape. The cloak was carried to a broker, and pawned for enough to liquidate her board-bill, which was immediately carried home and appropriated to that purpose.

Said she, "I consoled myself on this, *my first theft*, that my necessity was an excuse for the act, but it paved the way for my ruin. I began to feel that there was but two ways for me; one was to steal, the other, *to abandon myself to the town*. Of the two evils, I thought I chose the least." She had stolen probably twelve hundred dollars in value, sold it all to the brokers, and for the whole had received less than one hundred dollars.

I envy not the purchasers their ill-gotten gains had no owner appeared; but, as it proved, the speculation for most of them was not very profitable.

When Maria's term of service expired, she came out of prison with the good wishes of all her overseers, and was sent to the kind-hearted matron of the Home in Kneeland Street, who soon procured her a situation in a family in a neighboring city. I have no doubt her story was true; but she had been in prison, was disgraced in the eyes of the world, and had lost her own self-respect. She stole no more, but she was soon an inmate of a mad-house.

BEGGARS.

I NEVER was very partial to beggars, although I believe a hungry woman or child never went away from my door empty; but the bloated, red-nosed beggar, whose breath smells like a cask of decayed onions, never met with a very hearty welcome with me. But, opposed to the practice as I am, I one day found myself very deeply engaged in the same occupation; and although I never took much pride in relating my own exploits, yet I believe on that day I performed a feat of begging that will not find a parallel in Boston.

The cause that gave rise to the course I pursued was this. In the year 1856, when I had charge of Police Station No. 1, a few days before Thanksgiving, a poor woman came into my office and inquired if I could give her some work. I had no work for her; but her thin, pale face and a long-drawn sigh as she turned to go away, somehow made me feel kind of bad under my waistcoat, although accustomed daily as I was to witness cases of poverty and want. I called her back, and told her if she would leave her name and residence

I would try and find some work for her. To this she gladly assented. She told me where she lived, and that she had three small children, her husband having been dead about a year, leaving her destitute and in poor health. Said she, "When William was alive we were poor, but comfortable; we always had enough to eat, and something nice for Thanksgiving; but if I cannot get some work, we shall have to go without this year." I gave her a little change, and she went away wiping the tears from her eyes. As the poor woman left my office, I resolved that she should not go without a supper for herself and little ones on Thanksgiving Day; and as I sat thinking of the privations and sorrows that must weigh down the heart of that poor widow, it occurred to me that this was but one case of many that existed on my own Station, and within my own knowledge, where rigid necessity would allow but a scanty meal even on Thanksgiving Day.

But what could I do? I had not the means to furnish them all with a supper. But I did not feel satisfied with that argument; could not I do something? I knew plenty of people, many of whom, perhaps, would give something for such a purpose; but could I go out and beg? I could hardly beg for myself, were I ever so needy; but this would be begging for the needy. I would get laughed at for my pains. "Don't care; that wont hurt me;

the object is worth an effort, at least;" and my resolution was soon formed. I had no time to lose, and commenced on my new plan at once by drawing up the following document:—

"We, the undersigned, respectively contribute the sum of one dollar each, to be expended by Captain —— for the purpose of furnishing a Thanksgiving supper for destitute widows and orphans residing on Police Station No. One."

On the following day, at ten o'clock A. M. precisely, with my credentials in hand as above drawn, and with all the *cheek* I could summon, I sallied forth to try my luck. I took the precaution to secure a few names at the head of the list that were favorably known among the tradesmen on Hanover and Blackstone streets, and my work was well begun.

Having for several years been in a position to be pretty well known to the business people at the North End, and asking for but one dollar of any one for an object that commended itself to every generous impulse of the heart, I met with much better success than I had anticipated. My cause was so good, my encouragement so flattering, and I entered into the spirit of my business so deeply, that I forgot my own dinner, and continued my efforts till five o'clock P. M., when I repaired to my Station House to get breath, and take an account of stock; and I must acknowledge I felt not only a little proud, but somewhat surprised at my success, for till then I had not the least idea how much I had received. On counting my money, I found I had collected one hundred and thirty-nine dollars, of one hundred and thirty-nine persons, in seven consecutive hours, *averaging one dollar in about every three minutes.* (I would like to shake hands with the man that can beat that begging.) The next day I made a handsome addition to the fund, and the proceeds were appropriated to the purchase of such articles of provision as was thought would be most valuable and acceptable to those for whom they were designed.

In the mean time, my officers had assisted me in completing a list of those persons thought to be most needy and worthy, and the day before Thanksgiving, I had the pleasure of leaving at the door of over one hundred tenements (not forgetting the widow whose sorrowful story had given me the first impulse to beg) ample means to satisfy the hunger and gladden the hearts of those dwelling therein, for one day at least.

If those generous hearts who furnished the means for those little blessings, could have on that day witnessed what I witnessed, and enjoyed the pleasure of giving, as well as I did in distributing their generous liberality, I feel sure they would have thought it a good investment.

I have carefully preserved their *names* on that subscription list, but their deeds are written in a book that will last longer than mine.

A CHAPTER ON HATS.

Who that has enjoyed the advantages of dwelling in civilized society, that does not realize the importance attached to a fashionable, genteel hat.

It has been the pride and the ornament of the lords of creation from time immemorial. Long and loud, by legend and lyric, have its praises been said and sung, by rich and poor, old and young, bond and free, while its elegant figure has undergone every transformation that human ingenuity could invent; first assuming the form of a triangular cone, — then the shape of a genteel sugar-loaf, — next of an inverted dinner-bell; now it steps forth in the shape of an oyster keg, — next, the pattern of a brown-bread loaf, — next, perhaps, the copy of a pyramid, and then the fac-simile of a cheese-box, — or, mayhap, a thing without comparison in shape, yet still imparting spirit and life to its possessor, and still the admiration of all.

Neither has the character and position of this strange object been less varied than its form. First, it graces the head of a monarch, — then it is the habitation of a nest of young rats in a garret; to-day, the pride of an admiring multitude, — to-morrow, floating in a frog-pond, a roost for tadpoles, or lying hid in the depths of an ash barrel. Such has been its history in all ages of the world, and such its fate; and yet it has been but a prototype of its possessor.

No wonder, then, that an article which has attracted such universal attention of nations and communities in all ages of the world, should occasionally become an object of *individual* interest in our own day; and such was actually the case a few days since.

For many years past a highly respectable firm of hat manufacturers, "not a thousand miles from" *the State of Massachusetts*, have occupied an establishment where a salesroom was conspicuous on the ground floor, while the manufacturing rooms were in the stories above.

Of late one of the younger members of the firm, who has the supervision of the manufacturing branch, has on several occasions missed a specimen of his handiwork in the night-time, and thought the circumstances most singular; but being a prudent man he kept the matter to himself, and resolved to watch.

A few evenings since, at the close of work, a hat of peculiar beauty having been finished all but adjusting the lining, was left on the bench to receive a finishing touch the next morning. When the man opened his shop the hat was gone, and knowing that none but members of the firm had keys, he at once concluded that some burglar with false keys had entered the shop. He immediately reported his loss to the Police, and an officer was detailed to investigate the case.

Early in the afternoon of the next day, the young hatter came into the office quite out of breath, saying he had discovered his hat on the head of a man in the street, and had followed and saw the man enter a certain house. An officer went with him to the house, where the man and hat were found without difficulty. The man, who did not seem disposed to say how he came by the hat, was locked up for a thief, and the hat was retained for evidence, — the hatter declaring that he would swear to his property on a stack of bibles, and pointed out his marks, so that no one doubted his correctness.

After the prisoner had been in custody a short time a lady called to see him, and on being told why he was detained, she said the man was no thief, and was held wrongfully, for she herself had that day made him a present of *that hat;* and if anybody was accused of stealing it, she would frankly tell how she came by it. At her earnest solicitation the young hatter was sent for. He came, but he was not the man she desired to see.

"Is there not," said she, "another gentleman in your firm, that has grayish hair, and sometimes walks with a cane?"

"Yes," said the young hatter.

"Well, send for him," said she; "he is the man that I want to see."

There was some hesitation on the part of the young hatter; but the case began to grow interesting, and an officer went for the gentleman, who soon made his appearance.

"There," said the lady, "that is the gentleman, and this is my story. As I was taking a walk on last Friday evening, I fell in company with this gentleman. He bade me good-evening, and we passed on conversing together. When we got opposite a certain block, he said he had got to go in there a moment, and if I would wait, he would be my company further on. He took out his keys, opened the door, and started upstairs. I saw he was somewhat lame, and offered to assist him up; and, at his consent, I did so. When he came out, he took this hat from a bench and gave it me; I thought no harm, and carried it home, and to-day gave it to my friend who is now locked up for stealing it. Is my story correct, sir?" said she to the senior partner.

The gentleman, who had stood *transfixed* while she was telling her story, turned indignantly on his heel and walked out of the office without saying a word. The lady then turned to the young hatter, and demanded her hat and the release of her friend. The hatter thought it rather steep, but, on a little reflection, he said —

"I don't care to go to court, and, Mr. Officer, if you please you may discharge the prisoner and give her the hat."

CONFIDENCE MAN.

A CONFIDENCE MAN.

The detectives celebrated All Fools Day in the year 1862, by cribbing and showing up a celebrated rascal who has been both a rogue and a fool *all the days* of his life.

Chauncey Larkin, who has followed his trade under the name of Colonel Gorman, Colonel Dupont, Colonel Dudley, and Lieutenant Smith, having arrived at the Winthrop House last evening, and being wanted by the police in New York, was arrested by our police, and brought into the Office. When brought in he was dressed in a colonel's uniform, and was quite indignant, and said some big words; but on being confronted with some old acquaintances (for he had been here before), he caved in, and acknowledged that the day was propitious to his case.

In his possession were found various interesting papers from distinguished personages. One purporting to be from Mr. Johnson, United States Marshal for Kentucky, calling the attention of Governor Buell to the Henry Rifle Manufacturing

Company in New Haven, Conn., as suitable for a regiment of cavalry raised by Colonel Dudley. A second was from General Buell, directing Colonel Dudley to proceed to New Haven, and make arrangements for procuring rifles for his regiment. Of course these papers were all forgeries, to aid him in raising the wind. However, he contracted with the New Haven Company for one thousand rifles, but had obtained only a single pair, when his progress was arrested.

He had also several letters of a sentimental character, among which was one from the young ladies of a seminary in Brooklyn, N. Y., thanking him for a visit to their institution under the name of Colonel Dupont, and for his autograph, kindly written with his hand in a sling, which he pretended had been wounded in a late battle.

A few days previous to his visit at New Haven, he visited a celebrated military establishment in New York City, representing himself as Colonel Dupont, or rather Commodore Dupont, dressed in a colonel's uniform complete, excepting a sword and sash. He said he was commissioned by the War Department to select a model sword, and was fortunate enough to find one that exactly suited him. The firm felt highly flattered with his favors, and while in the store having casually remarked that he was to dine with General Scott that day, he was urged to accept the loan of the sword, and also of a beautiful silk sash, for the inspection of the brave old general and General Anderson, who was likewise to be a guest. He carried off the goods, and forgot to return them.

The same gentleman operated in Boston some dozen years ago on quite an extensive scale, under the name of Lieutenant Hunter, and at that time produced quite a sensation.

He purchased real estate, ships, merchandise, coal, produce, &c. &c., in large quantities, but did not take possession, although in most cases he managed to raise a little ready money by the operation. It was said that he went into one speculation in fancy stock that was not made public at the time, on this wise: A landlord who had just fitted up a crack hotel in the city, had been at considerable expense in furnishing a suit of rooms for bridal chambers, and which really presented a striking feature in the establishment. At the time the dashing Lieutenant flourished in this locality, these rooms had just been completed, but had not been occupied. This coming to the knowledge of Lieutenant Hunter, he at once conceived the happy idea of giving them a christening. Accordingly the dashing Lieutenant with his wife, one bright moonlight evening, jumped into the nearest hack, drove to the aforesaid hotel, reported himself as bridegroom and lady, just arrived from Providence; engaged the bridal rooms, ordered a splendid supper, and, with the exception of some round swearing, because the extra carriage with his servants and baggage did not arrive, all things went smoothly on. However, he consoled himself and his worthy host with the idea that by mistake these had gone to some other hotel, and, as it was quite late, he would let the matter rest till morning. As the couple were somewhat weary with their journey they retired to their splendidly-furnished chambers to forget the cares of life in general, and the perplexities of travelling with baggage and careless attendants in particular.

On repairing to the chambers at a late hour the next morning, to his great surprise and chagrin, our host found them vacant.

The next seen of Lieutenant Hunter was at City Marshal Tukey's Office, under arrest for swindling a merchant on one of the wharves out of three hundred dollars. For this he was sent to the State's Prison at Charlestown for three years.

After serving out his time in Charlestown he went to New York, where he was again caught at his old tricks, and sent to Sing Sing, where he served four years more. Where he has since been is not quite certain, but he now turns up again, "the same old coon."

Larkin is still a young-looking man, and is very active, although he must be rising forty. He will be sent to New York, where the courts will probably give him a little of the " sword " exercise, and send him again to his old home at Sing Sing.

When he rose to depart I saw the tears standing in his eyes, and as he took a very gentlemanly leave of those in the office, he remarked, " *This is All-Fool's day*, and I am a large stockholder."

THIEVES WITH A BAG.

"HE was a thief, and had the bag," was an epithet applied to one in olden time, and his name has come down to us in disgrace.

A thief is a thief, in any age of the world; but whether the bag and the way of carrying it is of modern invention, or patented by the old thief aforesaid, is not quite clear.

Be that as it may, the fact is evident that we have thieves amongst us at the present day who carry bags, and very big bags too, and female thieves at that; and honest shopkeepers in Boston (it is supposed there are some) are hardly aware to what extent they are fleeced by the walking warehouses that promenade our streets.

In most of the retail dry goods stores the method of showing goods to customers results in piling them up promiscuously in large quantities on the counters, and several pieces might not be missed till night nor even then, and it is more than probable that the footing up of the year's profit in many cases is seriously affected by the divers appropriations made by the *bagging fraternity* to the utter astonishment of the proprietor, and leaving perhaps a most cruel and unjust suspicion on some innocent clerk or salesman.

These female bag thieves — for they are mostly females — generally " go shopping " in pairs. One prices the goods, and while she engages the attention of the salesman, the other bags whatever she can lay her hands on.

The thief-bag is no great curiosity in itself, but, like most good things, is very simple and useful. It generally consists of about two yards of cotton cloth, doubled and sewed up at the sides, with a strong cord about the top, to fasten about the waist under the dress, with a pocket hole on one side. This, when well filled, answers all the purposes of the most approved balmoral. I have known a woman to secrete and carry off a whole web of cotton cloth in one of these bags.

In the summer of 1862, one of the officers brought in one of the professors of the art, who carried a bag, and it was well filled, too; but the bag was a little different from those above described. She wore a Florence silk dress of a costly pattern; the dress was made with a stout lining, forming a bag of the whole front part, which would hold at least six bushels. She was making her morning calls when arrested, but had succeeded in bagging about sixty dollars worth of ribbons, and a lot of laces, gloves, hosiery, &c., amounting in value to over one hundred dollars. These had all been taken at one store, and were not missed by the proprietor. What amount she would have bagged in the course of the day, had not her progress been arrested, it is impossible to say, but she had made a fair beginning. It was subsequently ascertained that she kept a *variety store* at the South End, and was retailing goods very cheap, — in fact, sometimes much cheaper than could be purchased of the importer or manufacturer, and no doubt she realized good profits at that.

This is by no means a solitary instance that came to the knowledge of the police, as numerous cases of the same nature occur every year.

The light-fingered gentry that carry the bag, as I have already said, are mostly females, who operate on dry goods stores; but cases among the other sex are sometimes detected, where overcoats with tremendous big pockets in the inside of the skirt, serve for the bag; and in relation to the dry goods trade, also, the rule, like all others, has its exceptions, as this class sometimes engage in the grocery and provision business to some extent.

I recollect a case that occurred on the 23d day of February, 1860. One Margaret (I will not mention the other name) was brought into the Station House by some citizens. She had got a little top-heavy, and fell in Blackstone Street. When brought in, her appearance looked a little suspicious, and on examination disclosed one of the cotton bags, worn as usual, containing the following schedule of contents, viz: One bottle champaigne, two glass tumblers (one broken), two earthen plates, two oranges, one apple, three boiled eggs, one pound of butter, one pound of sugar (loose), a double handful of black tea, five seed-cakes, two doughnuts, one pepper-box, one mustard spoon, part of a boiled potato, and two uncooked onions. Unaccountable as this may seem, it is true to the letter; but how or where she obtained them, I never could learn. She had probably made a grab in every grocery and provision shop and every saloon she had entered; but no one would claim any of the property, and she was discharged from custody when she became sober, saying, "it was a shame that a dacent woman cannot *go out shopping jist* without being insulted by the *Perlice*."

A TRIP AMONG THE SNOWBANKS.

Having occasion to make a short tour into the country, partly on business connected with my department and partly to visit some friends, I sallied forth one winter morning with valise in hand, and proceeded to the Fitchburg Railroad Depot. On arriving at the depot, just as the cars were about to start, I took a seat in a comfortable car, marked Cheshire R. R., and soon found my cage in motion. In a few minutes the bridge railings over Charles River, and the numerous shops and buildings in our sister city of pigs and pigeons, were receding from view with true railroad speed.

After indulging in a passing glance at the figures of some score of human beings that had taken up their temporary habitation in our flying house, some of whom were eagerly devouring the morning news, while others seemed deeply engaged in communion with their own thoughts, and seeing nothing that was likely to break the monotony of a quiet ride, I nestled myself into one corner of a double seat, so as to get as good a view as possible of external circumstances through a frosty pane of glass, and calmly resigned myself to the elements that had been brought into requisition for the benefit of myself and companions on this occasion.

The morning was cold, but beautifully fine, and the large fleece of snow that had so recently spread its white mantle over the landscape, had here entirely disappeared, and every object that from my isolated corner could reach the eye, seemed to indicate the early approach of Spring.

We hurried on apace, our iron-horse seeming to gain increased vigor as he puffed and snuffed the fresh north breeze, while I sat quietly indulging in the anticipations of sweet flowers and singing birds. After passing the good old town of Concord, some twenty miles on our journey, ever and anon there began to appear long, narrow, white banks, half hidden from view by the field fence, or gracefully encircling the woodland skirt, as if stern old Winter was still lingering, quite unwilling to take his final farewell.

As we passed further on, the white banks became more frequent, and of increased magnitude, till only here and there were to be seen small hillocks, occasionally peeping from their winter bed, looking for all the world like so many little islands dotting the broad expanse of ocean.

When we had proceeded so far northward as to bring to view the venerated Monadnoe, all vestige of earth had disappeared, and we were literally out of sight of land. However, nothing daunted, we ploughed our way along through the banks of snow until we arrived safely at the quiet little village of Bellows Falls, Vermont, at about half past twelve o'clock P. M., at which place my car ride was at an end.

This village, which lies just above Walpole, N. H., on the Vermont side of the Connecticut River, and which was named partly from an old Indian hunter, who flourished among the early settlers of Walpole, and partly from the beautiful falls in the river at that point, was some years ago selected as a site for an extensive cotton manufactory; but in consequence of unforeseen reverses, which occurred soon after, the enterprise was abandoned, and the large foundations then commenced still remain uncovered.

The falls in the river when the water is high, present a scene of much grandeur and interest; but at the time of my visit, the water being low, little was to be seen but a mass of ragged rocks partially covered with snow and ice.

At this place I took some refreshments with the obliging landlord of the Island House, and made preparations to take the stage for a nice snug village up among the hills about twelve miles to the eastward.

"*Stage ready,*" said a sharp but good-natured voice; and fearing I was about to lose my chance,

I dove through the open door of the hotel, from whence the voice came, and was speedily ushered aboard the aforesaid *ready* vehicle before I was fully aware of my exact whereabouts.

On looking about me to define my position (as politicians would say), I found myself not a lone tenant of the vehicle, three ladies having secured *preëmption rights* before my arrival. One was a lady of mature age, small stature, thin face, sharp nose, and gold-bowed spectacles. The second was a small woman, in dark dress, but so closely veiled I could not distinguish her features. The third was a large-featured, blue-eyed, rosy-cheeked lass of some twenty summers, with a fine pearly set of teeth, looking as if she could enjoy life in the fresh air, and apparently as full of fun as an egg is of meat. The rest of our freight consisted of some kegs of oysters, boxes, trunks, bundles, bandboxes, a bag of oats, buffalo robes, blankets and straw. And then *the stage*, — none but a backwoodsman would have recognized the *thing* by the *name;* and, familiar as I once was with country travelling, under any other circumstances, I should have been puzzled to know if I were not in the *wrong box*.

The stage consisted of two strips of timber about ten feet long, turned up at the front end. These runners were about four feet apart, and connected by strong wood beams, the ends projecting outside the runners, and fastened at each end by strong oak pins. On top of these beams was a stout board box, about eight feet long by four feet wide, and two feet deep, and secured by stakes inserted in the ends of the projecting beams, the stakes reaching about four inches above the top edge of the box. There were two old-fashioned high-back chairs in the hind part of the box, and two other seats consisting of strips of board laid crosswise with a hole at either end to receive the projecting stakes.

The team attached to the stage was a fine pair of bay horses, hitched on *tandem*, or one before the other, — and our stage was complete. I have been thus particular in giving a description, as it was an institution to which I was about to submit my *life*, if not my *fortune* and *sacred honor*. My observations were made while the driver was politely arranging the buffaloes and blankets for the comfort of the ladies.

"Driver," said I, "will you please give me an outside seat? Inside of a stage makes me sick; 't is a very unpleasant sensation, you know?"

"Certainly, certainly; take your choice of seats, sir; only accommodate the ladies."

"Thank you, sir," said I. And as the rear seats were occupied by the two elderly ladies, the next by the fair-cheeked funny damsel, whose ponderous hoop-skirt projected on either side the stage, and the only remaining seat seeming to be reserved for the driver, I thought my best chance was on the bag of oats just under the *lee* of the hoop-skirt, and there I resolved to make my *debut* in the coming performance.

"All aboard!" cried the driver (although there was no other person in sight); and springing on to the front seat, with reins in hand, he twirled around and above his head a long heavy whip which ended in a crack, that not only hoisted me four inches from my bag of oats, but also every foot of the fine bay ponies from their underpinning.

The sudden start elicited a groan from the ladies on the rear seat, a *tee-he* from her in the big hoops, and we were off at a speed that would have done credit to the most approved locomotive.

I believe I have given a pretty correct account of our travelling establishment, all but the superintendent, and I now had a chance to look at him. He was no inconsiderable personage in our enterprise, as the safety of our whole corporation was entrusted to his hands.

Well, he was a man about fifty years of age, medium size, broad shoulders, large head, covered with a profusion of bushy red hair, whiskers of the same color, with a peculiar formed nose, and mouth that seemed to indicate that his eye-teeth had been cut. His broad, good-natured face was well covered with freckles, and his twinkling gray eye denoted much good humor.

"Driver," said I, "you need not hold in them animals on our account. I reckon we can ride as fast as you can drive."

"I think so too," said the passenger on the middle seat.

"Don't be too confident," said the driver. "Disappointment lurks in many a prize." And his prediction proved but too true, for we had proceeded but a few hundred yards before we got *spilled out*, and left some distance behind.

Our road lay through a hollow, winding about between high hills on either side, and consisted mostly of a narrow canal dug out through ponderous banks of snow, shoulder high in many places. This canal was only wide enough for one team to pass, which made turning out very difficult. In some places it was necessary to dig into the deep banks at the side, where one team could switch off for another to pass, and sometimes advantage could be taken of a little rise where the snow was not so deep; but in all directions the crust on the top of the snow was of sufficient strength to bear a man.

It was at one of these *turn-outs* that our accident occurred, and to us it proved a *turn-out* in a double sense.

Our driver, on arriving at one of these points, had availed himself of the opportunity to let another team pass, and our tandem team being in high life, and not easily managed, sprang back upon the main track in such a manner as to separate our stagebox from the running part, and in the twinkling of an eye we found ourselves in an inverted position. To add to our misfortune, this turn-out had been chosen on the top of a little rise, where the snow was not so deep; it was also just at the turn of the road, and the consequence was, that we *inside passengers*, found ourselves with any quantity of lumber, baggage, and straw, making rapid progress down a little precipice, and all at once and all together bringing up against a fence at the foot, one mixed, heterogeneous mass. By hokey! what a mess! True to nature, my first thought was for myself, and after several severe struggles I found myself right end up, unhurt. Next for the ladies. The first two who sat upon the back seat had at first start toppled over backwards, and lay kicking among the blankets and buffalo robes wrapped about them. But where was the lady in hoops? Under the ruins, surely, and I dove for the pile; but before proceeding far in my efforts, I espied on the further side from me something in the form of a huge umbrella, that had been turned inside out by a gust of wind, and was swinging to and fro in the breeze like an inflated balloon endeavoring to escape from its moorings. I sprang to the spot, and peeped in at the top. Gracious heavens! there was a head in it! As I was about to reach in and part the ringlets that hid the features, a small voice saluted my ear, saying, "*Help me out!*" This was one end of our rosy-cheeked passenger; the rest was under the rubbish, and with some difficulty she was at length rescued from her unpleasant position.

After a few inquiries, we passengers, to our inexpressible joy, found we were all present and uninjured. But where was the team and the driver? Not in sight. However, in a few moments both made their appearance, together with the running part of our stage. When the stage-box, with its contents, had left its foundation, our driver with the team and what of the stage remained attached to the horses, had disappeared around a curve in the road.

"Well," said he, "thought you could ride as fast as I could drive."

"Blast your red whiskers!" said I, half inclined to think it was no accident. The lady in hoops nodded assent.

After some delay, we succeeded in arranging our furniture; and our stage again being *ready*, and we "all aboard," we again took a fresh start on our journey.

The lady passengers all left at the next village, and I being the only inside passenger, had ample time to reflect on the uncertainty of all sublunary things in general, and of tandem-team staging in particular. However, we pursued our journey without further accident, and about sunset we reached a thriving little village up among the hills of New Hampshire, where lies the homestead of my good old father, and where I was greeted with a hearty welcome.

After enjoying a night of refreshing sleep I arose with the sun, and sallied out to get a snuff of the fresh country air and take a look. I had not visited my native hills in *winter* for twenty years, and the scene now presented to my view was novel and interesting in the extreme. On every side, and at every point, as far as the eye could reach, the surrounding landscape was enshrouded in one continued sheet of everlasting snow. No fence appeared to mark the boundaries of the numerous fields that lay hidden beneath the frosty deep, and nought but an occasional intervening woodland, and now and then a human dwelling, appeared to break the sameness of this immense transparent sheet.

The bright, warm sun was shedding its rays obliquely on this earth-bound crest, imparting to the broad expanse the appearance of one endless ocean of glittering diamonds. Who could look upon that scene without experiencing emotions of admiration and devotion? My early days were passed here; then a like exhibition of Nature's handiwork would have passed my notice as commonplace. Then, at the return of each season I witnessed their beauties and enjoyed their sports with my companions; but a lapse of twenty years had wrought a change, not in the landscape, but in me.

Those who were my companions then, — where are they? Some are scattered to the four quarters of the globe, and many are sleeping in the tomb. I myself am an old man, and another generation now occupies the place once occupied by me and my companions, and I am a stranger in my native village.

Yet, standing here, with this familiar scene spread before me, brings to my heart the fond recollections of my boyhood, so deep, so real; and they come rushing back so powerfully as to fill the depths of my inmost soul with all their freshness and vigor.

"Am I not a boy again?" I asked myself, as I found the tears stealing down my care-worn cheeks. "These very tears bear me witness that I am yet a child. True, my old playmates are not here, but the hills, the valleys, the river, the woodland, the glittering silver landscape are here as they were, and the beautiful sun is still shining brightly down on them all; and although twenty years have passed since I last stood here, it seems but yesterday."

I trust I never was prone to murmur at the inscrutable ways of Divine Providence, but have ever felt it a duty, as well as a privilege, to improve and enjoy the blessings so bountifully bestowed upon us by that infinite Source of all good. And as I stood gazing upon the summit of the crest-bound hill on the opposite side of the river, the field of many a day's sport when I was young, I involuntarily exclaimed, "Young or old, if I live, I'll have a coast."

I prolonged my morning walk till a late hour, and returned with a keen appetite, and fancy that I did ample justice to a bountifully-spread table in the breakfast-room of my good old father.

After arranging some business I had in the village, I wended my way up a steep hillside, on the summit of which stood a venerable farmhouse, for the double purpose of shaking hands with some old acquaintances I thought I might find there, and also to find some one to assist me in carrying out my morning's resolution. Nor was I disappointed in my calculations, for on entering the door of that familiar old dwelling, "the latch-string of which was ever on the outside," I was greeted with the smiles of a dozen familiar faces, who with open hearts and extended hands bade me welcome.

"Just in time," said half-a-dozen voices; and so indeed I was just in time to make one of a most happy and interesting maple-sugar party, known only to those localities where the sugar maple-tree grows. And a glorious time we had of it too, — a time that I had coveted on many a returning spring since I had left my native hills, but a luxury that had this time escaped my anticipations, so intent had I been in the thought of a boyish coast.

After we had enjoyed a feast of warm maple sugar, and I had been asked and answered ten thousand questions, I carelessly remarked what an excellent opportunity the young people in the country have for coasting, adding, that where I lived, such chances would afford rare sport for young and old of both sexes. This was enough; the bait had taken beyond my highest expectations; and before I had time to put a serious face on the matter, I had received half a dozen challenges from as many roguish little nymphs to go out and *slide*. One little minx, not yet out of her teens, came forward and said, "I gueth you dathent ride with me, thir, down that stheep hill by the suthgar houth." This was a challenge I did not feel at liberty to refuse, and I said I dared to ride anywhere that any young lady dared to ride, and I would, too, if it broke my neck, — although, I must confess, I had my misgivings.

In a short time all the available *rolling stock* of the coasting company was in readiness, and all the stockholders and their guests were off to the coasting grounds, for a trial of speed.

Reader, did you ever participate in a regular country coasting expedition, where the hillsides descend at an angle of forty-five degrees, and as much steeper as you desire, all covered with the pure white snow, the surface hard enough to bear up an ox team, and as smooth and as slippery as the purest of glass? — where you can select a track of any length you choose, on which you can skim off with lightning speed into the long, deep valley a mile away; or where, by a circuitous course, you can wind around among the hills with your wooden horse, carefully guided by first one foot, then the other, till you arrive back almost to your first starting-point, where you can again commence the journey anew? — where red noses, rosy cheeks, bright, roguish eyes, and long flowing ringlets dot the hillocks as plenty as blackberries in August? — where little wooden clippers, whose capacity is extended by the addition of a board projecting behind, loaded to their utmost with merry life, are shooting down the giddy steep with the swiftness of an arrow, perhaps occasionally dropping a little lump of humanity, that, in spite of itself, tips end over end till it brings up at some convenient stopping-place? — or, mayhap, the bark, misguided by some inexperienced *foot*, leaps over some miniature precipice and lands its precious burden at the bottom? — where calico, satinet, caps, hoods, mufflers, shawls, tidies, leggings, cloaks, ringlets, big boots, heads, arms, feet, shins, and bodies are completely mixed up in the most incomprehensible and ludicrous confusion? — where the loud, merry laugh rings out from a score of healthy lungs from amid the throng of reckless adventurers?

Reader, did I hear you say that you had participated in these invigorating, soul-stirring exercises? If you have, I need not attempt to picture to you the pleasures and enjoyments of my coasting experience on that day. If you have not, any attempt of mine to enlighten you on the subject will be fruitless, for pen, language, or imagination, even, is quite incompetent to the task.

After enjoying my coast and completing my business transactions, I took leave of my friends and returned to my family and business in the city; and if I am really no younger or better, I fully believe I am, at least, no worse for my trip among the snowbanks.

COMMERCIAL STREET FIRE.

The 24th of February, 1862, was one of the most remarkable days occurring in our latitude, and one long to be remembered as the event of Commercial Street fire, which in a few hours swept away several millions of property.

In the morning came a thick mist, with snow and sleet, which, about noon, was followed with heavy rain. Early in the afternoon the clouds broke away, and it was quite warm; but later the heavens again became uncommonly dark, the air exceedingly close, and in a short time a most terrific thunder-storm burst upon the city and country for many miles around. The electric fluid in many places destroyed considerable property, and in several instances animal and human life. Just at sundown the shower ceased, and a most brilliant rainbow appeared in the east.

Early in the evening the wind shifted to the northwest, and blew a gale, and the snow and hail fell in avalanches; the wind strewed the streets with signs and window-blinds; chimneys and church steeples were blown down, and in several instances buildings were unroofed and much damaged.

About ten o'clock in the evening, while the elements seemed to be struggling in the wildest commotion, all at once the whole heavens were lighted up in one lurid glare. In a few moments the alarm-bells added their doleful notes, and gave warning that the dread Fire King was abroad on the wings of the storm.

The scene was the most sublime, the most fearfully imposing, my eyes ever beheld. A fire had broke out in the upper story of Mathews block, a large four-story brick and stone building, facing on North, Clark, and Commercial streets. This building, in the upper stories, was occupied for the storage of cotton, for sailmaker's goods and other combustible materials, and in a few moments the whole block at the top was wrapped in one sheet of flame. The firemen and a large force of police were soon on the ground, the former to extinguish the flames, and the latter to preserve life and property; but amid this terrible wreck of elements human power and greatness sank into insignificance.

The block was so high that the most powerful engine could not throw water to the top, and the weather had become exceedingly cold, the mercury falling from twenty-eight above to as low as zero, in about two hours. Under these difficulties, little or nothing could be done to arrest the flames in the block, and, in about half an hour from the discovery of the fire, the walls of the building came tumbling into the street.

The police had shut off the streets with ropes, and forced back the great numbers of persons who had collected in close proximity to the building, and, unquestionably, saved many lives.

The terrible wind, which seemed to gain new strength as the fire increased, drove the flames across Commercial Street into a stone block fronting on Eastern Avenue. These stores were also occupied mostly by combustible material, among the rest an extensive linseed oil mill, which burnt with terrific fury, and this whole block was soon a heap of ruins. A portion of the block on the south side of the Avenue, containing a large quantity of grain, was likewise destroyed.

The wind continued to blow a hurricane; snow was falling in an avalanche; boards, shingles, and cinders were flying in every direction; tremendous volumes of flame and smoke, swayed hither and thither by the tempest, now covered the adjoining building, and then, swaying over in an opposite direction, would seem to swallow up the sea of spectators that filled the streets, to witness the scene; red-hot columns of granite were tumbling into the street, hissing like serpents as they fell into the water, that was nearly knee deep. The loud cries of the firemen, the puffing and shrieking of the engines, and the crashing of falling timbers, all combined to form a *tableau* rarely witnessed.

More than ten hundred thousand dollars worth of property was destroyed. Some forty families were turned homeless into the street, two brave firemen fell victims to their fearful duties, and the morning light presented to the view one vast heap of smouldering ruins.

WOMAN'S REVENGE.

One evening in September, 1858, an intelligent-looking young lady came into the Station House, saying that she had shot a man in North Street, and, she supposed, had killed him; desired to give herself up to the officers, and very calmly seated herself and told me the circumstances.

Her story was the oft-repeated tale of seduction and desertion. The man she had shot had long been her suitor, and, under a solemn promise of marriage, had accomplished her ruin, and in her misfortune had abandoned her. In a fit of desperation she had procured a double-barrelled pistol, which she had loaded, both barrels, with powder and ball to the muzzle, one of which she designed for her seducer, and the other for herself. She had this evening crossed his path, and as he passed her she shot him in the back. The charge was so heavy that the woodwork of the pistol was shattered in splinters, and flew from her hand; she searched for it, and as people came running to the spot where the wounded man lay, she felt that she would soon be arrested, and hastened to the Station House, that the officers of the law might now do that which she had intended to do herself had she retained the other barrel of the pistol. She was fearfully calm, apparently rational, and her simple narrative bore the evidence of truth, and excited the sympathy of those that heard it.

When she first came in, officers were sent to investigate, and in a short time the wounded man was brought in, faint and bloody, and physicians immediately summoned. The ball was found to have entered the back, just under the left shoulder-blade, proceeding upward, so that it had not reached the vitals. The pistol was discharged just as he was stepping from the crossing on to the sidewalk; he was stooping a little as he raised himself up, which probably saved his life. The ball could not be extracted, but his wound was dressed, and he was conveyed home. The pistol was found, and is now in my cabinet.

When the case came before the Grand Jury, I took good care that all the facts of the case were made known. The jury found no bill, and the poor girl was discharged. She, with her offspring, are now sheltered by the roof of a kind father, and the wounded author of her sorrow now moves in respectable society; but he will carry that leaden memento of his perfidy with him to his grave.

MECHANICAL BAKERY FIRE.

On the night of February 5, 1859, at 11 o'clock, a fire occurred on Commercial, between Battery and Salutation streets, entirely destroying a large building recently erected and furnished for a Mechanical Steam Bakery. The building was of brick, with a granite front, six stories high, and extending back from Commercial Street some one hundred and twenty feet in depth, the front extending the entire length from Battery to Salutation Street, having been furnished with the most complete apparatus sufficient to make five hundred barrels of flour into bread daily. This establishment, together with several dwellings on Battery and on Salutation Street, was totally destroyed.

Several persons were severely injured by the falling of the crumbling walls of the bakery, before they could escape from their dwelling. One old man, who was too infirm to walk, was buried in the ruins of his house, but was finally rescued by the police and citizens, and conveyed to the hospital. Several were forcibly removed from their dwellings on Commercial Street, a captain of police actually carrying out by main strength an old lady weighing near two hundred pounds, very much against her will. She had barricaded her door on the inside, to keep the thieves from carrying off her little stock of furniture, and when told that her life was in danger, she replied, "It is all bosh that ye tell me; has not me landlord repeatedly told me that the house was insured?" But before she had been three minutes from beneath the roof, a falling wall from the bakery levelled every timber to the foundation.

The front granite wall of the bakery remained standing till the end walls had mostly crumbled down, when the police made an effort to clear the Square in front. This was not accomplished till we procured two long ropes, well manned, and commencing in the centre, we forced back the crowd each way, both down and up Commercial Street, which, amid loud oaths and imprecations from the spectators, was accomplished with no little difficulty. The Square, however, had not been cleared ten minutes, when the whole six-story stone front fell broadside into the street, and the space which was now covered with a huge mass of broken granite, ten minutes before was occupied by at least five hundred human beings, who, had they not been removed, would have been crushed to atoms. As it was, no one was injured, save one man, who had his leg broken by a stone, while standing on the opposite side of the street at Battery wharf.

After the fall of this wall, no more complaint was heard about the interference of the police.

It would be well for spectators at a fire to remember that the falling of a stone wall of a burning building is very different from a brick one; the latter comes crumbling down, while the former almost invariably falls by a broadside, like a plank reared on one end, and a respectful distance is much the safer place.

The loss by the Mechanical Bakery fire was estimated at $100,000; but the limits of devastation were most efficiently prescribed by the brave firemen, and many lives were saved by the prompt and energetic action of the police.

THE LOST TREASURE.

ONE day in July, 1858, an interesting, dark-eyed girl of some fifteen summers came into the Station House, inquired for me, and told me her story. Her father was a mechanic, and had resided at the North End many years; his business becoming dull, he was unable to get employment, and, as a last resort, he had enlisted in the Navy, to obtain means to keep his wife and family from the almshouse. He had been gone eight months, leaving his family in a small tenement in a place leading out of Snowhill Street.

A few days since, he sent home a draft on a firm in the city for his wages, and to-day, herself and little brother procured a check and drew from one of the banks in the city, some ninety dollars. They took the money, and with light steps and merry hearts started for home with their treasure, to pay up their bills and to procure the necessaries of life for themselves and their mother, she being confined to a bed of sickness, from which it was then probable she would never rise.

On arriving home the money was missing; it had been lost on the way, and it was their all. The children immediately retraced their steps, and made diligent search; but the money could not be found. They were advised to come to the Station House, and report the loss. When she had told her story, the big tears came stealing down her cheeks, and with a tone of anguish that would have reached harder hearts than mine, she exclaimed: —

"Oh, my poor mother! Can you, sir, do anything for us?"

I said I would try. I immediately sent out two trusty officers, with directions to make every effort within their reach to recover the money; but their most untiring efforts were fruitless. I next proceeded to Court Square, where, on the first corner, I found a group of good-fellows, familiarly known as *Reporters*, whose ears are ever open for an *item*, and whose hearts are ever alive with interest and sympathy for the unfortunate, and to them related the story. With the characteristic generosity of the craft, there came out in the evening papers a prominent notice of the loss.

About half an hour after the five o'clock edition had been circulated about the city, an Irish gentleman came into the Station House with paper in hand, and pointing to the notice, he said, "I have found that money, and here it is. Will you please take care of it, sir?" placing a roll of bills in my hand.

I looked at the money, and it was all there. It had been dropped on Salem Street, and picked up by this honest, kind-hearted gentleman, and was safe. We immediately proceeded to the residence of its owner; there, on the fourth floor of a tenement, in a small but neat room, we found the sick mother, pale and haggard; and there, too, were her children gathered about her. When we entered not a word was spoken, but sorrow and disappointment marked every feature in that little group. I went to the bedside of the mother, and told her that her treasure had been found by the gentleman with me, and we had brought it to her. She reached forth her emaciated hand and took it from mine, and the little ones drew closer about her bedside. Not a word was yet spoken by them, but the moistened eyelids and expressions of thankfulness resting upon the countenances of that little party, spoke in volumes that words could not impart.

For many years I had been accustomed to witness scenes of misery in almost every form, and I had supposed my own heart had become hardened by the frequent repetition; but I came away from that house involuntarily wiping the tears from my own eyes.

MY OLD GRAY CAT.

I FIND the following among my records of Police Recollections. It is, perhaps, a little out of place, but it is so true, and it calls up in my heart the recollections of other days in such deep emotion, that I hope to be pardoned for recording it here.

June 17, 1864. I have a pet cat, who has eaten of the crumbs of my table, this day, seventeen years. He is an old fellow, — not a tooth in his head this many a year, — yet he is as fat and sleek, as lively and playful, as when a kitten. He is, in fact, rather a curious old fellow for a cat, and I often think that he really knows more than he will tell.

After the close of my day's labor, no sooner does my footstep reach the threshold, than he is at the door to welcome my entrance with a *pert* or a *mew*. If I am in the house, he is uneasy unless he is with me, and hardly any closed door is proof against his handy paws till he reaches me; and then the antics and pranks that he will cut are anything but what would be expected of an old cat.

I sometimes think that many of his notions appear more like calculation than instinct. Often, when about to leave the house, have I found his long crooked claws inserted in my coat-tail, or deeply imbedded in the leg of my pants, endeavoring with all his might to prevent my egress, as if to say, " *Don't go yet.*"

He is but an old gray cat, but he has followed me, and shared my varied fortunes, for seventeen years. He is but an old gray cat, but he was a special favorite with dear and loved ones who now lie mouldering in the tomb. In his early life his friends were my friends; *but among them there are now none left, — no, not one!* He seems to be the only living link that binds me so tenderly to those who have left me to battle the ills of life alone; and often, while looking at him, I find the big hot tears stealing unwittingly down my furrowed cheeks, as memory wanders o'er the scenes of other days.

He is but an old gray cat, but why should I not care for him in the wane of life? He will die one of these days, — *and so shall I.*

CHURCH ROBBERY.

As I was about to leave the Office one evening, a gentleman came in and inquired for an officer. He was a tall, straight, well-built man, with a large round head, the moral and intellectual well developed, rather sharp features, quick, pleasant eye, that did not seem to evade your own; his hands and countenance indicating an indoor life, his whole bearing bespeaking the perfect gentleman.

I at once saw that he was no ordinary customer, so I invited him to take a seat, and gave him my whole attention. After looking at me a moment in quite a familiar, but rather ludicrous manner, he laughed, without uttering a word. Was the man insane? No; the intelligence and self-possession shining out in that blue eye could not be mistaken; he was not insane, neither was he a rogue nor a fool.

After waiting what seemed to me a long time, (each of us looking the other square in the face,) finding he still hesitated, at last I said—

"Well, sir, what can I do for you?"

"Well, sir," said he, in a rich, mellow voice, "I have called on rather a curious errand. I am Mr. ———, the Rector of ——— Church, and to-day being *Good Friday*, a collection was taken up for charitable purposes in my church, which probably amounted to some two hundred dollars, for my people are wealthy and liberal. That money, sir, has been stolen from us, and in a manner which appears so ludicrous — (and the novelty of the thing getting the advantage of his dignity, he laughed outright,) — excuse me," said he, "but the thing is so queer!"

"A till thief, of the first water," thought I, running over in my mind the whole catalogue of that branch of the profession, wondering who among them all was mean enough to rob a contribution-box. "Please tell me all the circumstances," said I.

"I can tell you very little of my own knowledge," said he, "except that the money was collected, and is gone; but, as I have it from my people, it was this way: As usual, on *Good Friday*, the collection was taken up by six messengers. After passing through the house, the boxes containing the contributions were placed on the chancel rail till the close of the service, all but the one passed by the messenger in the gallery. At the close of the meeting, while all were busily engaged, some in making their egress from the house, and others in stopping a moment to speak with a friend, some one walked up to the chancel rail and deliberately emptied the contents of the boxes into his own pocket. I was in the robe-room at the time," said he, " and distinctly recollect hearing the change chink as it was turned out of the boxes. The young sexton came down from the gallery at the time, and having no suspicion of wrong, also emptied his box into the same pocket with the rest ; and just as our *new treasurer* turned to walk off, an old gentleman of the congregation stepped up and remarked that he had not given what he intended, and wished to add another five-dollar bill, which was politely accepted, and the newly-installed official walked quietly away, before any of the proper officers had noticed what was going on. Did you ever hear of anything so supremely ridiculous?" said he; and he again showed a fine set of white teeth. " I really think the rascal is deserving some credit for his impudence, but I would like to recover the money, if possible," said he. " But I do not wish to make the matter public; I desire you not to publish the robbery in the papers."

I said the case should be managed as he desired, and calling one of the officers, gave him instructions relative to the matter, and the reverend gentleman departed

Next morning the gentleman sent me word that the whole suspicion was a mistake, — that the money was taken by one of their own people, and it was all safe. Then it was my turn to laugh, and I really wished the good man who gave me the case the evening before had been present for my benefit. But I was heartily glad it turned out to be a mistake, and that I had the opportunity to make the acquaintance of a highly-accomplished and respectable gentleman under no worse circumstances.

THE NEW YORK
PUBLIC LI...

ASTOR ...
TILDEN F...
R

PICKPOCKETS.

PICKPOCKETS.

Of all the thieves that disgrace the name of man, the pickpocket is the meanest. Yet mean as he is, it is not uncommon to hear members of the craft boasting of their skill. In former times this class of thieves were comparatively small and included active young men only. I recollect reading an account of a pickpocket operation at Faneuil Hall many years ago when *Town* Meetings were held there. A young fellow was caught in the act, beat almost to death by the bystanders, and afterwards sent to the Penitentiary. The crime was looked upon with great disgust then, and pity we have not a little of their discipline now. But picking pockets has since become a profession and includes not only *active young men* but males and females too of every age, sex, and color, from the boy and girl of eight years to the man and woman of sixty.

Some officers seem to think it prudent to give notice when a pickpocket is seen in a crowd, and immediately cry out "Pickpockets, look out for your wallets!" &c.; but this is the very thing he should not do, for no sooner comes such word of caution than every man's hand almost involuntarily goes to his wallet, indicating to the wily thief (who stands by unknown to all but the officer) just where the coveted treasure lies, and really saves a good deal of his valuable time which would otherwise be consumed in *sounding*.

I have said that the profession now includes almost every age, sex, and color. A few months since, our fellows brought in two girls, well-dressed and sprightly, aged *thirteen* and *fourteen* years only, who were as busy as bees in rifling the pockets of a crowd of ladies who were standing about Scollay's Building awaiting the cars; and a short time since the police arrested some dozen boys all in *round caps*, who had a regular organization for pocket picking. They were from eight to fifteen years old, and one of the number, aged but ten years, made his boast in the Police Office, that he had *gone down twenty-five pockets in less than six weeks*, — and he probably told the truth.

The place selected by these juvenile operators is generally some crowded thoroughfare, the vicinity of a fire, and places where a crowd may be found in a street.

Another class of the profession, consisting of well-dressed females, may be found any pleasant afternoon in popular retail salesrooms, places of amusement, and horse-car offices, while others frequent omnibuses, horse-car platforms, and every other place affording opportunity.

A crowd and a lot of *tobacco-smokers* on the platform of a horse-car offer peculiar facilities for *losing watches*, wallets, and breastpins; the smoker and picker working together most admirably; the former stops your breath and closes your eyes with his fumigations, while the latter helps himself to whatever you may carry about your person, with perfect impunity. And I confess that I never see a *thing in pants*, puffing his nauseating fumes (from a receptacle for aught that is known coated with some loathsome disease) into the face of every lady and gentleman within his reach, without thinking the pickpocket's *assistant* is at hand, and people will do well to look to their wallets.

One day in March, 1862, a lady from out of town went into an auction store on Federal Street to make purchases, and while there missed her wallet, containing about thirty-five dollars. She suspected a man who had stood near her, but he was not to be found; and, like a sensible woman, she came immediately to the Police Office, made known her loss, and gave a description of the suspected thief.

A detective immediately started out, and was fortunate enough to get the trail, — followed it up, and found his game in his own room on the third floor of a house in Purchase Street, just as the old thief had replenished his stove with the stolen wallet. The wallet was secured and the money found on his person, and when taken before the lady both he and the wallet were fully identified.

The old thief, for he was a man above sixty, stoutly denied the charge, or that he was at the auction store, but the evidence was too positive to admit of a doubt. He said he was a German by birth, but his name plainly indicated another nationality and was probably a borrowed one at that, for on investigation it seemed to be impossible for him to tell the truth.

He was small in stature, very dirty and ragged, and looked much more like a *rag* than a *pocket* picker, and would no doubt have been discarded by the more genteel members of the profession, although he operated with good success.

Michael, for that was the name he gave, wound up his career with a round turn. At eleven o'clock he sustained a good character; at twelve arrested for pocket picking; at one locked up in City Prison; at three tried and convicted of larceny, and at four serving out a six months' term at the House of Correction.

One afternoon an old lady came to the Office with a sad countenance, and told her story. She was apparently sixty-five years old, looked tidy but careworn and feeble. She said she was formerly a resident of Boston, but for several years past had lived at Lynn; the family consisting only of herself and maiden daughter, who had a long time been an invalid. Her husband had been dead many years, and her only means of support were what little labor she could perform; and, said she, "You don't know how hard it is for us to get along."

In consequence of her unfortunate condition, an old friend of her husband had interested himself in her behalf, and secured for her the benefit of the Pemberton fund, which is raised by a legacy in the will of a gentleman of that name for the benefit of indigent widows, amounting to ten dollars semi-annually.

She had come to Boston to-day and drawn her money, and after securing her treasure had stepped into the horse-car office at Scollay's Building and took a seat on a settee to await the cars for home. While there she had her pocket picked of all her money and was left penniless.

Like reports often come to the Office, but this case seemed peculiarly painful. True the sum was small, — only ten dollars, — but it was all the old lady had. Its receipt had been anticipated by numerous little wants — those bills must be met, and the loss of the money sank deep in the poor old widow's heart, and all hands in the Office were deeply interested.

On investigation, it appeared that the old lady

thought she had kept her hand continually on her pocket while in the car office; nor could she hardly be made to believe that she had removed it at all while there, although she undoubtedly did, as will appear.

When she took a seat on the settee in the car office, two other ladies, one about her own age and one much younger, took a seat beside her on the right. While sitting there, she noticed a spool of cotton on the floor rolling along and unwinding at her feet, and, woman-like, she stooped, picked it up, rewound it (which of course took both hands) and passed it to the lady next her on the right, supposing it hers. No, it was not hers. She then passed it to her companion, but it was not hers either, and as there seemed to be no owner the old lady put it in her pocket and thought no more of the matter, not once dreaming of the opportunity she had given the pickpocket beside her while winding up the thread.

In a few moments " Cars for Prattville " was announced, and the two ladies hurried away. Soon the cars for Lynn also were at the door, and the old lady arose to go, when she discovered her loss, which she immediately made known in the office, but no trace of the missing money was to be found. She had exchanged her treasure for a spool of cotton, without the least idea of the trick that had been played upon her with such skill and success.

The lady pickpockets were never detected, but the old lady did not go away from our Office penniless.

IN the summer of 1862, several ladies who lost their portemonnaies on Washington Street, reported noticing an elderly female well-dressed and wearing *gold-bowed specs*, who abruptly jostled them on the sidewalk. Indeed, so common were these complaints, that the officers gave the unknown the name of *Madam Specs*, and made it a specialty to look her up; and one afternoon two of them who were on Washington Street *tumbled* to the veritable old lady herself.

The officers represented her as being one of the most industrious and reckless *pickers* they ever saw. She would stop at a window apparently for the purpose of looking at the goods inside, but really to watch every one that passed. When an old lady came along (she seemed partial to ladies of her own age) she would *break* for her sometimes in a smart run, get alongside and immediately commence on the pocket as they walked on. Some would notice her and edge off. If so, she would again stop at the first window and watch the next chance, all the while appearing as careless and as eager in her labors as if they were ever so legitimate.

She was not, however, very successful in her work on the day in question, having in the course of half an hour made some dozen attempts and securing but one wallet containing but about five dollars for all her trouble, and no sooner had she done this than she found herself in custody.

The old lady wore a new black silk dress with a profusion of flounces, a nice straw bonnet and veil, carried a parasol and large reticule, wore a black kid glove on her right hand, the left, with which she operated, being bare. Ladies usually wear their pockets on the right side, I believe, making it necessary for the pickpocket to use the left hand, and the old woman well understood the theory of "handling her work without mittens."

When at the Office, old woman as she was, for she must have been near sixty, she showed the most shrewdness of any thief I ever saw. When asked, she would not even give her name, nor could you draw a direct answer to any question whatever. Thieves, shrewd as many of them are, generally talk too much for their own good, often dropping a word that eventually leads to their own conviction, and it is a tough customer that will sit quietly under the inquisition of a shrewd officer without lessening his chances of escape if really guilty. But not so with *Madam Specs*. Not the movement of a muscle, or a sound could be drawn from her.

In her possession was found a few trifling articles such as *a spool of cotton*, a few pearl buttons, and the stolen purse which she had taken the last grab. If she had *raised* anything more on that day, she had an accomplice to receive the funds, but probably she had none.

Madam Specs was locked up for the night and shown up at the Office next morning, but no one knew her. At the close of which she quietly said, "What do you expect to make out of all this?" which was the only remark she was heard to make while in custody.

The lady who owned the purse refused to appear in court against the old thief, and the officer who had charge of the case very reluctantly suffered her to go. I am not aware that she has since been seen in Boston.

A CHARM GAME.

A WELL-KNOWN legal gentleman came into the Office one day, and requested me to render some assistance in ferreting out a *lady rogue*, who had been playing a deep-laid game on a highly respectable lady in a neighboring city.

It seems that a lady of wealth and the highest respectability, had formed a matrimonial connection with a gentleman every way her equal, and considerably younger than herself. After a time, although everything passed on smoothly, the lady began to have misgivings that the disparity in their ages might prove a source of inconstancy on the part of her liege lord; and the germ of distrust once having taken root, soon branched forth with amazing rapidity, and notwithstanding no earthly cause could be assigned in her own mind, the thought soon became insupportable. The lady was naturally of a marvellous turn, and she soon formed a resolution to apply to a certain female fortune-teller of considerable notoriety, who, Madam Rumor said, dealt in charms.

Well, to the fortune-teller she went, and opened her case, which was entered into with much spirit and interest.

The fortune-teller, after a long consultation and a frequent recurrence to the cards, finally decided that although the case was peculiar and extremely difficult, yet it was, if carefully managed, perfectly practicable and sure of success, and, notwithstanding the seeming disparity in age, that the affinity of spirit might be formed without a blemish, if the lady herself would keep the charm. They were to form a profound secret, to which of course the lady so deeply interested yielded a ready assent.

Then for the process: the lady applicant must carefully collect together anything valuable belonging to her husband, the smaller in compass and the higher in value the better, especially if ever worn by him or carried near his person, — watch, jewelry, money, or anything valuable. "Keep them closely near your person for a few hours, and then send me word, and I will come to you. You must keep them near you, but I, being the medium, must touch them, and then I will instruct you what to do."

The deluded lady treasured up every word, as if they had fallen from the lips of an angel, promised the strictest secrecy, and hastened home to make preparation. Before many hours she had collected gold watch, jewelry, money and keepsakes amounting in value to something over two thousand dollars, and the *charm queen* was forthwith informed, and made her appearance, bringing with her a nicely-wrought little box, in which to deposit the treasure.

The property was carefully placed in this box, the charmer being particular to touch each piece. The box was then locked, and a peculiar seal set thereon, so that it could not be opened without breaking the seal, the lady owner placing the box carefully in her own trunk, where no hand must pollute it for three weeks; and during that time the charmer was to retain the key. At the close of the specified time the charm queen was to return and deliver up the key, when the charm would be complete. The charmer departed, and the lady rested in peace.

At the expiration of three weeks, the fortune-teller did not make her appearance. The lady began to grow a little uneasy, and made inquiries, but could learn no tidings of her friend; but having carefully examined the box, and finding the seal unbroken, she felt no alarm for the safety of her property. As time rolled on and no charm queen appeared, and feeling that she had faithfully kept her secret and performed all that was required, she thought she might as well open the box, and replace the money, jewelry, &c., in their accustomed places, before the husband missed them.

She accordingly proceeded to break the seal, and, as she had not the possession of the key, to pry open the box; but on doing so — oh! horror of horrors! the valuables were gone, and in their place she beheld a box of pebbles. The *charm game* was at once apparent; she had been most cruelly duped, and her treasure was gone. The wily charmer had brought two boxes, and had managed to place in the hand of her confiding customer the box of pebbles, while she had walked off with the box of jewels, having ample time to gather up her traps and remove to parts unknown.

The lady, of course, was in a dilemma, and she could not long conceal the circumstances from her husband; but how the case became fully developed, the deponent saith not.

However, diligent search has been made for the charm-worker, as yet without success. If she manages as shrewdly in avoiding detection as she did in securing her booty, she will not soon be brought to justice.

While in the act of making a record of this transaction some months after its occurrence, a gentleman and lady, both of prepossessing appearance, walked into the Office and inquired for me, and gave me their names. I had never seen them before, but they were the duped parties of whom I had been writing. They came to make inquiries of what had been done relative to their loss; but our efforts having been closely limited by their counsel, for fear of exposure, and the guilty party not having come to our city, we had done very little in the case.

The people did not appear like persons likely to be easily imposed upon, yet so it was, and apparently very mortifying too. The gentleman seemed to take the matter very coolly, and remarked that misery loves company, and it was some consolation to know that his family were not the only fools at his own place of residence, " for," said he " ours is not a solitary case, nor the most provoking one of the kind that has occurred in our own immediate neighborhood."

LIQUOR LAW DISCLOSURES.

Of the many evils that have taxed the ingenuity and the patience of the philanthropist and the legislator, the manufacture and sale of liquor has not been among the least. The liquor law has been enacted, established, amended, reënacted, reëstablished, modified, remodelled, suspended, and reconstructed, from time immemorial.

The present law, which, from its similarity to one made for the Pine-Tree State, is called the "Maine Law," was passed in Massachusetts in 1855, and was then supposed by its friends to be the best that could be made. At the time of its passage, the question assumed somewhat a political character, and some are so ungenerous as to hint that *the spirit* still enters into the canvass of our municipal matters; but as the temperance people hardly ever have an exclusively separate candidate, the idea may be erroneous.

However, when the Maine Law came in force in 1855, the order from the City Government to the Police, went forth to *execute*, — not the liquor, but the law. Nevertheless, I believe there *was* some of the liquor worthy of condemnation, and some men probably *punished* a good deal of the article.

Well, when the order came, *Geevus* (poor burgher), loaded down with instructions, *struck out* to perform his duty, — and an up-hill business he found it. The opponents of the law (and they were a majority in Boston), of course, threw every possible obstacle in the way, and those in favor of it, I must say, seemed not over-anxious to aid us and " come up to the help of the " police against the mighty. This made our progress, to say the least, *a little slow.* However, in a few weeks many good cases were presented for the investigation of the Grand Jury; the police, in all cases, making themselves witnesses, and there their powers ended. The result is not yet forgotten.

Notwithstanding the serious necessity of some method to regulate the great evil, or of the grave character of our work, circumstances would occasionally grow out of our attempts to execute the law, in themselves the most ludicrous and annoying.

One provision of the law makes it the duty of an officer, if he finds a person intoxicated in a public place, to take him to some proper place to be kept till sober; from thence to be taken before the Police Court and complained of. Further provision is made, that if such person shall then and there fully disclose the name of the person who sold him the liquor, and all the facts relative thereto, said defendant shall be discharged, &c.

Well, one day, while one of our officers was perambulating North Street, he found a poor body lying drunk in a public place, *contrary* to law, and, faithful officer as he was, he commenced the performance of his duty. Next morning poor Pat found himself at the bar of justice, — and he was not alone in his dilemma, by a long chalk.

The practice of the clerk then was to first read the complaint for being drunk by the voluntary use of intoxicating liquor, and then pertinently inquire of the poor culprit if he wished to disclose. Very few ever responded to this invitation in the affirmative, and, on the morning in question, not one seemed to be willing to place his fault at another's door. Pat anxiously watched them, one by one, as they were fined three dollars and cost, and trotted off to the Tombs below. When his name was called by the worthy clerk, he sprang from the prisoner's stand with the agility of a cat, and sang out at the top of his voice —

"Hauld on, hauld on, misther Consthable! Ye grady spalpeen, don't let me hear another word from your mug at.all, at all; it is meself that will disclose to the jidge, his Honor. And now will yer Honor hear me, Misther Jidge? Didn't I mate Dennie, me first cousin, jist come out from the auld counthry, Mr. Jidge? And when I was so glad to see him, did n't he come along wid me to the warehouse, Misther Jidge, and by the help of Masther Walker's gimlet and a fine bit of sthraw, did n't we take a wee drop of the crather free gratis, Misther Jidge! And now, Misther Jidge, I am not like the spalpeens just here who gets drunk on three cent liquor, Misther Jidge. And now have I not disclosed according to law, sir; and if ye plase, Misther Jidge, I'll be going jist."

The venerable magistrate could not see the point, and poor Pat was fined three dollars and cost, and sent down with the rest.

Another case, that will serve to illustrate, and also to show the ingenuity of an old rogue when half-seas-over in an attempt to free himself from limbo, may be seen in the following: —

An old fellow, whose Christian name was Uriah, and who had been up for almost every offence known in the catalogue of crime, was seen by an officer early one morning seemingly inclined with a very *prying curiosity*, at the door of a dry goods store in Hanover Street; but being a little top-heavy, he made but poor progress. After watching his movements awhile, the officer brought him in.

"Well, Uriah," said I, "you did not meet with much success this morning, I learn; from present appearances it must be in consequence of that article you have in your hat."

"In my hat!" said Uriah, starting up from the railing on which he was leaning. "What is in my hat?"

"A brick," said I.

"You mean I'm drunk," said he, apparently quite willing I should take that view of his case. "Well," said he, shutting up one eye and squinting at me with the other in a most comical manner, "*I admit — I admit* 't is the thing in my hat, and if I disclose, will ye let me up; it 's the law, sir, an' I know ye will. Well, sir, I have been down to the *Home*, you know, and one of the good people there, no doubt meaning well, gave me something that is the cause of all this trouble. Yes, it is in my hat, as you say, sure enough; but I will disclose, and then I am free — 't is the law. I will disclose, and here it is," staggering back, pulling off his hat, and drawing therefrom a copy of the Maine Liquor Law in pamphlet form. "That 's the thing," said he, — "that 's what used me up; and now I 've disclosed, you 'll let me go. It 's the law;" and over he tumbled upon the floor, but not half as drunk as he pretended. He was, however, put in the cell, and kept till he was quite sober.

POLICE DESCENTS.

ALL communities may be said to have their peculiar standard of morals, and there must, of necessity, be different classes in the scale, as the higher, middling, and lower, and in speaking of either we have a comparative reference to the others. If we say a man is good, we mean that he is up to the standard, which, in fact, only means that he is better than many others — for no man is good, " no, not one ; " and, on the other hand, if we say a man is bad, we still speak comparatively, meaning that his character is below the average. If there was nothing wherewith to form a comparison, there could hardly be an appreciation of either good or evil, and a good man once said, " Were it not for the evil, I had not known the good."

It has also been said, that the standard of morals is lower in large cities than in the country, where the population is more sparse, and that the standard depreciates as the population increases. I can hardly believe this, however, for such doctrine would tend directly to encourage a life of celibacy and hermitage, where morals would hardly be counted as valuables; and if it is said, also, that there are not as good men, and women too, in cities as there are in towns, I shall demur to this whole batch of opinions.

However, it cannot be denied that a spirit of licentiousness is spread abroad through all large cities, where *influence* for evil keeps pace in a great degree with the increase of population, and which, like a lingering humor, often concentrates and breaks out at different points in the system. Or, if it is smothered by conservative treatment, it may for a time disappear from the surface, yet ever ready again to break forth anew in a different locality. Nor has our own city been an exception to the general rule.

Some people seem to think that licentiousness is almost a necessary evil, and argue that a household, or a community, who would preserve a healthy condition, must have their *sink*, or their *cesspool*, and some cities in the old world have adopted this principle, and attempt to regulate by license what they say they cannot prohibit, and when we come to look about us in relation to these matters, we can hardly see that the execution of our own laws of prohibition fully accomplishes the desired result.

In early times, the laws of our Puritan Fathers

were very severe on the licentious and vicious. So much so as to appear to us in some instances quite ridiculous: but that such evils did exist, even among the *Puritans*, is evident from the fact that it became necessary to make laws in relation to them, and more than that, the record reveals that there must have been a very curious standard of morals in Boston at these times. The time was, when, if a gentleman kissed a lady, he subjected himself to a fine of three pence at least (provided always that the offence be proved), it is presumed that this law did not prove *prohibitory*. Or, if a woman was suspected of any little improprieties, she was liable to be set high up on a stool in the broad aisle of the church on Sunday, there exposed to the gaze and derision of the whole congregation; if this were the universal practice at the present day, should we not require large churches and very *broad* aisles?

Since Boston became a city, the evils of licentiousness have sometimes shown themselves in such formidable array as to set at nought, for a time, the powers of the executive; and, in some instances, the evils have become so obnoxious that the better portion of the citizens have felt compelled to take the matter into their own hands. The demonstrations on what was called "The Hill" at the West part of the town, the *Tin Pot*, and The Beehive at the North End, were of this nature.

In demonstrations of public displeasure, it was not the practice for those engaged in them to make any arrest, but the *executors* generally amused themselves by pulling down *shanties*, and breaking up furniture, and allowing the tenants to "flee with their lives."

Since better Police Regulations have been inaugurated, these extreme measures have not been deemed necessary, or, if they were, parties have been careful not to carry them into execution. But yet, evil has not been entirely suppressed, as the records of Ann Street and some other localities bear abundant testimony.

In the year 1851, the purlieus of Ann Street had become so notorious and troublesome, that the City Government found it necessary to adopt some measure to work a reform, and, under the direction of City Marshal Tukey, a new plan was set on foot to " spring a mine."

About this time, for several weeks, might be seen the forms of two stalwart fellows (with neither badge nor baton) continually passing up and down the sidewalks in Ann Street, peering into dance-halls and cellars, and carefully taking notes of the various passing transactions; and on the evening of the 23d of April, the grand finale was brought out by a tremendous Police Descent.

The police officers who were detailed for this important duty, had been at work accumulating evidence against the numerous disturbers of the public peace, and violators of law, and had procured warrants for the arrest of some two hundred persons. At nine o'clock in the evening of this day, the whole police force, consisting of some fifty men, and about the same number of the watch department, started out from the Watch House on Hanover Street, and proceeded directly to Ann Street, where each had his work assigned. In about half an hour one hundred and sixty-five persons, of all ages, sexes, nations, and colors, were in custody in the Watch House for the various crimes of piping, fiddling, dancing, drinking, and all their attendant vices, — and from thence were marched off in pairs to the Leverett Street Jail. The next day, this horde of depraved humanity was before the Police Court, and sentenced for their crimes. Some three, some four, and some six months, to the various Reformatory Institutions.

For many weeks afterwards, the great reform in Ann Street, and the efficient and well-judged action of the police, was spoken of with admiration and praise. But the poor miserable victims of vice and misfortune, who had been taken from the street and sent to prison, were yet alive, and when their sentences had expired and they were set at liberty, they must go somewhere; they dare not go home, to their respectable friends in or out of the city; they had been in felon's cells, and would not be received and aided to reform where they were known. They dare not go back to Ann Street; the eagle eye of justice was there watching their return; they must go somewhere where they were not known, and a few weeks afterward they were scattered as domestics in the families of respectable citizens throughout the city and its suburbs. They had not reformed. During their confinement they had not the time nor opportunity for that great and important work. But they necessarily carried with them, more or less, the tastes and the feelings that they had acquired in Ann Street; and I firmly believe, that many a Christian father, and pious mother, has shed the bitter tears of grief over a fallen son or daughter who was little aware how or when the first seeds of immorality were sown in the heart of their child. What else could be the result of such family associations? At any rate, the house robberies and burglaries for a period of time directly after, increased to a most alarming extent, and those even who at first were the admirers of the grand Police Descent, began to speak in doubt of the propriety or benefit of such measures. That was the end of Police Descents of a similar character for many years.

In the fall of 1858, the writer was entrusted with the supervision of another Descent in Ann

Street, on a little different principle from that in the year 1851, and it is hoped with better results.

During the time the Station House was undergoing repairs, in Hanover Street, in the summer and fall of that year, the nymphs of Ann Street had been gaining ground both in spirit and numbers, and the officers thought they could count fifty or sixty new faces on the street, and the old stock had not diminished. Many of the new arrivals were young, and quite a number had been taken from these haunts of vice, and sent home to their friends in the country. But most of such were soon back again, and it was evident that something more potent than moral suasion was necessary to convince them of the error of their ways. After consulting with the kind-hearted Judge Wells, of the Police Court, and taking instructions from the Chief of Police, the officers at Station No. 1 were set at work to look up the evidence, and in a few days fifty-four warrants were obtained for as many of the poor deluded specimens of female humanity dwelling in Ann Street.

On the evening of the 22d of October, as the clock on the old Cockerel Church struck nine, forty policemen without uniform quietly left the Station House by different routes, and in less than thirty minutes there were fifty-one women in custody in our guardroom. Such a sight, under such circumstances, it was most painful to behold.

These girls were mostly young, and many of them had been in the city but a few months. Most of them were good looking, and under other circumstances would be considered handsome. They were taken in custody at a time when they had but just completed their toilet (the best they could raise) for the evening dance and debauch. To an unpractised eye they might have been mistaken for an assembly of beautiful and accomplished young ladies, for they were now quite sober and reserved, *rum* not having had time on that night to accomplish its accursed work.

But to one who had often been an eye-witness to their lewd and wanton behavior, and who well knew their loathsome haunts of filth and vice, the scene was heart-sickening indeed.

I spoke to them separately of their home and friends, to learn something of their history, and then told them collectively my design.

The next morning the fifty-one were at court, most of them having realized the sweets of a prison for the first night. On the opening of the court, the good judge was informed of the nature of their case, and was asked if not inconsistent with the requirements of justice, to give all who were found guilty of the charges preferred against them, a good smart sentence, with a suspension, to enable them to leave the city for their parents and home. To this the kind-hearted judge readily assented, and forty-seven of the number gladly accepted the opportunity.

With the aid of the officers, I believe they all fulfilled their agreement, and it is sincerely hoped that most of them left these dens of infamy forever.

I never had cause to regret the course I pursued in assisting to execute this Police Descent.

CHOLERA IN 1854.

In the summer of 1854, the city of Boston was visited by that dreadful scourge the Asiatic cholera; and although our northern climate is not so congenial to the fearful malady as more Southern cities, yet its ravages here were amply sufficient to carry terror and dismay to every household.

The New Police Organization had gone into operation in May of that year, and having the charge of the North Station, it fell to my lot to be much amongst the disease, and a most unpleasant, not to say dangerous, duty it was. I hope never to pass through like scenes again.

At the first appearance of the disease, fear seemed to seize almost every heart, and the Police were expected to do what no one else cared to do.

I cannot say that I was free from a lingering dread myself, but I formed a resolution that, come what would, I would not neglect my duty to the poor suffering beings about me, nor would I ask a subordinate officer to go where I dare not go, or do what I dare not do myself; and I assisted with my own hands in removing more than fifty bodies, of the dead and dying, where necessity for the safety of others required it. In some instances, where life had departed but a few hours, the corpse would be so swollen, that the largest coffin could not contain it; in others the flesh would actually fall to pieces, a putrefied mass, before it could be properly laid out, the stench arising therefrom being almost suffocating.

Most of the sickness occurred in filthy or overcrowded localities, yet the disease found its victims in all parts of the city.

In looking over my memorandum, made at the time, I find the following, in substance, omitting names.

The first case that occurred was on Sunday, June 11, in rear of what was then No. 6 Fleet Street. Hearing that a man had died there very suddenly, after making examination, I called the city physician.

The man was lying dead in the yard; had been sick about eight hours, — and another man was dying in the room from which the first had been removed. The physician immediately pronounced these marked cases of cholera. The second man died while we were there, and a woman was also taken sick. The room where these men died was over a shed, low posted, poorly ventilated, and occupied by thirteen persons.

By direction of the physician we summoned help and removed the last body from the room; it being so much swollen, that we had to put it in a box and take it out of a window; the bodies of the two men were immediately buried, the people removed, and the room closed. The day was extremely hot and muggy, and our work was anything but desirable.

These cases aroused the city authorities to action, and preparations were immediately made to remove and accommodate the sick at a hospital on Fort Hill, and the most stringent sanitary regulations were adopted.

The next day the weather became cooler, and for a few days no more cases occurred, but in about two weeks the weather became sultry again, and the disease broke out anew.

June 25. A laborer died in Keith's Alley, after an illness of eight hours; his body was too much swollen to put in a coffin, and was buried immediately.

June 26. A sailor on board the schooner "Cossack," at Lewis wharf, was attacked and removed to the hospital. The city had now provided a team with a spring wagon and bed, for the removal of the sick, which was driven by a faithful and efficient man. The same day, a woman and child died in Keith's Alley, and were removed immediately, and the house was cleansed and closed.

June 27. A woman died at 41 Portland Street, and the body was removed immediately.

A laborer was cut down in Mechanic Street, was carried home to Causeway Street, where he died in about six hours, and was buried immediately.

June 28. Several cases of smallpox occur. A woman in Arch Place is taken sick and cared for.

July 1. A woman died in Keith's Alley, sick but six hours, body putrid before we could remove it. Several others being sick in the house, the occupants were removed to the hospital. One poor woman died in the carriage on the way. The house was cleansed by fumigation and closed.

July 3. A child at No. 150 Canal Street, died this morning, sick but ten hours, and in the evening the mother was cut down and died in six hours; we removed these bodies to the Dead House in the night, and smoked the rooms.

July 5. The weather was very hot and damp, and to add to the general gloom, several cases of sunstroke occurred at the North End. One man fell in the street and was brought into the Station House apparently dead. Three others were also struck down and brought into the Station House in the course of the day. In each case medical attendance was procured, and the sufferers were carried home or otherwise provided for. Fear seemed to act as an auxiliary to the contagion, and when these people fell in the street, it was supposed to be an attack of the dreadful scourge; but the cases mentioned were decided by the physicians to be sun-stroke. The city physician and Superintendent of Health were in constant attendance, and with great care and skill, rendered the most important services in their profession. Their duties were highly responsible, and we took our directions from them.

At this time our Station House had more the appearance of a hospital than a prison. Several of those brought in on that day, died.

July 6, two women were taken down with cholera at 231 North Street; one died in six hours, and the other was removed to the hospital, where she lived but a few hours. We removed the body of the first, and cleansed and closed the house. A woman died at 212 North Street, sick but five hours; while we were removing the body a woman named Mary McGuire, aged fifty years, in a fit of *delirium tremens*, jumped from the chamber-window to the ground, a distance of twenty feet; we took her up for dead, and carried her to the Station House, but she recovered, not being seriously injured.

A laborer died at No. 6 Battery Street; this evening we removed the body. I shall long remember the sad work of those two days.

July 7. A man was brought into the Station

House from Mechanic Street, insensible; it proved to be sun-stroke — he recovered in a few hours.

A man died of cholera at No. 10 Hanover Avenue — sick twelve hours — his wife was sick in the same house — his body was removed. The house being neat, and no others sick there, she was not removed.

July 9. A woman, at 231 Hanover Street, died to-day after an illness of twelve hours; assistance was rendered, but the body was buried by the friends.

July 13. A child at the Beehive in Endicott Street died, being sick fifteen hours. The father died the same evening, after an illness of ten hours. The wife was also taken about the time the husband died. The bodies of the father and child decayed very fast, and were removed by us that night, and the mother was removed to the hospital.

The Beehive consists of two blocks of wooden buildings, end to the street, separated by a narrow passage, each block containing twenty-four rooms. There are, in these forty-eight rooms, forty-eight families, and two hundred and eight persons. By the direction of the Board of Health, we removed the families in one block.

July 14. A man died at No. 116 Friend Street — sick ten hours — the body commenced to putrefy immediately; we carried him to the Dead House.

July 15. A report came that there was cholera at No. 92 Endicott Street. On going there, I found no cholera, but something that required my attention. A woman was lying on the floor *dead* drunk, and beside the drunken mother lay an infant child nearly naked of clothing, but half covered with lice. Another woman was lying drunk in the room, which was filthy in the extreme. I learned that the family consisted of the mother, six children, and three boarders, and they all occupied but two rooms. Why the cholera had not found them I am at a loss to know. The whole were however removed; the mother to the House of Industry, where the father had already gone, the children to the Almshouse, leaving the boarders to select new quarters.

A man was taken with cholera at 406 Commercial Street; we removed him to the hospital, where he died next day.

A man died at 155 Charlestown Street — sick fifteen hours — we removed his body. A woman died at No. 119 Friend Street — sick but ten hours — body immediately became black and putrid, was very difficult to remove. A man was brought to the Station House intoxicated, attacked with cholera while there, removed to the hospital, and died in a few hours.

From this date, up to about the first of August, the weather became cooler, the atmosphere more clear, and the disease seemed to abate. There were several cases of smallpox, and some deaths by ship fever, but these diseases, fatal as they are, had lost their terrors during the prevalence of the cholera.

August 2. The weather again became sultry, and cholera began again to appear. A woman died at No. 18 North Bennet Street, — sick sixteen hours, — she was buried by friends. A woman was removed from Jefferson's Block to the hospital. A member of our own Police Station died at his residence, No. 1 Bennet Avenue, after a most distressing illness of twelve hours; his body turned black immediately after death, and it was necessary to bury it without delay. We also removed a woman in a dying condition from No. 554 Commercial Street.

August 7. A case occurred this morning which tended to add to the horror of our duties. An old man, who occupied a room on the second floor, No. 84 Cross Street, had been absent from his room some eight days; this was not particularly noticed by the other occupants, as he was frequently absent some days at a time. For a day or two prior to this day, the people in the house had noticed an offensive smell; this morning it was found to come from this man's room; his door was tried, but found fastened, and notice was given at the Station House. I went down and procured a ladder, which I placed on the outside and went up and raised the window to the room, but a stench met me that I could not withstand, and I came near falling from the ladder. After the foul, confined air had somewhat escaped from the room, I entered the window. I there found near one corner of the room a man standing erect, leaning backward a little with one foot on the round of a chair standing near, with a rope about his neck attached to a hook overhead. He was as stiff as a bronze statue, and his features were so blackened and decayed that no one could recognize them, yet I knew from the figure and dress that it was the body of the missing man. He had in all probability hung himself and remained in that position about eight days. My eyes never beheld such a sight, — I hope never to see such another. The coroner was called, who took charge of the body.

August 8. A woman died of cholera at No. 131 Charlestown Street. We removed the body and cleansed the room.

August 11. A man died at No. 129 Charlestown Street — sick twelve hours — body decayed so as to make the burial of immediate necessity. A man died at 163 Charlestown Street — sick but ten hours — body so swollen we could not put it in the coffin, and removed it in a box.

August 14. A man came to the Station House

for lodging, while there he was attacked with cholera, and taken to the hospital.

A woman at No. 1 Crescent Place, and two others at No. 6 Battery Street, were removed to the hospital.

August 17. We removed a man from Page's yard to the hospital.

August 21. Several persons were sick at a place called the Platform, in Causeway Street, many of them having gone there to be sick with their friends, rather than go the hospital. We commenced an investigation, found twenty-nine families huddled together in a very small place, and as filthy a place as I ever saw. I was an unwelcome visitor, and the occupants would have driven me out had they dared. I found several persons sick, and by direction of the Board of Health removed, five persons and a child to the hospital. The people there were very determined, and the sick were removed with much difficulty. The next day the Board of Health passed a special order to clear the premises, which was accomplished with great difficulty, some of the occupants making a strong resistance. True, it seemed a hard case, but no one who saw the premises could doubt the necessity.

There were many cases of a less serious character taking place on our Station, which are not copied in this account, in which it became my duty to lend a hand, but these last mentioned were about the last cases of cholera occurring in Boston this year.

During the prevalence of this dreadful malady nearly the whole police force on my district were continually employed in caring for the sick and dying, and removing the dead, and on no occasion do I believe that any man shrank from his task. These noble fellows, many days in the discharge of their fearful duties, were meeting death face to face in its most fearful form, and the disinterested sacrifice offered up by them is worthy of a lasting remembrance.

In pursuing my own duties through this ordeal of disease and terror, I could take little precaution. I sometimes took a few cloves in my mouth, and sometimes after being a long time exposed to the most insupportable stench, and experiencing a dizzy nausea, I have taken a few drops of laudanum in a spoonful of brandy, but I ate no green thing. No one could go where I went and see what I saw without dread. I knew by sad experience the indescribable suffering attending this fearful disease, having had an attack that nearly cost me my life a few years previous. THE CHOLERA — no pen, no tongue, no thought, no imagination can depict its terrors. 'T is death and desolation stalking abroad at noonday

SMALL MATTERS.

One afternoon in the month of January, 1856, a man who enjoyed the reputation of being a well-to-do and respectable citizen, came to the Station and required the services of an officer in ferreting out some thieving operations that had been consummated in his house, freely expressing the opinion that the theft could be readily traced to Bridget, the domestic.

As such cases were not uncommon, an officer was detailed to accompany the gentleman to his house to make the necessary investigation. On arriving at the house and instituting an inquiry, the officer found that the lady of the house had been out to the provision store and purchased two quarts of small apples, which were placed in the hands of Bridget to prepare for pies. Bridget had paired and sliced them carefully, and made them into two pies, having two apples left. This was not satisfactory to the mistress, and Jerry, the half-grown son, gave it as his decided opinion that two quarts of apples would make at least three pies, and Mrs. thought so too. In talking the matter over in the family, although this was the first suspicion, yet it was carried by a majority that in this case at least, Bridget must have been dishonest.

After settling that point satisfactorily, it was further decided that if Bridget was so dishonest as to pilfer pie apples she would take something else, which she certainly had many an opportunity to do, although nothing had been missed; but when it was recollected that Bridget had in her chamber a large, suspicious-looking trunk, the inside of which had been seen by none of the family, and when in consequence of all these circumstances, Bridget's room had been quietly visited, and that trunk was found to be locked, the landlady declared she could stand such "*carryings on*" no longer, and on consulting the husband they concluded to call in the officer.

The whole case was explained to the officer in presence of Bridget and the whole family, and ended by a demand to have a search instituted inside of that suspicious trunk. It would have been hard to tell which was the most astonished at the proceedings, Bridget or the officer.

But Bridget, who, by the way, was neither a thief nor a fool, scanned the features of the officer for a moment, and detecting nothing malicious there, but rather perhaps an indication of contempt for her accusers, and an expression of sympathy for her, in her unprotected condition, she promptly said, "Come up to me room," and up went the whole injured family followed by the officer.

On reaching her room Bridget threw open her trunk, exclaiming, "WE hear enough. Now there, mem, ye may sarch me ould duds an' ye will, and much may ye find among 'em; but I tell ye, mem, two quarts of yer little pesky wormy apples wont make more than two pies any way."

The injured family appeared satisfied, and the officer quietly retired from the house, and in a few days the honest, hard-working Bridget found a better *place* at better pay.

VALUE OF CHARACTER.

There are seemingly many people plodding their way along through life without any just comprehension of the value of a good character. The rich can live without it, but it is the poor man's capital, and by him, above all others, it should be held and cherished as a jewel above price.

Although this feeling, or rather want of it, is much too common among mankind, yet I am happy to know that it is by no means universal, and I have seen some laughable, as well as grave instances, plainly indicating that the value of a good name is often well understood in the very humblest walks of life.

On a certain occasion, an honest laborer came to the Station House and requested me to take charge of a trunk which he said belonged to one *Kitty Quadd*. It had been left with him while Kitty was absent in the country. He was about to move, and the trunk was a burden, and he wished to leave it with me for safe keeping till Kitty's return. To accommodate him I took the name of the owner, made a schedule of the few articles in the trunk, and set it away in the property room for safety.

About two months after, a buxom Irish girl called at the Station House, saying that her name was Kitty Quadd, and she was told that I had her trunk. After asking her some questions, to see if it was right, the trunk was brought out and delivered.

Kitty's eyes glistened with joy as she beheld her treasure, but said she, " It's not the value of me clothing, sir, but it's me character that's there, me character it is." And hurrying her hand into the pocket of an old dress as she lifted it from the trunk, she drew forth a dirty piece of paper with much apparent satisfaction. " This is it, an' sure enough it's safe it is, and it's yerself that shall read it too, for yer kindness," said she.

I unfolded the paper and read as follows: —

" This certifies that Kitty Quadd is a good domestic, capable of doing all kinds of work, *but she will get drunk when opportunity offers.*" (Signed) Mrs. S —."

" Pretty good, Kitty," said I.

" Pretty good; and well ye may say that," said she, folding the paper and placing it carefully in her bosom. " Pretty good it is; it is me character sir, and 't is well earned too; but it is well worn, and I am going to get Biddy Harrigan, me first cousin, to copy it;" and she marched off with her trunk and her character, as happy as a queen.

A WEDDING IN THE TOMBS.

It is generally known to the citizens of Boston, that there are numerous small-sized, convenient little rooms in the basement of the Court House on the easterly side, with brick walls and iron-grated doors, with a bunk, a pail, and a tin cup for furniture, where persons of almost every age, sex, and color find entertainment, in consequence of a neglect to conform to the various rules and regulations established by the usages and customs of the society in which they dwell. These various apartments constitute what are familiarly known as the Tombs; and although the name might impress a stranger with grave sensations, yet there are times when the name would hardly be suspected from the character of the tenants. For although the name might seem to indicate to the contrary, it is nevertheless inhabited by live men and women, where coffee and white bread are plentifully served out every morning for breakfast, and I have even seen it turned into the drawing-room of a bridal party. The circumstance was on this wise.

In the summer of 1861, it happened that a lad who we will call Arthur Clarke, and a lady we will call Johanna Hickey, were quite intimate. Johanna at first thought it was only between herself and Arthur, but by and by there began to be indications that there might erelong be a *third* party in interest.

Johanna began to be fidgety, but Arthur was in no hurry to marry. Johanna did not feel inclined to pocket the insult, and at her suggestion Arthur one morning waked up in the *Tombs*. On a little reflection, Arthur concluded he *was* ready *to marry*, and Johanna being nothing loth, there seemed to be no obstacle to interpose. A certificate of intention was procured by some friend of the parties, and precisely at twelve o'clock noon, Arthur and Johanna met by appointment in the superintendent's office. The good-natured Esquire Beal volunteered his services, and in presence of several witnesses the ceremonies commenced. The bride and groom were placed side by side, fronting the desk, which was occupied by the worthy Justice, who, with certificate of intention in hand, and uncovered head proclaimed, "Has any person aught to say why Arthur Clarke and Johanna Hickey should not be joined in wedlock, let him say it now or ever hold his peace hereafter." All were silent. "Do you, Arthur Clarke, take this woman to be your lawful wedded wife." Arthur winked. "And do you, Johanna Hickey, take this man to be your lawful wedded husband." Johanna smacked her lips. "If you mutually assent," said the Justice, "you will take each other by the right hand." Johanna stuck out a paw, but Arthur had no right hand, that was gone, but he presented his left, which seemed to answer the purpose. And now said the Justice, "By virtue of the power vested in me by the Commonwealth, I pronounce you man and wife, *and what God hath joined together let no man put asunder.*" Arthur and Johanna looked at each other as if they did not quite understand the last sentence, but neither attempted to make any inquiries in relation to the subject, but remained motionless, to see what came next.

After a while Arthur began to examine his locomotive apparatus, as if to satisfy himself of the power of the new shackles with which he had been bound, and whether they were as potent as those he had left at the cell, and apparently becoming satisfied on that point, he took a bee line for the door. Johanna soon followed in his wake and both disappeared, leaving the spectators gaping at the door that closed behind them.

That proceeding may have vindicated the majesty of the law, but whether Esquire Beal's last remark was correct, I was always in doubt.

OLD BUILDINGS.

During the summer of 1859, the City Government widened North Street, by removing some buildings and cutting off others on one or the other side of nearly the whole length of that ancient thoroughfare.

Many of these old houses, for most of the buildings were dwellings, were objects of much interest, as they were one after another about to disappear, both on account of their peculiar structure and apparent great age.

Having considerable extra police duty in that locality, on account of the work of widening, in common with others I took much interest in the history of these ancient relics and old landmarks, as they were disappearing forever, and during the progress of their removal I made some observations which I thought might be worthy of note.

Although many of the houses bear the marks of great age, yet to fix the date of the building of most of them with any degree of certainty was quite impossible. Deeds can be traced back, showing the locality and names of owners of most of the estates to an early date, but when buildings now standing were erected is quite another affair. Most of the older class of buildings were built one or one and a half stories high, with various additions to one end or the other, and at top in after time, but often the addition will show greater marks of decay than the original, and the age of either is an equal uncertainty.

By close observation, however, it is evident that something may be gathered from the kind of material used, the style in architecture, and manner of building at different periods, to indicate the age of both wood and brick buildings.

The former, the low-studded, two-story structures with heavy oak timbers, the second story projecting far over the sidewalk, with Lutheran windows, oak clapboards, and triangular floor timbers, denote the greater age of this class of buildings. Specimens of this style are still to be seen at Nos. 19 and 27 North Square, corner of Moon and Sun Court Streets, Salem, opposite Cooper Street, and in some other localities in the city.

Something a little more definite, however, may, I believe, be gained relative to the age of brick buildings, not only from their peculiar structure and style of architecture, but from the size of the bricks, the composition of the mortar, and the different styles of the walls at different periods of time. The first walls laid in Boston were in clay mortar, mixed with a lime made by burning shells, which can at this late day be easily detected by close observation. This mortar was used in the " Deacon Phillips's Old Stone House," Cross Street, " Noah's Ark," corner North and Clark Street, " Old Province House," Province House Court, " Old Reed Store," Change Avenue and Basement, " Old Feather Store," Dock Square.

The first brick houses also were built of imported bricks, which are somewhat larger and thicker than those first made in New England.

There have been several different styles of laying brick walls since the first settlement of Boston, which more clearly indicate the age of brick buildings. These styles are called bonds, and consist in laying " *headers* " and " stretchers " alternately, as they appear in the outer surface of the wall, a " header " being the end of the brick appearing on the face of the wall, and a " stretcher " the edge. The styles consist in laying the headers and stretchers in different form, and have been known to masons at different periods as the " English Bond," " Promiscuous Bond," " Flemish Bond," " Tile Bond," and " Modern Flemish Bond," each of which was the style of laying brick walls in buildings at different periods.

These styles may be better understood by the following table, which shows the front in the different Bonds in brick walls : —

ENGLISH BOND.

This style consists of a course of stretchers and a course of headers alternately, and was in use from 1647 to about 1723.

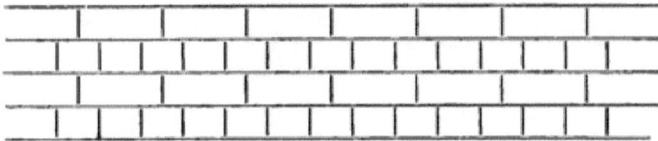

PROMISCUOUS BONDS.

The Promiscuous Bond consisted of a course of headers, and from three to eight courses of stretchers, according to the fancy of the builder, and was in use from about 1720 to 1770.

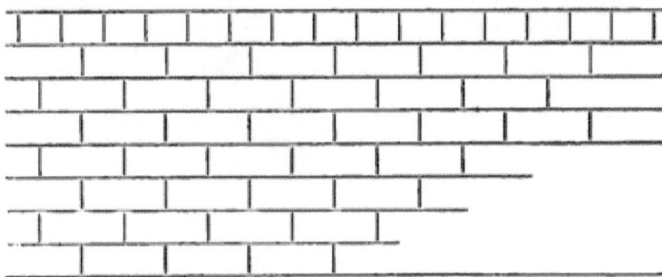

FLEMISH BOND.

The Flemish Bond is a header and stretcher laid alternately in the same course, each course being laid alike, and was in use from about 1770 to 1810.

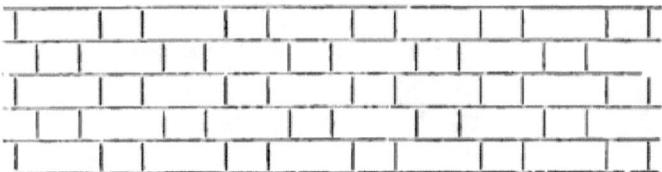

TILE BOND.

Tile Bond every course alike at the surface, laying a tile or eight-inch square brick in place of a header, in use from about 1820 to 1855.

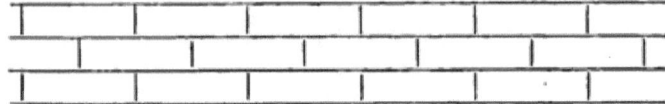

MODERN FLEMISH BOND.

The Modern Flemish Bond consists of a header and a stretcher alternately in one course, and the next eight or ten courses being wholly stretchers, when a header and stretcher are again laid. This style has been in use since about 1855.

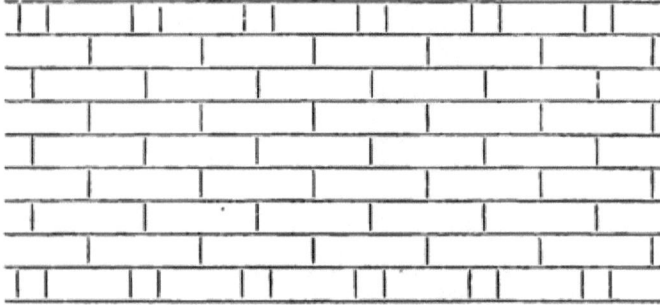

The following table shows the style of bond and the date of erecting the buildings named: —

ENGLISH BOND.

1647, Noah's Ark, corner North and Clark streets.
1679, Old Province House (Ordway Hall).
1680, Basement Old Feather Store, Dock Square.

1687, Old Reed Store, 'Change Avenue.
1712, Part of Old Town House, head of State Street.
1723, Christ Church, Salem Street.

PROMISCUOUS BOND.

1720 to 1770, No. 6 Margaret St., Nos. 21–3 Richmond St. Nos. 21, 23–73 Charter St., Nos. 125–148 Prince Street.

FLEMISH BOND.

1773, Brattle Street Church.
1729, Old South Church.
1795, Old Part State House.
1804, Parkman Church.
1806, Lynde Street, Chambers Street, and Belknap Street churches.
1809–10, Park Street and Baldwin Place churches.

TILE, OR IRON BOND.

1822, Old Hancock Schoolhouse.
1824, Charles Street Church.
1826, Green Street Church.
1828, Bennet and Salem Street churches.
1835–6, Merrimac and Pitts Street churches.
1838, Streeter's Church.
1843,5, Canal Block and Maine Depot.
1848,9, New Hancock Schoolhouse, &c. &c.

MODERN FLEMISH BOND.

See buildings since 1855.

From the commencement of building brick buildings in Boston to about the year 1710 to 1720, there seems, so far as can be known, to have been but one style of laying bricks; that style is called the English Bond, and was laid so as to show on the face a course of headers and a course of stretchers laid alternately throughout the building. Although several specimens of this bond are shown in the table, yet I know of but two buildings now left standing entire, viz: the old Town House, built in 1712, and partly destroyed by fire, and rebuilt, preserving the same style, in 1745; the other, Christ Church, in Salem Street, built 1723. A part of the walls only of some others in the table now remain. There were many to be seen in North Street before the street was widened.

The Promiscuous Bond, which was in use from about 1720 to 1770, consisting of a course of headers and three, four, five, six, or seven course of stretchers, are met with much more frequently than the old English Bond, but yet the buildings have a very aged appearance.

The Flemish Bond in use from about 1770 to 1810, are much more common, being seen in nearly all the principal streets. The Tile, or Iron Bond, from 1820 to 1850, came in use about the time faced bricks were first manufactured. This bond has the appearance of continued courses of stretchers, the bond being formed by laying in a flat piece of iron between the courses, which are not seen on the outer surface or by the use of square tiles, being the same as two bricks struck together.

A building which was removed near the foot of North Street, in the course of widening that street, attracted much attention in consequence of having circular openings through the outer walls, and by some was thought to have been some military fortification in former times. The building was but eighteen by twenty-seven feet in size, three stories high, and the walls but one foot thick, and seemed much better adapted to use as a dwelling-house than a fortification. The circular windows are no bar to this opinion, as such may still be seen at numerous churches and stores both of ancient and modern date

DEACON PHILLIPS'S OLD STONE HOUSE.

The Old Stone House, which for more than two centuries had nobly withstood the ravages of time, has at length disappeared. It stood on the east side of Cross Street, about half way between North and Hanover streets, and when removed was one of the oldest buildings in Boston.

By whom this venerable pile was erected is now unknown, but old Deacon Phillips, of the Second Church, dwelt within these strong walls many years. Mr. Phillips died Dec. 22, 1682, at the good old age of seventy-seven years, leaving his lands and other worldly estate to his grandchildren, making reservation for Sarah, " the wife of his old age," and for his only daughter, Mary, the wife of George Mountjoy, of Piscataqua.

The estate passed down in the possession of the Mountjoys and other descendants of the deacon, until it came to Edward Proctor and others. In the year 1793, William Williams became the owner, who sold it to Thomas Williams in 1810, and Thomas sold it to John Sullivan in 1816, since which time the history of the estate is well known. The estate has been leased to Mr. John Cochran, and by him underlet to various Irish families, for more than thirty years.

When *Goodman Phillips* resided here, his neighbor toward Middle Street was Mr. John Turell; on the north was George Burrill; he had no neighbor on the east, his estate extending to Fish Street by the sea.

A short time before Deacon Phillips died, he sold from his estate a houselot just southeast of his stone house, to Mr. Christopher Clarke, and other portions of the estate have subsequently been sold off on North Street.

Some of the owners of the Old Stone House in more modern times have made an addition of a third story, consisting mostly of brick, and also changed the external appearance by covering nearly the whole of it with boards, clapboards, and shingles.

Credulous persons have been willing to believe that the old mansion was once used as a prison, and many have called it the Old Jail, but there is no evidence that it was ever used for that purpose. On the contrary, from the time of Deacon Phillips down, nearly all the tenants are known. The locality of the jail also, from early date, is shown to have been in Prison Lane.

Although no evidence does exist that the Old

Stone House was ever used either as a jail or fortress, yet in raising such a formidable and costly structure as this must have been for that day, it would seem that the proprietor intended something more than a mere dwelling-house. It will not be forgotten that the early settlers of Boston, from the commencement, in 1630, to the termination of King Philip's war, in 1676, were in constant dread of attacks from the French and Indians. So much were the people in fear, that beacons, batteries, and fortifications, were thrown up and maintained for the protection of the colony.

The Indians, who generally made their depredations under cover of darkness by stealth, quietly landing from their canoes, performing their missions of plunder and murder on private families, and as quietly retiring, were the especial dread of the inhabitants, long before the war of extermination was commenced with the Wampanoag Indians.

At the time of the erection of the Old Stone House, it is quite probable that neighbors were not so plenty as at subsequent periods; the house was also located near a convenient landing-place for a hostile foe of the character most to be dreaded; and it may not be an improbable supposition, that the construction of these strong walls was a result growing out of these circumstances, although perhaps never used for the purpose for which they were in part originally fitted.

After the death of Mr. Elisha Goodnow, who was owner of the estate for many years, it was conveyed by his executor to the city of Boston as a legacy in Mr. Goodnow's will; and in the month of April, 1864, the estate was sold at auction for the benefit of the city, and the Old Stone House was removed, not leaving one stone upon another.

The removal offered a good opportunity to examine the character and material of the original building.

The Old Stone House at first consisted of two wings of uniform size, joining each other and forming a right angle. Each wing was forty feet long, twenty feet wide, and two stories high, the wings fronting the south and west. There was one door in the end of each wing on the first story, and a single circular window in the second story over the doors; there were also two circular windows in each story of each wing in front, but neither door nor window in either wing in the rear. The foundation walls were four feet thick, or more; the walls above ground were two feet in thickness, and built entirely of small quarried stones unlike anything to be seen in this neighborhood, and were probably brought as ballast from some part of Europe. They were laid in clay mortar throughout.

The timbers were of live oak, sixteen inches square, and are in a good state of preservation.

The upper story, which was added, was built of English brick, and laid in lime mortar, and some of the circular windows had also been filled with the same material, new doors and windows having been opened through the thick stone wall.

But the Old Stone House has disappeared, and another of the very few ancient landmarks of old Boston will be seen no more forever.

The stone which formed the walls of the Old Stone House, of which there was a large quantity, was removed to form the underpinning of a new Methodist Church on Saratoga Street, East Boston.

NOAH'S ARK.

This ancient building, which could, in 1860, be seen at the southwest corner of North and Clark streets, claimed to be a rival in antiquity with the Old Feather Store in Dock Square, the Old Deacon Phillips's Stone House in Cross Street, and even the Old Hewes House in Washington Street, all of which have since been taken down.

It is believed that this brick house, which for many years was known as Noah's Ark, was built in the year 1647, and if so, it had then been standing two hundred and thirteen years. It is quite certain that it was built previous to 1650, and was in possession of a widow as administratrix, her husband having died in 1648, leaving her in care of this estate and a family of five children; and it will be hardly supposed she would undertake to build a house of this magnitude within two years of her husband's death, and that, too, before the estate was divided.

Again, the house was built by a way, of a rod wide, which had not been fully completed, early in 1646, Walter Merry being ordered to build his part near the Battery, before the 15th of May of that year, under a penalty of twenty shillings.

The owner of this building improved a shipyard on his estate in 1646, and was familiarly known among his contemporaries as Captain Thomas Hawkins. He was a man of wealth and enterprise, and an extensive shipbuilder and owner for those days.

In 1643, Capt. Hawkins with one Captain Gibbons, fitted out four ships with sixty-eight men, for the celebrated DeLatour expedition against D'Aulnay. The ships were the Seabridge, Philip, Mary Increase, and Greyhound, which sailed from Long Island, July 14, and it was said " that no ships of like burden had gone out before."

In 1645, Captain Hawkins built the Seafort, a beautiful ship of four hundred tons burden, and himself went master in her to the coast of Spain, where he was wrecked, losing part of his crew; he sold what was saved of the wreck to the Spaniards, and returned home.

In 1646, Captain Hawkins once more visited the coast of Spain, and was again cast away, but escaped with his life, and returned home, where he remained with his family during the year 1647, at which time, it is believed, he built this brick mansion-house, importing the bricks from London in his own good ship the Greyhound.

1648. The restless spirit of Captain Hawkins again carried him to sea this year, when he was again cast away, and lost his life. (*See* Winthrop, by Savage, vol. 2, page 357.)

Captain Hawkins left a widow, Mary, four daughters, and one son, viz: Elizabeth, Abigail, Hannah, Sarah, and Thomas. Mary, the widow, was married twice afterward, first to Mr. Robert Fenn, who died, and she again married Henry Shrimpton. Elizabeth married first to Adam Winthrop (who died); then to John Richards. Abigail was married first to Thomas Kellond, and again to John Foster. Hannah married Elisha Hutchinson, and Sarah married James Allen. Thomas is said to have come to an untimely end.

In 1645, "Edward Bendall granted to Captain Thomas Hawkins, shipwright, a certain parcel of land situated in Boston. the bounds thereof beginning forty feet to the northward, from the lot which was Mr. Robert Thompson's, and so by Major Nehemiah Bourn's lot, running with a straight line, according to Major Bourn's pales, run from the seashore toward the east, and unto the railes of Christopher Stanley towards the west, the south side running nearly parallel to this." Dated 30, 11, 1645. (*See* Book-possessions, page 23.)

The above-described lot of land contained all the territory now bounded by a line commencing at the south end of Dr. Charles French's apothecary shop, No. 367 Hanover Street, thence easterly, by the south line of said shop across North Street, through Matthews Block to the water on the south, by Bartlett Street on the north, by Hanover Street on the west, and by the water on the east.

North Street was then " the way of a rod in breadth," from Gallop's point to the Battery. It was afterward known as Fore Street, and changed successively to " Ship Street," " Anne Street," " Ann Street," and " North Street."

Clark Street was an eleven feet passage-way left between Mr. Hutchinson and Mr. Richards in 1682, to accommodate Thomas Kellond, and it was then known as " Kellond's Passage," then " Shrimpton's Passage," " Hawkins's Lane," " Foster's Lane," " Clark Lane," and " Clark Street."

Bartlett Street was opened at a later date, and was first called " White Bread Alley," from a bakery located there.

As has been shown, Captain Hawkins probably built his brick house in 1647, and his widow is found in possession in 1650. On the 12th day of April 1650, the selectmen ordered that the way of a rod in breadth, formerly granted, from Gallop's Point to the Battery (by the water side), being intercepted by widow Hawkins, *her brick house*, it shall turn up from the water side through Mrs. Hawkins, her garden, and so by Mr. Winthrop's house, between Major Bourn's house and his garden, before Mr. Holyhoke's to the Battery." (*See* Town Records. vol. 1, page 89.)

The way did so turn up, and the western line "of the way" of the part that turned up, and the east wall of Mrs. Hawkins's house was within ten feet of said way. (*See* Fleet's plan, drawn in 1663, on which this brick house is designated.) Mr. Fleet's plan of the premises was found among papers of the late James Ivers, formerly warden of King's Chapel, among other old papers that came into his possession from early proprietors of the Hawkins estate.

It is probable that this "turn up of the way," as ordered by the selectmen, was in part for the accommodation of Mr. Winthrop, Mr. Bourn, and Mr. Holyhoke's houses, which were built just below, but stood a little further west than Mr. Hawkins's house. It is believed that a part of Mr. Winthrop's house is still standing in the rear of 344 North Street.

1653. Mary Fenn, formerly widow of Captain Thomas Hawkins, and his administratrix, returns an inventory of her late husband's estate, including "the *brick house* and lands in Boston, and asking for a division of the estate; which request was granted in 1654, she receiving for her share the house and lands in Boston." (*See* Probate Records, vol. 3, page 101.)

1655, April 9. John Aylet conveys by mortgage to William Hudson, *vintner*, "all that house and wharf belonging to the same, which is commonly called or known by the name or sign of *Noah's Ark*, situated, lying and being, at the north part of Boston, late the inheritance of Captain Thomas Hawkins, but now in possession (or occupancy) of John Viall." (*See* Reg. Deeds, vol. 2, page 244.) There must have been a conveyance of this estate by Mrs. Fenn to John Aylet, between the years 1653 and 1655, but as no record is found, however, the identification is beyond dispute. Thus, as early as 1655, the brick house of Captain Hawkins is occupied by John Viall, who kept an ordinary, or inn, as it was known by the name of Noah's Ark.

In early times, places of business were known by the peculiarity of signs, rather than by numbers of the street. In this case, the proprietor had placed over his door for a sign, the model of a ship; but people said the model looked more like an old ark than a ship; hence the name. This was still occupied as a noted cake and beer saloon, and known as the Ark or Ship Tavern within the memory of some now living.

1656, May 6. William Hudson conveyed by mortgage his interest in the "Noah's Ark" estate to William Phillips, described in the mortgage of Aylet to Hudson, which was not redeemed. (*See* Reg. Deeds, vol. 2, page 289.)

1657, June 1. William Hudson, holding a right by Aylet's forfeiture, in conjunction with William Phillips, who held the mortgage from Hudson, conveyed by Deed to Mary Fenn, "All that garden, dwelling-house, and wharf, commonly known by the name or sign of *Noah's Ark*, formerly the inheritance of Captain Thomas Hawkins. since of John Aylet of Boston, by him mortgaged to William Hudson, and by him to William Phillips." (*See* Reg. Deeds, vol. 3, page 86.)

1657, July 1. Mary Fenn conveyed by deed to George Mountjoy (Mariner,) "All that parcel of land situated in Boston, butting on the sea on the east, by Alexander Adams on the west, and by land of said Mary on the south, and on the south, being at the water side forty-three feet in breadth, and at the upper end *above the highway* thirty-five feet, and in length from the water side to the land of Alexander Adams, on the west, with the dwelling-house thereon, commonly called or known by the name of *Noah's Ark*." (*See* Reg. Deeds, vol. 3, page 88.)

This is the first division of the Hawkins estate found on the records, in which the bounds of the house lot is well defined.

1663, July 24. George Mountjoy conveyed by deed to John Viall (vintner), "All that messuage, dwelling-house, garden, and wharf commonly called or known by the name or sign of

Noah's Ark, bounded by the sea forty-three feet, at the upper end *above the highway* thirty-five feet, and extending from the sea to Alexander Adams on the west." (*See* Reg. Deeds, vol. 4, page 272.)

1682, May 19, in deed of Elisha Hutchinson to John Richards, the brick house of John Viall is mentioned as one of the boundary lines to an adjoining estate. (*See* Reg. Deeds vol. 12, page 185.)

1688, July 17. John Viall mortgaged to Abigail Kellond "All his tenement at the north part of Boston called *Ship Tavern*, bounded North by building yard formerly of Thomas Hawkins, now of John Richards, south by land of Abigail Kellond, east by the sea, west by land of Abigail Kellond, *measuring in breadth at the sea forty-three feet, at the upper end above the highway*, thirty-five feet &c." (*See* Reg. Deeds, vol. 15, page 30.)

1695. John Viall conveys by mortgage to John Foster and wife, " All his tenement at the north part of Boston called the *Ship Tavern* (bounded and described as heretofore), and being in breadth forty-three feet at the sea, at the upper end *above the highway* thirty-five feet, &c." (*See* Reg. Deeds, vol. 17, page 148.)

1713, May 14. John Viall and wife conveyed to Thomas Hutchinson (the governor's father) by deed, as follows: " This indenture, made the 14th day of May, Anno Domini, 1713, in the 12th year of our Sovereign Lady Anne of Great Britain,

France, and Scotland, Defender of the Faith, between John Viall of Boston, within the county of Suffolk and *Province* of *Massachusetts Bay* in New England, *Taverner*, and Mary his wife on the one part, and Thomas Hutchinson of Boston, aforesaid merchant, on the other part. That the said John Viall, for divers reasons him thereto moving, and more *especially for the sum of nine hundred and fifty pounds* of lawful money to him paid, conveys (&c.) All that certain messuage or tenement commonly called or known by the name of the *Ship Tavern, heretofore as Noah's Ark*, containing a large brick dwelling-house (&c. &c.), lying at the north part of Boston, *a part above* and a part below the highway or street called Ship Street, and bounded west by land of Thomas Hutchinson, formerly Alexander Adams, thirty-five feet extending easterly across the street, being forty-three feet in breadth at the water side. (*See* Reg. Deeds, vol. 34, page 80.)

1714. Thomas Hutchinson had a permit from the selectmen, to build a dwelling-house on that part of the John Viall estate formerly occupied by him as a brewhouse. This old brewhouse was the one in which Mr. John Viall brewed his beer, which was then of world-wide reputation. (*See* Town Records, vol. 2, page 280.) Matthews Block at the corner of North and Clark Street, now covers the ground where the old brewhouse stood, the new building having been erected in 1853. It was burnt down and again built in 1861. The dock had been filled in, and that part of Clark Street was opened in 1714. The building below Clark Street was never known as Noah's Ark, as some have supposed.

1739, Oct. 10. "In the 13th year of King George III., Thomas Hutchinson (father of the Governor) made his will, dividing his large estate between his two sons, Thomas and Foster, and four daughters. Sarah Welsteed, wife of Rev. William Welsteed; Abigail Davenport, widow; Hannah Mather, wife of Rev. Samuel Mather, and Lydia Rogers, giving his wife Sarah the income of most of his real estate during her life. In this will is found the following —

"Item. I give and devise to my daughter Hannah Mather, wife of Rev. Samuel Mather, her heirs forever, my *brick house* and land in Ship Street, which is now rented to Thomas Warbeat and Thomas Power, the income whereof I have given to my wife during her natural life. (*See* Reg. Probate, vol. 34, page 261.)

Mr. Hutchinson owned the brick house called the Ship Tavern, and from the wording in the will "my brick house," it would appear that he owned no other of that description. Warbeat and Power also occupied the Ship Tavern.

1785, May 24. Rev. Samuel Mather makes his

will, in which he makes mention of his wife Hannah, his three daughters, Elizabeth Mather, Sarah Shaw, and Hannah Crocker, his little granddaughter Hannah Mather Crocker, and a son in England, who appears to be disfranchised (probably in consequence of Revolutionary troubles). (See Reg. Probate, vol. 84, page 235.) This reference is important only in showing the heirs of Hannah Mather, who are interested afterward in the brick house in Ship Street, given them by their grandfather, Thomas Hutchinson.

1788, March 22. Elizabeth Mather, single woman, makes her will, in which she bequeaths to her sister, Hannah Crocker, wife of Joseph Crocker, "All my right, title, and interest, in all the property, real and personal, which I have received from my father, Rev. Samuel Mather, my mother, Hannah Mather, my aunt Sarah Welsteed, and my cousins Nathaniel and Sarah Rogers, all late deceased. (See Reg. Probate, vol. 87, page 221.)

This will included her share of the brick house in Ship Street. It is said that the other sister, Sarah Shaw, died without issue, and her share of her grandfather's gift, reverted to the surviving heirs of her mother, Hannah Mather, the son being in England and disfranchised. By Elizabeth's will, Hannah Crocker became the sole owner of the estate called the Ship Tavern.

1794, Dec. 9. Hannah Crocker (widow) conveys by deed to Benjamin James (brewer), "All that dwelling-house and land thereto belonging, situated in the north part of Boston at the corner of Ship and Clark streets, so called, and bounded as follows: From Ship Street, thence running west on Clark Street, eighty-two feet; thence southerly on land of Messrs. Dolbeare & Lavis, forty-six feet four inches; thence easterly on land of Mr. Tate fifty feet; thence northerly by Tate's land, two feet four inches; thence easterly on said Tate's land, forty-five feet six inches to Ship Street; thence on Ship Street to the first-mentioned bound." (*See* Reg. Deeds, vol. 189, page 2.)

This conveyance includes more than the original Noah's Ark estate above the street. That estate and much more of the adjoining land, it will be recollected, formerly belonged to Thomas Hutchinson; since his purchase of John Viall, in 1713, all the territory mentioned in this deed was undoubtedly included in his bequest to his daughter Hannah and her heirs in 1739.

From the date of Benjamin James's purchase of the Noah's Ark estate of Hannah Crocker, in the year 1794, to the present time, 1860, it has been in possession of him and his heirs, being now in care of John W. James, Esq., of this city, who is a son of Benjamin, and joint heir to the estate.

This estate, which is now known as the James Estate, was for many years a keepsake in the family of Hannah Crocker, as a gift from their Grandfather Hutchinson, and many interesting incidents connected with the place were communicated by her to persons now living. The Old House is still standing. It was at first but two stories high, the additional story having been built by Mr. James. It was built of the large English brick, with shell and clay mortar, and the bricks were laid in the old English Bond style, the first style of laying brick walls in New England. The house had Lutheran attic windows, deep projecting eaving, low-arched wall windows with sliding sash, triangular flooring timbers, and finished in the heavy style of the times when it was built, although the interior has undergone repeated alterations, yet the walls probably preserve nearly their original appearance.

The original building was thirty-two feet front, "on the way of a rod in breadth," now North Street, and twenty-eight feet wide on Clark Street; but in widening North Street in 1855, a part of the first wall was removed. Before widening the street a large crack was to be seen in the front wall, which — tradition handed down from John Viall through Hannah Crocker, says — was caused by an "earthquake in 1663, which made all New England tremble." Mr. Viall occupied the house, and history records the event of the earthquake that year. Mrs. Crocker used to say, that her grandfather Hutchinson spoke of a casket of papers, that was said to be placed under the corner-stone of this house when built. If so, they would no doubt be extremely interesting at this day; but I never could learn that any such papers were ever found.

Mr. Samuel Yendell and Mr. John Childs, highly-respectable citizens, and in 1865 residents of the North End, the former ninety-one and the latter about eighty years of age, said that Noah's ark was among their earliest recollections. Mr. Yendell remembered this house eighty-five years distinctly, and said it was the same, and looked as old when he first knew it.

Although many generations of men have passed away, and change has placed its mark on all surrounding objects since Noah's Ark first rested on Boston soil, yet the venerable relic still remains a monument of olden time, and its identity is beyond dispute.

There is something deeply interesting associated in the memory of these old houses; they were the homes of our ancestors, and that thought alone makes them sacred. They are mouldering links that connect us with the past. Our fathers, — where are they? Their memory, even, is fast fading away.

I have been thus particular in tracing the records of this old building, because there are several others, for each of which it is claimed that it is the oldest in the city. This *brick house*, with the peculiar name by which it was so early and so long known, affords facilities for tracing its identity enjoyed by none other; and I think I have shown beyond question that Noah's Ark was built in the year 1647, seventeen years after the settlement of Boston.

A STAMPEDE.

In the month of October, 1855, rumors were in circulation that in the witching hour of night, *something* was to be seen, *somewhere*. Young men and middle aged, old men and gray, knownothings and knowsomethings, were on tiptoe. The countenances of some wore a broad grin; that of others indicated anxiety and caution. Some, who seemed to rank with the knowing ones, were observed with thumb to nose, the digits of the same hand performing certain ominous gyrations; and some even were overheard to utter the unintelligible word *Moakus*.

Geevus, who had both an eye and ear to business, and is ever ready for the chances, in this case was not idle, and one of them, a little more curious than the rest, was out several nights *prospecting*, and with a little strategy and disguise, he had the good fortune to see and hear even more than he had anticipated. In consequence, arrangements were made for a reconnoissance in force the next Saturday night.

Well, the next Saturday night came, and with it a most powerful rain-storm, the water pouring down in torrents, which, however, only tended to favor the design of the expedition.

About nine o'clock on the aforesaid Saturday evening, just as the church bells were chiming the hour, a figure closely wrapped in a dark cloak, who had for a short time occupied a deep doorway, noiselessly and unobserved mingled with a crowd of some dozen young gentlemen as they came round the corner of Cooper and North Margin streets. The party were from a highly-respectable public house up-town, and evidently on an errand of some interest, but seemed to care very little to attract particular notice.

The whole party hurried noiselessly down North Margin Street a few rods, when all hands disappeared round a corner down a dark alley, which was entered by a flight of old wooden steps.

Rap, rap, rap, sounded the knuckles of some one of the party on a rickety old door, the first on the right. Up came a window in the second story, and out popped a woolly head, just discernible from below, that seemed of itself to make darkness visible.

"*Whose dar?*" said a gruff, female voice.

"*Moakus*," said one of the party below.

"Yah, yah, yah," said the voice, "*dat you — dat you*. Jus stop dar one minute — I'ze dar jus one minute:" and down went the window again.

In a few moments the portals of the establishment, which were secured with a large wooden wedge, were thrown open, and the whole party entered. Inside the darkness was intense; but the guide that opened the door piloted the party up the winding stairway, till all arrived safely in the reception-room on the third floor.

"Dis way — dis way, gemmen; dis de 'ception-room. Walk right in — done be 'fraid; walk right in;" and in they all hustled.

The room was a large, square one, neither ceiled or plastered, with little furniture, lighted with two old oil lamps, and looked about as dark as the proprietor.

"Gemmen, all in — all in," said the proprietor, "dat's right — dat's right;" and taking the hat of one, she began collecting the admission fee. "Only quarter dollar, gemmen — jest quarter apiece. Put it right in de hat — dat's right, put it right in de hat;" and the gents shelled out their quarters without hesitation.

When this operation was in progress, the figure in the cloak, which had attracted no attention, slid quietly out the door, down the stairway, and unbolted the outside door (which had been carefully fastened after the party entered), passed outside and took a convenient position for further observation.

As the figure in the cloak passed out of the establishment, two other portly individuals, who seemed to be in waiting, stepped in and passed quietly up the stairway into the reception-room, without attracting notice, the company inside being too intent on witnessing the exhibition to trouble themselves about external circumstances.

When the performance was well in progress, the countenances of the whole party having been well observed, a tremendous foot-stamp on the floor attracted the attention of all present, and mantles falling from the shoulders of the two individuals revealed the forms of two stalwart fellows dressed in blue frock coat and bright buttons, standing in their midst, one of whom proclaimed, in a plain, clear voice, that the performance of the evening was now closed.

A clap of thunder in a clear sky, or the ghost of Hamlet's father in corduroys, would hardly have produced a greater surprise on our little party of sportsmen. For a moment silence reigned supreme; and then commenced a retreat, a stampede, — and such a stampede as is rarely witnessed. Such a scratching, snatching, scrabbling, puffing, hunching, punching, rolling, jumping, tumbling, "Such a getting *down* stairs," and out of doors and windows, never entered into the fruitful imagination of the author of "Paradise Lost."

Those who were the *innocent cause* of this tremendous fright, stood looking calmly on until the last coat-tail had snapped round the corner, and the sound of retreating footsteps was lost in the distance, and then two very sable individuals were carefully conveyed to the Lockup.

GIVING A DESCRIPTION.

One of the greatest perplexities encountered by the Detective Police Officer, arises in consequence of the vague and erroneous description given of persons who it is desirable to find. Descriptions are often given, that are no more like the persons intended, than Cleopatra was like an Orang Outang, or the great American traveller is like the celebrated *Big Dick*.

Descriptions are not unfrequently given by different individuals, of some intimate missing friend, so different from each other, as to cause delays and mistakes enough to provoke the most cool and self-possessed officer. In fact, it is but too well understood by every detective, that he will hardly find two persons that will describe the figure of a stranger alike, although seen at the same time, and under the same circumstances.

My own observation leads me to believe that but comparatively few persons can give a good general description of others, unless led to make observations for that purpose by occupation or profession;

and then, when an officer once gets a good description, the difficulty of picking up your man among the tens of thousands of persons that throng the streets is no easy matter, even if you have the good fortune to get in sight of the right one.

I recollect one time of being sent out by my superior officer, to hunt up a pickpocket ; a general description was given of him, which would answer for half the men in the streets, but the mark that was to *fix the fellow*, was a *round top gray cap*, a very uncommon article, it was said.

I started out, with all the confidence I could summons, to find that *gray cap*, with the rogue under it ; but before I had proceeded half the length of Hanover Street, I was completely discouraged, and I soon returned to the Office, ready to swear on a stack of Bibles, that, of all the men I met, one in every ten wore that same style of cap.

But to the Descriptions. I recollect a case which, although literally true, may yet be thought a rather *tall* illustration of my subject. One day in the summer of 1862, there came a tall, careworn-looking lady into the Office where I was in charge, and proceeding cautiously up to my desk, asked in a loud whisper if I was the man. I quietly nodded assent, and she took a seat at my elbow ; and after carefully adjusting the folds of her dress and bonnet strings, she remarked that she had called on very important business, and desired the strictest secrecy. After being assured that her confidence would not be betrayed, she proceeded.

"Well, sir," said she, "I have lost my son;" and she covered her face with a clean white handkerchief.

"Indeed, madam," said I, at once touched by the apparent depth of her grief. "Pray, madam, what were the circumstances attending his death?"

"Dead!" said she, springing to her feet, "you don't tell me he is dead."

"Oh no, no, madam," said I, "but I understood you to say you had lost a son."

"Well, so I have," said she, resuming her seat; "but he *aint* dead; I should feel better, though, to follow him to his grave, than to have him run away, as he has, and leave his poor heart-broken mother. Oh dear, dear! for one so young and so tender to be sacrificed so soon!"

"Well, madam," said I, "what can I do for you?"

"Oh, sir, you can take his description, and hunt him up for me. They told me if I left his description, you would surely get him for me. He is surely in some recruiting office."

"Well, madam, give me the description," said I, "and we will try. What is his name?"

"Timothy Browning," said she. "But he enlisted by another name."

"How old?"

"Fourteen."

"How tall?"

"*Eight feet five inches*," said she.

"Eight feet five," said I. "Don't you mean five feet eight inches, and that would be extremely tall of his age."

"Do you think I don't know my own son better than a stranger?" said she, apparently a little vexed.

"Certainly, certainly, madam," said I. "Well, fourteen years old, eight feet five inches high. What complexion?"

"Light hair and black eyes."

"Rather uncommon," said I. Well, is he slim?"

"No, he is thick-set and full face, and he wears a *No. 9 Boot*, a cap, and gray coat and pants," said she. "But he is not dressed so now, for he was seen coming out of the Recruiting Office yesterday with some other boys *about his size*, and dressed in military uniform."

"Any other peculiarity?" said I.

"That's all," replied the lady.

"Well, let us see if I have it correct," I said.

"MISSING — Timothy Browning, (has taken some other name,) age fourteen, eight feet five inches high, thick-set, full face; was seen coming out of a recruiting office yesterday in military uniform, with several other boys about his size; wore a No. 9 Boot."

"That's correct," said the lady. Any one would know him by that description." I thought so too, and I promised her my best efforts; but I never found him.

TOUGH CUSTOMERS.

DURING my police life I have had many thousands of persons in my custody, the books at Station No. One alone showing a record of some sixty thousand names, during the seven years I had charge there; and it may readily be supposed that among so large a number, we found some very *tough customers*. *Tough* they were, many of them, and I know no reason why they might not be called *customers*, for they have done a good deal of business in our line, — called often at our place of business, and we furnished them with a good deal of what they very much deserved. Among the many I will name a few.

One day an officer found a man lying insensible in Haverhill Street, procured a carriage and brought him to the Station House, apparently in a dying condition. A physician was immediately sent for, who at once commenced applying *restoratives*. First, he let a stream of cold water fall some distance upon his temples; no movement was produced. Next, he applied a sponge saturated with hartshorn to his nostrils; not a muscle was seen to stir. The doctor looked puzzled, but after carefully feeling his pulse, he said there was life, and he would try the lancet. Accordingly he drew forth a sharp-pointed instrument, and opening a vein, the red fluid flowed quite freely.

At this stage of the proceedings the dying man sprang to his feet, and swore with a terrible oath that he would stand this nonsense no longer, and he pitched into the kind-hearted doctor right and left.

He said, he did n't care a fig for the water, or the smelling-drops; but when they came to butcher a fellow in the cellar of a watch-house, it was more than he could stand, and he believed the rascals would soon had the knife in his throat, and he would have been a dead carcase in the medical college.

The fellow was hurried into a cell for the safety of the doctor. After being there a few moments, he very calmly requested to be let out, that he might give the doctor what he deserved; and, said he, "If I am not let out immediately, I'll be shot if I come out till I get ready."

He came very near being as good as his word, for we did not get rid of him for two days, in which time he neither ate nor drank, and then he was only taken off by force, on virtue of a warrant charging him with being a vagabond.

Dick O'Brien was not one of the very worst of roughs, if you could catch him sober. Some one has said, " when wine is in, wit is out." If he had said, " when Medford rum is in, Dick is a quarrelsome blackguard," it would apply better to his case.

Dick had taken lessons in the *manly art*, and by some means had acquired the title of " The Irish Pet," of which name he was very proud, and allusions to it in a tone of disrespect has caused more than one *row* in North Street. Sometimes, too, when Dick had indulged pretty freely in his favorite beverage, without any provocation, he was inclined to indulge in his favorite sport, to the great annoyance of all peaceably disposed persons.

One evening in September, 1855, the Pet had been tasting rather heavily, and getting a little out of sorts because he could not get more without money, he posted himself at the corner of Richmond and North streets, evidently intent on mischief; and by way of *opening the ball*, he at first selected a young darkey who came up street, and gave him a tremendous punch in the head. The blow was a severe one, but the darkey seemed to think it all a joke, and went off grinning, while Dick stood rubbing his knuckles with pain.

Dick's next attempt was on a country looking chap, who came round the corner, who, when he saw Dick's well-aimed blow nearing his knowledge-box, just threw up his arm, and Dick's fist passed harmlessly by; but at the same time he laid his open hand on Dick's cheek with such force, that his heels were noticed high in the air.

When Dick regained his feet, the countryman was nowhere to be seen, and Dick went back to his corner swearing vengeance against all mankind in general, and any that might approach him in particular. In a few moments after Dick had again taken his position, peaceable and unsuspecting John Bigney came along, and caught a terrible blow from Dick's fist, which laid him senseless in the street with a broken shoulder, and a stranger who hastened up to see what was the matter, got a sidewinder, which only left life enough in him to cry *watch*, and the cry being repeated by several others in the neighborhood, soon brought up two of the *guardians*.

Dick was too proud to run, and too well-garrisoned to be taken without a siege; but he was eventually obliged to surrender in disgrace, and carried into the enemy's camp minus every rag of regimentals.

Next day Dick was sent to the House of Correction one year, for a felonious assault.

One evening a little old colored woman came into the Station House, and very politely asked for a night's lodging. On being questioned in relation to her name, age, and residence, she said she was a citizen of the world, was nine hundred and eighty years old, and her name was Kill Time.

She was evidently old and tough, but very smart and lively, and was neither drunk nor crazy; so she was taken at her word, and the record made on the books. After being furnished with some bread and cheese, she took her lodging-room in the basement, for which she expressed her thanks, and seemed to enjoy herself remarkably well.

When she turned out next morning, she was as bright and as chipper as a school girl, and when about leaving the house was again asked her age.

" Nine hundred and eighty," said she.

" And what is your right name ? " said one of the officers.

" *Kill Time*," sir, was the reply ; and she departed with a low courtesy.

EARLY one morning in the month of December, 1855, one of the officers heard the cry of " watch," apparently in a stifled voice, emanating from a yard in rear of a lodging-house on Union Street, and hastened in that direction. On reaching the spot, the officer found the cry came from the lungs of one John Diver, a big lump of a drunken loafer, who had come over from Cambridge the night previous, and whose head held more rum than brains.

John had taken lodging in the house at a late hour, and after retiring, "the spirits" or some other power, suggested to him that he was in a very bad locality, and dangerous withal; and, to add a peculiar interest to the case, John imagined he saw myriads of hideous monsters, who, with enormous horns, protruding eyeballs, and extended jaws, were about to put an end to his corporeal identity, *uncooked* and *unseasoned*.

John at once resolved not to surrender without an effort, and following up his resolution, he performed some feats that highly illustrated his name, and which would have done honor to the veritable *Sam Patch* himself, although Sam, very unlike John, always kept right end up.

At first, John dove out of bed, — then, down two flight of stairs, — then, through a glass window in the upper part of a door into the street, — next, through the panel of a gate into the back yard, every jump head foremost; and, last of all, he jumped his head into a swill barrel, where the officer found him kicking and struggling with all his might to make further headway.

Why John had not beat out what brains he had left is more than can be well accounted for, yet he was not materially injured. When rescued by the officer, he entertained the idea that he had barely managed to escape from Purgatory, and walked off to the Station House with his new guide with a very good grace.

One evening a neighboring shopman came rushing into the Station House in breathless haste, demanding the immediate assistance of an officer, saying that a terrible customer had just entered his store with a loaded pistol in hand, and threatened to shoot every one within his reach. Said he, "myself and clerk have barely escaped with our lives."

An officer was on the way at once, and soon returned with the would-be assassin in custody, closely followed by the affrighted shopman and several neighbors.

The desperado was a little drunk, but not turbulent, and submitted to be searched without a murmur. After carefully examining his pockets, the officer drew from the one under the left arm, the supposed deadly weapon. As it came in sight a shudder seemed to run through the crowd of bystanders, and the shopman exclaimed, "That's it; look out, it's loaded!"

On examination, however, the weapon proved to be but a sweet potato, about the size and something in the form of a small pocket-pistol, but certainly possessing none of its deadly qualities. The rascal of a prisoner stood grinning as we examined the weapon, and when I turned to speak to the shopman, he had gone, and his friends were retiring one by one.

I HAVE in my mind a pair, one of each sex, who dwelt together for some years, who would not suffer in comparison with the toughest set I ever saw, especially the female specimen, for she was the tougher of the two.

It was shortly after the great Police Descent in Ann Street, and a large number of the same class had *fled from the wrath* in that street, and taken up quarters at North End block. There were at this time some fifty rooms in this block, occupied by as many different families, if you could call them such, and they were made up of the very toughest class of human beings I ever met. Add to this the numerous roughs visiting every night from other localities, and the crews of two men-of-war's men, whose vessels lay in the harbor, and who were not slow in prospecting about this locality, and it made up one of the most interesting little colonies ever known in the puritan city of Boston.

Well, Shoddy, as he was called, and Mary Lovina, were perfectly at home here, especially as far as rum and fight was in the play; and it was said that when outsiders were a little scarce, Shoddy and Lovina would occasionally get up a brush between themselves, just to keep the hand in.

In these family exercises, the drunker of the two generally got the worst of it, although they contrived to keep the account along about even. In fact, the pair were so troublesome, that, strange as it may seem, they really annoyed the neighborhood, bad as it was, and it became necessary to make an example of both Shoddy and his wife.

One night two of us went down with Constable Stratton, who was armed with a warrant to make the arrest. We went to Shoddy's room and made known our errand, and both he and the wife being somewhat accustomed to similar visits, took it all as a matter of course, and although both were pretty drunk, they immediately began to prepare. Mary Lovina, during her preparation, stepped into a small side-room. While thus engaged, all at once Shoddy cried out, "She's gone," his eyes sticking out most wonderfully as he gazed at an open window that led from the side-room down into the street. I looked just in time to see Mary Lovina's hands slip from the window-sill. I sprang to the window, but she had gone, sure enough, out of the window down to the sidewalk, a distance of twenty-two feet, having fallen partly into an open cellar-way, her body lying across the sharp edge of the cap timber, partly on the sidewalk and partly down the stairway, and apparently a lifeless corpse.

We hurried down as quickly as possible, took her up and carried her into the house for dead; but on feeling her pulse it was found she still had life. A physician was sent for, and after a while she began to revive, and, strange to say, not a bone had been broken. She finally so far recovered, that, at the physician's suggestion, she was conveyed to the hospital at South Boston, although it was supposed that she had received internal injuries, indicated by volumes of blood from the mouth, and could not live. But Lovina did live, and in about ten days so far recovered as to be brought over to the Police Court, and sentenced to the House of Correction six months for common drunkenness.

Lovina was placed under the kind care of Captain Robbins, and took her post among his pupils; but before ten days had elapsed she had eluded the eye of her overseer, crawled over a board fence ten feet high, and made her escape, — after which I heard no more of Shoddy or Mary Lovina for some years.

However, in the year 1858, some six years after, the pair turned up again in an alley-way leading out of Friend Street, as purely Shoddy and Mary Lovina as ever, and at their old tricks, — getting drunk and pummelling each other as in former days.

But poor human nature cannot always bear up against the storms of adversity, and Lovina, getting a little tired of life, one day went down to the Boston and Maine railroad wharf and jumped overboard. She was so ugly she could not sink, but floated off upon the water as buoyant as an old bonnet. She was picked up by a boatman and set ashore, swearing vengeance upon the poor boatman and her ill luck, and steaming up the wharf in a paroxysm of rage. I have never seen her since, but, in her prime, I think she stood at the head of her class.

John Brown, *unlike him of song*, was a character of very little note, were it not for his big burly head and ill temper. John was a rough, however, of considerable muscular power, and was always to be found at a cock or dog fight, or a bar-room brawl, and he not only dealt out many hard knocks, but now and then he managed to get one himself.

One evening John kicked up a row in the pit at the National Theatre, and got put out. He immediately made his way up to the third circle, and demanded admittance there. Just at that time I was passing the theatre, and thought I would step up and see if there were any new faces among the *profession*, as there were usually a good delegation of that class to be found in the third circle. As I came up the stairs to the door, John was making preparation to pitch into the doorkeeper for refusing to admit him without a ticket, and seeing there was likely to be trouble if John remained, I turned my back to him (he had not noticed me), and taking a good hold with each hand on the bottom of each leg of his pantaloons I started down stairs. From indications behind me, I came to the conclusion that John's underpinning had given way, and that he was playing the part of a boy coasting *belly bump*, only he was "*advancing backwards*" at a tremendous speed; however, I kept steadily on, without once relinquishing my hold of the pants, down one flight of stairs, and then another, till I fairly reached the sidewalk, when I suddenly released my hold, sprang across the street to the opposite sidewalk, and turned round to see the result, leaving John sprawling, face downward, looking very much like a frog on dry land in hot sunshine. The officer in the lower part of the theatre, who had put John out of the pit, hearing the racket, ran out upon the sidewalk to see what was the matter, and reached the spot where John had lain just as he had regained his feet. John, supposing poor *Geevus* (who was the first man he saw) to be the cause of all his trouble, pitched into him and made the claret fly at short notice. *Geevus*, who was not a cripple, returned the compliment in fine style, and with the butt end of a heavy cane he floored poor John instanter, and with help ready at hand lugged him off to the Station House. I followed on to see how matters progressed, but nothing further interesting coming up, I quietly went my way, and next day I saw in the papers that John was sent to the House of Correction six months for an assault on an officer in the discharge of his duty.

THE OLD ELM ON THE COMMON.

This venerable representative of olden time, which has lived to witness the rise and fall of empires; the birth, progress, and decay of nations; which has withstood the fury of the storm and the ravages of time for many generations "*still lives.*" Its widely extended roots still grapple with mother earth, in all the tenacity and vigor of manhood. Its massive trunk, supported by iron strengthening-bands, still stands firm and erect, and its numerous branches, with here and there the stump of an amputated arm, are still stretched forth toward heaven, as if in *supplication* to the Father of Life, and in veneration of the handiwork of the great Creator.

Although the old tree bears unmistakable marks of great age, yet the exact date of its origin is now unknown. In the year 1854, Dr. Smith, then Mayor of Boston, caused a fence to be erected, enclosing and protecting the *Old Elm*.

This fence is of octagon form, made of cast iron, and is one hundred and twenty feet in circumference, although it falls far short of enclosing the area shadowed by the branches of the tree. On the iron gate at the entrance of the enclosure, is a tablet containing a short history of the tree, in raised letters, as follows: —

> THE OLD ELM.
>
> This Tree has been standing here for an unknown period. It is believed to have existed before the settlement of Boston, being fully grown in 1722, exhibited marks of old age in 1792, and was nearly destroyed by a storm in 1832. Protected by an iron enclosure in 1854.
>
> J. V. C. SMITH, *Mayor.*

Although the foregoing account of the supposed age of the tree is entitled to great credit, yet the Hancock family, who have always had a deep interest in its history, have a tradition that differs somewhat from that upon the iron tablet.

I have seen an affadavit of Madame Scott, formerly the widow of Governor Hancock, which says: —

"Mrs. Hancock, the wife of Thomas, who was uncle to the Governor, has often told me that her grandfather, Hezekiah Henchman, when a boy, transplanted the great elm from the North End to where it now stands. Mrs. Hancock has often pointed at the old tree, and spoken of the circumstance, and it was a matter of notoriety in our family."

Mrs. Hancock used to say that she could remember when the tree was not fully grown.

Madam Scott was said to be a highly educated and accomplished lady, and was living in about the year 1818, being then nearly eighty years of age.

Mr. Thomas Hancock, uncle of the Governor, was a bookbinder and bookseller, served his time with Colonel Daniel Henchman, and married his daughter Lydia. Mr. Hancock lived in Queen Street, in the house afterwards occupied as the Brattle Street Church Parsonage, which was given that Society by his widow. Mr. Thomas Hancock was the patron of the Governor, who inherited a large portion of his estate.

Colonel Daniel Henchman, the father of Mrs. Thomas Hancock, established the first paper-mill in New England, at Quincy, Mass. He was the son of Hezekiah Henchman, the boy who is said to have transplanted the tree.

Hezekiah was the son of Captain Daniel Henchman, the emigrant, and was probably born about the year 1658. The family removed to Worcester in the year 1674, and, if the tradition is correct, young Hezekiah probably transplanted the elm previously to the removal to Worcester. Which account of the origin of the Old Elm is correct, or either, I shall not attempt to determine.

The old tree is said to be a native elm, whose roots extend much further and deeper, and lives much longer, than the English elm, many of which have been blown down or decayed while standing on the adjoining malls, while the native of the soil remains unharmed and thrifty.

The combination of incidents and memories, in ten thousand ways associated in the history of the venerable old tree for the past two hundred years, would fill a volume of the deepest interest.

IMPERTINENT POLICEMEN.

Policemen are often funny fellows, and not only so, but they sometimes have the faculty of asking some very impertinent questions; nor is this fault confined to patrolmen alone, but is sometimes indulged in by officers of higher rank. Instances of this character from any source were always annoying to me, especially where the subject relates to matters of a grave nature, or are designed to call in question the official integrity of the officer of any other department, as I think the interest of the public is best subserved by each department confining itself to its own legitimate duties.

However, we should not look for perfection among men; but I am willing to confess, I should commence in the Police Department to take the first look.

One bright winter afternoon, when for once the sleighing was fine in Boston, one of the Captains of Police had the impudence to send me the following communication.

Mr. ———

Dear Sir: Having a leisure hour, I have taken the liberty to send you an account of my doings in one of the courts this forenoon, and in return desire you to send me your opinion of my success.

I had four cases in court, of a nature and result as follows, viz: No. 1. A thief stole four pair of boots, valued at sixteen dollars. Plead guilty to the charge, fined eight dollars without costs. No. 2. A young boy, but an old thief, stole five dollars from a money-drawer. Caught in the act. Boy said he was coasting on the Common at the time, — pretty sister swore he was in the house all day. Conflicting testimony, — boy discharged. No. 3. Till-tappers accomplice, — no warrant. No. 4. Brutal fight, — broken heads, — mutual assault, and mutual damage. One fined six dollars and costs, the other discharged.

In my perplexity and chagrin at the Captain's impudence I returned him the following answer.

"Dear Captain, in your note this day,
A leisure hour to while away, —
You gave a sample of your readings
In our Court of special pleadings;
Where, in his glory and alone,
Sat Justice, smiling on the throne.

"In No. 1, for stealing leather,
Admit without proceeding further,
'I did it,' pays one half the debt,
The balance cash, eight dollars net.

"Then No. 2, 'the noted thief,'
What if he steals cash, bread, or beef;
Pray, has he not good claims on grace,
With a pretty sister in the case?

"Now tell me plainly, as your friend,
What right have you down at *North End*,
To pick up strangers, just for sport,
To worry and perplex the court;
Should you not strive its cares to lighten,
When sleighing's tip top out to Brighton?
Despise not honors, fame, or pelf,
For you may yet be Judge yourself."

The Captain sent me no more communications of a like nature.

ADVICE TO A YOUNG POLICEMAN.

My Friend: You have recently been appointed, and are about to assume the responsibilities, of an office the duties of which are much more varied and difficult, and the trust of which is of much more importance to the public and to yourself, than is generally admitted.

You are to assume the duties of an *executive officer* of criminal law, of the ordinances of a great commercial city, and as a conservator of the public peace. Your acts will at all times be subject to the observation and the animadversion of the public, and on the stand-point where you commence, and the course which you pursue, depends not only much of the welfare of the community in which you move, but the credit of the department to which you belong, and your own success as an officer and a man.

At the commencement, do not forget that in this business your character is your capital. Deal honorably with all persons, and hold your word sacred, no matter when, where, or to whom given. If you are entrusted with the care of a beat, do not play the loafer on it by lounging in doorways or on corners, or leaning against lamp-posts, but patrol your district continually; make it your business to know what is doing on every part of it, as far as practicable, without unnecessary interference; let no person or circumstance escape your notice, and be able at all times to give information respecting any circumstance of importance occurring thereon. Learn the people residing or doing business on your beat; protect their property; make yourself useful, and aid them in all their lawful pursuits, and by an upright and straightforward course, and a close attention to duty, endeavor to merit the good will of all good citizens. You know not how soon you may need their aid, and their favor will add much to your power and influence to do good. But in the pursuance of your duties, as much as possible avoid laying yourself under special obligation to any one; let your services rather place others under an obligation to you. You know not how soon your duties may peremptorily demand that you *act* in opposition to some individual interest.

Lend a willing ear to all complaints made to you in your official capacity; the most unworthy have a right to be heard, and a word of comfort to the afflicted, or of advice to the erring, costs you nothing, and may do much good.

In ordinary cases, if you find yourself in a position not knowing exactly what to do, better do too little than too much; it is easier to excuse a moderate course than an overt act. But if an act of great violence has been committed, secure the offender the first possible moment; delay increases his chance of escape; there are always plenty of willing hands to care for the party he may have injured.

Whenever it is necessary to make an arrest, and you attempt to do it, *don't fail;* but use no more force than is necessary to protect yourself and secure your man.

If you have a prisoner in custody, *keep him before you*, do not trust him behind; he might escape, or he might injure you, and, besides, bystanders might mistake you for the criminal, being in his place. If an arrest is necessary, so is care and caution.

A warrant directed *to the Police Officers of the City of Boston*, may be executed by you, none other. Such a warrant legally carries you through any door within your precinct where the offender may really be; but before executing any warrant, *read it*, and see what are its directions and requirements; and when executed, have your prisoner at court at its first sitting, never omitting to make your return on your warrant over your own official signature, else you have made a false arrest, and may be held liable.

The offences for which persons may be legally arrested without a warrant, are, felony (crime punishable in State's Prison), assault and battery *in your presence*, persisting in disturbing the peace, and drunkenness. Simple larceny is not included in the statute, but common practice will, I think, justify an officer in taking a person charged with that crime to the Station House, for the direction of his captain. Other cases may occur, which will require much good judgment and discretion to determine what is proper.

If you are called to the witness-stand, give in your evidence clearly and distinctly, but as briefly as the whole facts can be stated. On no account let any personal feeling creep into your testimony, nor ever disgrace yourself in the eyes of the court, or prejudice your case, by a show of malice, or an attempt to color the facts; and *never* give as one reason that you made an arrest, that "*he was saucy.*"

No officer can be successful or efficient in the execution of his duties, unless he understands the requirements of the laws and ordinances. Spare no pains in posting yourself in these matters; recollect that by virtue of your police warrant, you can only serve a criminal process. Every Police Officer should be familiar with the law or ordinance he is to execute, and he should also know enough of the civil law to distinguish between the two.

Visit the courts as often as practicable, and make yourself familiar with their rules and practices, that when called as a witness, you may not appear a stranger.

Carry with you at all times a memorandum-book, and let it contain some record relative to your duties every day; it will be of great value as a reference.

Let promptness mark all your acts; don't be the last man at roll-call, or at your post of duty, nor leave your post without orders; and never keep a person waiting for you one moment after the appointed time.

In whatever duty you engage, set your mind and your *face* to the work, and while on duty, never suffer yourself to appear like an idle spectator. Make promptness a rule for yourself, and require it of others.

School yourself on all occasions to keep *perfectly cool;* maintain a perfect control of temper, come what will: one that can govern himself, can control others. Never degrade your position by placing yourself on a level with a drunken man or a man in a passion, by suffering his abuse to get you in a passion also.

Remember that in your official duties, you are continually and eminently exposed to the ten thousand snares and temptations in city life. I charge you, as you value the character of the Department to which you belong, as you value your own character and happiness, and the fondest hopes of your friends, *beware, be ever on your guard;* " be not deceived, nor led into temptation." Select your associates with care. " A man is known by the company he keeps;" you will learn to so judge others, and others will so judge you.

Treat all persons kindly; avoid discussion in politics; pay your honest debts, and lay up what you can spare for a sick-day. And, finally, in whatever duties you engage, either in public or private life, let all your acts be guided by a common-sense view of men and things that surround you.

I might say more, but should I, you would still have to go out and *learn* your duty.

CONSCRIPTION RIOT.

The opening of the spring of 1863 witnessed the renewal of hostilities between the loyal and the seceding States with redoubled vigor. The last session of the Congress of the United States, in anticipation of this event, had clothed President Lincoln with extraordinary powers to meet the emergency by passing the so-called Conscription Act, for drafting men for three years or during the war.

Early in June, under this law, the President issued his proclamation, calling for three hundred thousand men. The enrolment was to consist of two classes, — first, those between the ages of eighteen and thirty-five, and all unmarried men between thirty-five and forty-five; the second class comprised all married men between the ages of thirty-five and forty-five, — the first class to be exhausted by the draft before the second were to be drawn.

In this law various exemption clauses were provided, among which was the commutation fee, whereby the drafted man was entitled to exemption on the payment of three hundred dollars.

It has ever been a difficult task to please everybody where life or money is at stake; and where partisanship is in any way involved in the case, the undertaking is much more difficult; but whether this was a case in point, I shall not stop to argue. One fact is patent, however, there was much opposition to the draft even in Massachusetts, and the three hundred dollar commutation clause was a theme for many an eloquent animadversion.

However, Provost Marshals were appointed in the several congressional districts in all the loyal States, who, with their assistants, were to supervise and execute the enrolment and draft under the direction of a Provost Marshal General.

The quota of Massachusetts amounted to something over eighteen thousand men, of which Boston was to furnish about thirty-three hundred. The head-quarters of the Provost Marshal, comprising the southern wards, Roxbury, and Brookline, was at No. 22 Summer Street, and that of the northern wards, Cambridge, Chelsea, and Winthrop, were at No. 106 Sudbury Street. At the former, Marshal George A. Shaw; at the latter, Marshal William G. Howe.

The marshals immediately commenced to canvass their districts, and on the eighth day of July following the enrolment was completed, and drafting commenced in Boston.

The names and residence of those belonging to the first class were placed in an octagonal, or circular globe, revolving by a crank.

After several revolutions of the wheel by one of the assistants, another, who stood by blindfolded, thrust his hand into a slide door at the top of the wheel and drew forth one ticket, which he held up and passed to another assistant, who, after reading the name aloud, passed it over to the clerk, when the name and residence were recorded, and the man whose name was on the card was *elected*.

In this manner the draft was proceeded with day after day, till, as was supposed, a sufficient number of names had been drawn to fill the quota, allowing an excess of fifty per cent to make up exemptions.

Many spectators were present, all seemingly deeply interested in this new kind of lottery; and when one who was present chanced to draw something more than a blank, he would immediately receive the hearty cheers of the bystanders, and start off, if not quite satisfied, yet apparently convinced that life is a lottery, and it is not always the most fortunate that draws the prize.

So far as Boston was concerned, there was yet no indication of a design to interfere with the draft, although some persons in high places spoke of the conscription as unconstitutional, unjust, and oppressive, and others avowed their determination, if drafted, to neither go, pay, nor furnish a substitute.

On the 14th of July, the draft for the Boston districts was completed, and the assistants were sent out to notify those whose names had been drawn to appear at the Marshal's Office and undergo the surgical examination.

At this time, and for about two days previous, a most fearful riot had been raging in New York city, got up and carried on by those opposed to the draft in that locality, with a most fearful sacrifice of life and property; and there began to appear certain indications that the same dreadful contagion lay hidden beneath the surface in our own city. The fact that the mob were in the ascendent in New York, which was loudly heralded through the streets in the hourly newspaper issues, by no means served to allay the turbulent spirit here, which was fast ripening for action.

About one o'clock in the afternoon of this day, two assistant Provost Marshals from the Fourth District were distributing their notices in Prince Street near the Gas Works, and went into a house to serve a notice. The woman supposing they had come to take her husband away, followed the marshals into the street, hurling at their heads every article within her reach, and screeching like a raving maniac. In an instant the street was filled with infuriated men and women, each vieing with the other in revenging their imaginary wrongs. The two officers were set upon, bruised and beaten in a most inhuman manner, barely escaping with their lives. Several citizens, also, who attempted to reason with the mob, were badly injured, and a store at the junction of Endicott and Charlestown streets, through which the assistant marshals succeeded in making their escape, was damaged and robbed.

This was the commencement of a scene such as has not been witnessed in Boston since it became a city. At the first alarm several policemen, who were on duty on their respective beats in the neighborhood, immediately hurried to the scene of disorder; but their presence only excited the mob, who immediately commenced an onslaught, and the officers, being but few in number, and arriving at opposite points, made but a sorry show with the several hundred madmen that filled the streets.

Several officers from Stations No. One and No. Two were struck down, and so severely hurt that for many days their lives were despaired of, and others were materially injured; in fact, all the officers present only escaped death on the spot in consequence of the anxiety of the mob on the outside to press into the centre, literally forcing away those who were dealing death-blows on their fallen victims, thereby themselves defeating their own object, and giving the officers an opportunity to crawl away with what little of life remained, the enraged mass in their progress overrunning and trampling under foot many of their own number, without regard to age or sex.

When the rioters had lost sight of the officers, they ran howling through the streets like so many demons, in quest of some object on which to vent their fury, and meeting with nothing seemingly worthy their notice, a large number headed for the Hanover Street Station House, and in a few moments a mass of many hundreds were crowded together in that locality; but as no one was in custody, and nothing appearing there to furnish fuel for the flame, they offered no violence. The violent exercise so lately indulged in, the day being hot, might also have had its influence in cooling their ardor.

The whole transaction as above narrated probably occupied not more than twenty minutes, and word immediately came to the Central Office of what had transpired.

The news was not wholly unexpected, but it was not looked for so soon; anticipation of trouble had been entertained when arrests began to be made of conscripts for non-appearance after being duly notified; but we had not got to that. However, the moment the news came, an order calling together the police of the Second Station was given, and the writer, who was at the time in charge of the Central Office, started for the North End. On reaching the Station House in Hanover Street, he found a collection of some two thousand persons, of all ages and sexes, standing in the streets, but they were perfectly quiet, strikingly so. There were some dozen officers at the Station House, but no person had been arrested, neither was there any apparent cause for the gathering. The writer had been in charge of that Station for several years, and the crowd being principally North End people, he was probably known to a greater part of those present, and he took the opportunity to go out upon the steps and say to those present that no one was in custody at that House; there was no cause for excitement or alarm, and earnestly begged of them to retire quietly to their homes or places of business. But it was like talking to trees; the crowd listened in silence, and some near by would step back a few paces, but it did not number one less, while the indication of those upturned faces seemed to forebode no good.

The writer then left the steps and passed quietly among the people, speaking with many that he knew; but he soon learned for a fact, what he had before suspected, that very many were armed with various weapons. This, together with the general appearance of the crowd, what they had already done, with now and then a suppressed threat that met the car, but too plainly indicated that there was "*mischief in the meal*," and there was no time to lose in preparing for it. To attempt to clear the streets with the force at hand was worse than useless; ten or twelve men could not control the hundreds there collected, with the temper they plainly possessed, and to attempt and fail, would likely be a signal for a general outbreak; we were not ready for that. If there was no excuse offered the outbreak would not likely occur till favored by the darkness of night; that would give time to prepare. *But should the Police suffer that crowd to have exclusive possession of the streets that afternoon without an effort?* After consulting with the captain of the Station, the writer started for Station No. 2, in Court Square, for more officers, with a determination to clear those streets at all hazards. But he was not to go alone, and at least fifteen hundred of every age and sex (*there was little diversity of color*) formed a most uncouth escort up Hanover Street, without, however, offering any abuse save a continued round of shouts, half complimentary and half defiant.

The company was none too pleasant, but it effected a most desirable object little calculated on at the start, namely, successfully removing the crowd from the Hanover Street Station House, and which superseded the necessity of returning with a force from Station No. 2. The mob, however, or at least a part of them, followed to Court Square; but that locality soon grew a little uncomfortable for them, and quiet was restored for the time.

It was now nearly two o'clock. His Honor the Mayor, the Chief of Police, and members of the City Government were at once fully aware of the responsibilities resting on them, and from that moment no one was idle. It was well known that a lawless mob were at that moment bidding defiance to law and order in the city of New York. Were we to have its counterpart in our own city, and not be prepared to meet it?

Our Police force were immediately prepared for their work, and armed with weapons suitable for the occasion. Fire-alarm bell signals were so arranged as to call the whole Police force, or any part thereof, to either part of the city; sentinels were placed at various points, and scouts to all parts of the city were passing to and fro from the Central Office. Officers were patrolling every part of the city, ready to pass the word if any disturbance occurred, and the whole force were ready for duty. Nor was this deemed sufficient. Orders were immediately issued by the Mayor to call out the State Military, who were ordered to be in readiness at their Armories without delay, and a detachment of Regulars, numbering about one hundred and seventy-five men, were also sent up from Fort Warren.

It was nearly three o'clock P. M. when the first step of preparation was taken; at six o'clock the authorities were ready for any emergency.

The crowd of persons that gathered at the north part of the city early in the afternoon, did not entirely disperse after leaving the Hanover Street Station House, but were seen in squads at different points in that part of the city; but no further outbreak occurred during the afternoon.

No arrests had been made of those engaged in the riot in Prince or Endicott Street, for the reason that no identification of the guilty parties could then be made, the officers being too seriously injured to leave their beds, and citizens who knew, not daring to open their lips.

At six o'clock the military companies of the city had quietly repaired to their respective Armories, one by one, and every Police officer was at his post.

It was the design of the City Government to make no unnecessary display, and to pursue no course that could be construed into a menace which might add fuel to the flame, but to be prepared to crush at a blow any demonstration that could be made, no matter at what point or how formidable; but they were prepared none too well or too soon, as the sequel will show.

About seven o'clock in the evening, the Regulars from Fort Warren came down Hanover Street, leaving a detachment at the Armory in Marshal

Street, and passed with the remainder down Salem and Cooper Street, without music, so as not to attract a crowd. On their arrival at Cooper, that street was densely filled with an excited mob, armed with pistols, clubs, paving-stones, bricks, and other missiles; but the military steadily proceeded to the Gunhouse, where a Battery was already in quarters.

The Regulars had hardly reached the Gunhouse, when a perfect shower of missiles were hurled at them and the building. Sidewalks were torn up by the rod by women and children, and carried forward to men and boys in front, and the mob commenced a siege in good earnest. Various persons in the streets who had been attracted by the tumult, were knocked down and severely beaten, the Rioters seeming to be determined that none but their own gang should remain in the neighborhood. A Lieutenant of the Battery, who arrived alone just after the Regulars had entered the Gunhouse, was struck down, trampled under foot, and dragged out towards Endicott Street for dead.

When the Battery entered the Gunhouse, which was as early as six o'clock, the commander had requested a Police officer of the First Station, who lived near by, to stand at the North Margin Street door of the Gunhouse, which was open, and allow no citizen to pass. The officer remained at this door till about the time of the assault on the Lieutenant of the Battery. The mob having collected on the Cooper Street side, where the Regulars entered, when the Lieutenant was attacked, some one informed the Police officer, and he communicated the information to the military commander inside the Armory, who immediately dispatched a Lieutenant with a file of men to go out and rescue the Lieutenant. About this time the outside on North Margin Street began to grow a little warm, and the Police officer, with his father, an elderly gentleman, who had been standing near, both stepped inside the Gunhouse. The Lieutenant and his command at once left the house, by the North Margin Street door, and charged round into Cooper towards Endicott Street, where they found the Lieutenant of the Battery lying senseless in the gutter. They took him up and attempted to return; but the mob had filled in the rear so densely and determined, that the soldiers were obliged to charge on them with fixed bayonets, to again reach North Margin Street, on their way back to the Gunhouse. As the military filed into North Margin Street, the mob made a furious attack on the rear with bricks, stones, clubs, and a plentiful discharge of pistols. The attack was so furious that the Lieutenant ordered his men to wheel and fire, to preserve their own safety. This only seemed to increase the fury of the assailants, and they being apparently well armed, and vastly superior in numbers, the Lieutenant thought prudent to retire inside the Gunhouse as soon as possible.

As soon as the military were under cover, the mob seemed to feel that they had gained the ascendency, and renewed the attack on the Gunhouse, on the Cooper Street side, with redoubled fury. Every window and some of the doors in the lower part of the house were soon broken, and the mob were improving all opportunities to fire upon those inside, through the broken doors and windows; but there were preparations made by the military that the assailants outside had not counted on. These were held in reserve till urged forward by the most pressing necessity. When the command of the Lieutenant retired inside, two brass field-pieces were brought forward and manned, one at the Cooper Street door, which was closed and barred, the other at the North Margin Street door, which was still open. Both were charged to meet any emergency, and flanked by the infantry, with loaded Springfields. In a few moments the Rioters had demolished all but the double door on the Cooper Street side, and those heavy oak doors were fast giving way. It was supposed to be the intention of the mob to storm the house, secure the firearms, and turn them upon whoever might interfere with their progress. In that emergency there seemed to be but one course for the military to pursue; at any rate self-defence was justifiable, and at this moment this was the only question at issue, and that, to be effectual, must be acted upon without delay. The commander was not long in forming a determination, and just as the Cooper Street door was giving way, the order was given to the Artillery men to fire, and a brass cannon swept all before it. The mass of human beings outside surged back; but they soon recovered, and came rushing forward again; but they were promptly met by powder and minnie ball in such profusion that they again fell back, and sullenly retired from the near locality of the door for the time. At the time the Police officer and his father retired inside the Gunhouse, they both stood for a moment near the North Margin Street door; but as soon as the cannon were placed in position, by the advice of his son, the old gentleman went over upon the back or west side of the room, where some soldiers were standing, as a place of safety. His son last saw him, alive, standing there; he was on the left of three soldiers, facing the Cooper Street door, and was noticed and spoken to by one of them. He was unwittingly standing just in range of a front window and side door, both of which had been broken in, and at that point he was shot by a ball entering his body near the left breast and coming out under and just back of his right arm.

He fell dead at the feet of the soldiers. This was a few moments before the cannon were discharged.

The dead man was immediately taken up by the soldiers, and removed upstairs, with others who had been wounded in the fray, where he was recognized by his son.

Word was immediately conveyed by a messenger to the Central Office, but the extent of the difficulty was not then fully known. A posse of Police, however, were forthwith sent to Cooper Street, under the charge of a competent officer; but on arriving in the neighborhood, and learning the true state of affairs, he reported back to the Central Office. While making his report, a scout arrived bringing intelligence that the cannon had been discharged in Cooper Street, and the mob were heading up town. While he was speaking, a second messenger reported the mob rushing up Salem and Endicott Street, crying out, "*To Dock Square, boys — to Read's Store! We'll give 'em New York!*" &c. The idea at once occurred that they were rushing to the hardware stores, for firearms and ammunition. The officer who was first sent out was ordered to proceed at once, with all the Police force at hand, and clear Dock Square at all hazards; and then came the ominous sound of the alarm bells throughout the city, eleven strokes three times repeated. At seven o'clock the assault on the Cooper Street Armory was commenced by the Rioters; at eight o'clock the field-piece was discharged; at fifteen minutes past eight the signal alarm was given; and in less than fifteen minutes more Mayor Lincoln, at the head of the Cavalry and Infantry, was on his way from Court Square to the scene of disorder.

The Police who had been sent to Dock Square were doing their work nobly; they reached the Square before the Rioters had much time to secure arms or ammunition. For a time they were struggling against fearful odds in numbers, but the alarm bells brought reinforcements in a few moments.

The Rioters had reached several stores in Dock Square, where they demolished doors and windows, and secured a small quantity of firearms; but they were rushed upon by the Police, who were well armed, and driven from the stores.

Another gang had attacked a store in Faneuil Hall Square, where a large quantity of arms was known to be kept; but here they met with no better success, being there also furiously attacked by the Police. Although most of the mob beat a retreat when they were met with powder and ball, yet there were some master spirits who stood their ground, and fought desperately. One man, who had a musket, cried out to his fellows, "Don't run, like cowards, but let us give the dam' Yankees hell!" He discharged his piece at one of the officers, and then with his musket clubbed, rushed upon him. He however missed his aim. and broke the breach of his piece on the sidewalk ; he struck again, and bent the barrel of his piece over the officer's head. He received one bullet in his arm, and another in his head, before he was arrested, and fought desperately after that. He was afterwards recognized as a ringleader at Charlestown, Endicott, and Prince Streets, early in the afternoon, and also at Cooper Street, in the early part of the evening.

Another ringleader was also arrested near Dock Square, about the same time, who was brandishing a large knife, and boasting of his daring deeds during the evening. But few arrests, however, were made at that time, the Rioters being so strong in numbers that the Police could hardly afford to diminish their own force to carry off prisoners.

The military force, headed by the Mayor and Chief of Police, reached Dock and Faneuil Hall squares soon after the affray between the Police and the mob, and the Rioters were driven from that locality, the military holding possession till next day.

At about half past twelve o'clock, a fire alarm was sounded in District No. One, — the Cooper Street Armory had been fired. Previous to this, the military from this place had removed their armament to Dock Square; the dead and wounded had been removed to more convenient and proper places, and the house had been closed; but the incendiary had applied his torch in the rear of the building, and the flames were beginning to make headway. Four Police officers, however, were immediately on the spot, broke in at the door of the Armory, and commenced to extinguish the flames. They were immediately attacked with bricks, stones, and pistol-shots by those still lurking in the neighborhood; but these compliments were returned with such promptness and vigor that the assailants, who were not now in large numbers, and who had been treated to a like entertainment on the same ground earlier in the evening, thought it prudent to retire, leaving the officers to turn their attention to the fire, which they kept in check till the fire department arrived.

The names of these brave and determined men, who, at the risk of their lives, prevented a conflagration on that already fearful night, should be given here; but where so many officers merit so much as was really due them for that night's service, the names of all cannot be given, and justice seems to forbid a distinction.

Although the organization, if there was one, had been substantially broken at Dock Square and elsewhere during the evening, yet fragments were still lurking about the streets, evidently bent on mischief, and the Police and military were constantly on the alert.

About two o'clock in the morning, word came to the Central Office that an attack was to be made on the property of a worthy citizen at the extreme north part of the city. Although these reports were numerous during the night, it was deemed prudent that none of them be unheeded, and in this case a squad of Police was despatched to that point. They arrived none too soon to prevent the mischief intended; the attempt was made, but the military soon reinforced the Police, and the attack resulted in breaking a few panes of glass, the waste of a few rounds of ammunition, a few broken heads, and the arrest of another ringleader. This was the last effort made by that mob, so powerful in numbers, so determined in its action, so fearful in its intentions.

Among the many who were on that night, and subsequently, arrested for participating in the riot, were five ringleaders, who were charged with the murder of a citizen at the Cooper Street Armory, on the well-established principle of law, that where persons acting in concert commit a crime, each is responsible for the act committed by either of the others. These five were held for trial without bail; their names are a matter of record in the courts, and I have no desire to harrow up the feelings of their friends by repeating them here.

Taking into account the great number of persons engaged in this riot, the fury and determination that seemed at all points to pervade their ranks, the amount of property destroyed was comparatively small, but the sacrifice of life was much more fearful.

Of those who suffered in defending life and property, and in the preservation of the peace, were two men in the service of the General Government, seven in the service of the city, two or three of the military; and a number of unoffending citizens were severely beaten and otherwise seriously injured, and one quiet, worthy old man was shot dead. But the destruction of life among the Rioters will ever remain shrouded in mystery; the public journals subsequently made mention of eight that were killed, but it is believed that many of the dead were hurried away by their friends, whose untimely end was not made known to the public; and it is said by those who had good opportunities to form an estimate, that many more than is generally supposed fell victims to their own imprudence and folly on that fearful night.

One instance, which may serve to show the spirit of the mob, even before the military had shown them any resistance at Cooper Street, is worthy of note.

A gentleman who is universally known in Ward One, and who, perhaps, possesses as much influence with a majority of the inhabitants there as any other one man, was lying on a sick-bed at the time the riot commenced in Cooper Street. His anxiety was so great that he called his carriage and hurried there. On arriving at the Armory he was set upon, his carriage upset, himself thrown out, and with some difficulty he made his escape around the nearest corner.

Had the authorities known the precise time and place the attack was to be made, they might, perhaps, have been better prepared to prevent so great a sacrifice of life; but this it was impossible to know. Rumors were rife in the afternoon that demonstrations were to be made at the Provost Marshal's head-quarters at East and at South Boston, and at various other places. It seemed necessary to be prepared to meet the emergency at all points. The Mayor was early at the scene of disorder, but the disturbance was so great that he could not for one moment be heard, and was obliged to give way to save himself from harm. The conquest of a mob is ever without limit; the destruction of life and property, fire, pillage, and carnage, are its legitimate work. The Conscription Riot in the city of New York is an example. Nothing but force, and that of the most powerful character, can arrest and stay its progress. Too much credit cannot be awarded to the Mayor of our city, who so promptly prepared to meet the crisis, and to the Chief of Police and others who planned, and the men who executed their important trusts on that eventful night. Had either delayed, or faltered in their duties, who can count the cost, — who can foretell the consequences? They are, indeed, too fearful for contemplation.

A confidence in the loyalty and law-abiding character of the Boston people might have justified an opinion that the unprecedented preparation made the afternoon preceding the riot was unnecessary and uncalled for; but the events of the evening but too well justified the fears entertained by the most timid.

And if there is anything wanting to show the estimation entertained by the citizens of Boston towards the worthy Chief Magistrate who so nobly stepped forth to protect their lives and property, and to preserve the good name of our city in that trying hour, I would point to the succeeding municipal Election, in which those very acts of his on that occasion were made an issue, and where on that issue the people rebuked his opponents by giving him a majority of their suffrages, too overwhelming to be misunderstood.

Whether the Conscription Riot in Boston was the result of a regular and extensive organization, reaching far beyond the limits of our own city or State, for the purpose of aiding the Rebellion, or whether it was only composed of a combination of men limited within the bounds of Boston and the suburban towns, or whether it was only a spontaneous outbreak, which is at any time liable to happen in all thickly populated places, is a question not well understood.

Each position has its advocates, and neither, perhaps, are without reasons to sustain their theory. Without attempting to offer my own views on the subject, it may not be irrelevant to inquire, Why was it that fire, rapine, and murder, were on that day laying desolate the hearths and homes of peaceable and unoffending citizens in the city of New York? Who were the fiends in human form whose hands were then reeking in the blood of innocent women and children, while the hitherto strong arm of the law was powerless to save or protect?

And who is responsible for these deeds of wholesale carnage and murder? Have not the same poisonous seeds been strewn broadcast throughout the length and breadth of our land, and by the self-same hand? and what would have been the result in our own beloved city, had not those turbulent spirits been crushed at a blow? The subject is too painful for contemplation.

For several days succeeding the Riot, great fears were entertained by many of the citizens that a concentrated demonstration would be made at some point by the Rioters, and preparations were kept up not only in Boston, but also in many of the adjoining towns to meet the emergency, should one arise; but no further outbreaks occurred, and for some months Boston was never more quiet and orderly.

THE DRAFT.

EARLY in the summer of 1863, much interest and no little excitement was manifest throughout the Loyal States, in consequence of the Conscription, or Military Draft, which our Government found it necessary to resort to in order to fill up the thinned ranks of our army.

But even in good old Massachusetts, there were those who so far forgot their duty as men, and their loyalty as citizens, as to openly denounce the act which was forced upon the Government, as unjust, unconstitutional, and uncalled for; thus lending their aid and influence in opposition to the measure, and the means of sustaining our cause, and putting down the Rebellion.

This course, so persistently pursued by some of our people, naturally produced much discussion and no little ill-feeling among those whose interests certainly were, and whose principles ought to be the same; and it is a matter of no surprise that he who was so hardy as to boldly denounce the Draft, should be looked upon with suspicion and distrust by all loyal men.

"Hang the Draft," *said I*, as I one day emerged from my house, with swollen eyes, flushed face, and an empty stomach.

"There is secession for you in good earnest," said a large, portly gentleman, who was passing my door at the moment, and who stopped and gazed me square in the face just as I had relieved myself of the odious sentiment.

He was a man apparently fifty years of age (so old as not to be mistaken for under forty-five), and the contempt got up in his countenance, for my especial benefit, I must confess took me a little aback.

"I have heard," said he, "that we had secessionists in our midst, but little did I think to meet with so flagrant a specimen of disloyalty in open day. Do you know," said he, "that this very Draft of which you speak so disgracefully, is what has become eminently necessary to save our beloved country from desolation and ruin? Do you know, sir, that this measure has become the last resort of the good and true men who hold the destinies of our Government, to raise troops to put down this cursed Rebellion? Do you know, sir, that *I* (and here he straightened himself up to his full height) would sacrifice *my* life, *my* fortune, and *my* sacred honor, in this the cause of my country, and that he who is not with us is against us, and that you, sir, and all like you, who are not only traitors at heart, but stand here and boldly proclaim your disloyalty, should ere now have been inmates of the prison at Fort Warren, with an Ex-Mayor Brown and a Marshal Kane? Indeed, sir, I can but hope that this very Draft may bring forth your own name as a conscript in the cause of which you speak so contemptuously."

"Stop, stop, stop, for heaven's sake, my good friend!" said I, imploringly. "Don't, for pity sake, annihilate me, and send me to endless perdition, without judge, jury, or benefit of clergy; and don't, don't for mercy's sake, sacrifice your own valuable life; for *you, as well as I, are too old to be drafted.* Sacrifice your property, sir, if you please, but be careful of your *honor*, sir, for that is an article so rare and valuable, that its possessor ought not to relinquish it without an equivalent. But, sir, as you seem to take a deep interest in my case, I presume you will do me the justice to listen a moment to my side of the question, and if you don't eventually come to my way of thinking, I will be your willing disciple ever after."

"Convert me to disloyalty, sir!" said he, with disdain. "No, sir, never!"

"Hold, hold" said I; "not too fast; wait a moment, and hear me; don't condemn me without an audience. Perhaps, sir, I am not so disloyal as you imagine. People who think alike, sometimes quarrel by misunderstanding terms. Now, sir, please for one moment listen to my case. You see, sir, I live here in this house, and generally succeed in living quite comfortable. I have a nice little family of a good-natured wife, a fine fat baby, and an excellent cook, and we usually find something wholesome to eat. This day, sir, I came home to dine rather late, with a keen appetite and in fond anticipation of masticating a portion of a rib of roast beef. Well, sir, on arriving home, imagine my disappointment and chagrin at finding babe in convulsions, wife in tears, — cook skedaddled, house full of smoke, and no dinner; and all in consequence of the inefficiency of a new thirty-dollar stove I had set up in the morning, the flue of which persistently *refused to draw*. And now, sir, if any moral man, or devoted Christian, can conscientiously console himself under such circumstances without emphatically denouncing *that draft*, he is a more loyal man than I am."

The portly gentleman turned on his heel, and walked hurriedly down the street.

THOMAS SEMMES.

Under the administration of City Marshal Tukey, who was truly one of the smartest executive officers I ever knew, the Police were not usually overstocked with information in relation to his intended movements. Shrewd and sly in his nature, his plans were deep laid and secret. If he gloried in any one thing, it was in getting up a surprise, which usually proved a surprise, *in fact*, not only to some unlucky offender, but to the public also; and to his tact in planning, and not less to the secrecy with which he managed his plans, may be attributed most of his success.

When Marshal Tukey gave an order, it was short, tart, and to the point; every man knew what it meant, and no questions were asked. If any officer did not obey, it was but a word and a blow, and the blow usually *took off the delinquent's head*.

If an officer obeyed orders, be they ever so reckless or at fault, no matter; the Marshal would back him up to his utmost.

In the year 1851, the day Police under the Marshal numbered about forty men; we reported to him at his office at eight o'clock A. M. and two o'clock P. M.; from thence we separated to cover our respective beats throughout the city.

When we assembled at the Office, little Johnny Crocker, the clerk, called over our names, and read to us any orders or notices there might be. We did not usually see the Marshal, who was in an adjoining office, unless we had a question to ask, or he a special order to give.

When he had something to say to us, you could see his office-door open slowly just before Crocker had finished the call, and then that peculiar Roman nose and keen black eye of the Marshal's would make its appearance. Then came the order, short and quick, and he was gone, — *and so were we too, very shortly.* There are yet a few who will recollect this picture, but very few of that forty are Policemen now.

One morning in the month of March this year, the Marshal made his appearance at the door, and in a low voice gave the following order: "*Officers north of City Hall, will pass the north end of the Court House every hour while on duty; officers south, will pass through School Street same; no questions asked or answered;*" — and the Police dispersed. The nearest part of my beat was a mile from the Court House, and the twelve hours which we were on duty made me twenty-four miles travel. The reader can judge how much time I spent on the beat, for if I had been within reach of a "crock of gold," I should have left it to conform to the order. Day after day I travelled the ground over till I was actually ashamed to be seen, and I went every different route that was open till I felt that I had worn them all out. I often met and passed my brother officers, who were on the same mysterious errand, and I could read in their eye what seemed to say, what the d—l does all this mean; but we all remembered the order, "no questions asked or answered," so we passed each other in silence.

Some two weeks passed away without any countermand, and we began to think this was to be regular duty, when one morning (it was the third day of April), I came by the north end of the Court House, as usual, where I was met by a smart, good-natured little fellow, who belonged to the Office, and who the Marshal familiarly called Esquire. He told me to go quietly to the Office, at which place the whole force congregated within the hour, and where the long pent-up secret was soon disclosed.

Thomas Semmes, a colored man, was in custody at the Court House, and was to be tried on charge of being a fugitive slave, belonging to a Mr. Potter, in Savannah, Georgia.

This was a new order of things to us, and although the whole military force was at the command of the Government, it was deemed expedient to substitute the Police for guarding the prisoner and preserving the peace.

Semmes had been arrested by two officers of our department the night previous in Cooper Street, and had made rather careless use of a very ugly looking knife which he carried, and he gave one of the officers rather an ugly looking mark in the hip; but he was in safe quarters now. Semmes was about twenty-two years old, medium size, and black as ebony. His master had taught him the brickmaker's trade, and had (it was said) made provisions for him to purchase his freedom, which his brother had already done, and which he could do in about two years; but, like some men of different color, Tom was reckless, and took to gaming and strong drink, and besides, he had an idea that he had as good a right to himself as anybody, and so ran away, came to Boston, and took up quarters in Richmond Street.

Here Tom took up his old trade of gambling and drinking, got into a quarrel with another darkie about a white woman, who gave information to his master, and poor Tom got arrested. While in charge of the officers during trial, which lasted nine days, he proved himself worthy the reputation he had gained in Richmond Street, for he could smoke and drink his keepers blind drunk (of course, I do not mean to say he did that); but it was hinted that Tom had plenty of small bits of change, which he obtained by some process with cards, and one day I saw him take three dollars on a bet that he could take a man's vest off from under the coat and leave the coat on. However, we green hands had little chance to lose our money with him, as we were posted outside. I, for one, stood on a flat rock at the north end of the Court House twelve hours a day, and on the same substance inside six hours a night, each twenty-four hours, and slept on the soft side of a pine board the other six, for nine days. I wished the black rascal had stayed at home, or kept *dark* in Richmond Street; and I have since sometimes wished that some fellows who have obtained Police appointments on account of ill health or *laziness*, had the chance I then enjoyed.

Well, after it became pretty certain that Semmes was to be sent back, the Police began to *drill* for the expected occasion. As good luck would have it, we had one man in the Department who "understood military." He was a tall, athletic fellow, familiarly known as "Captain Sam," and when standing at the head of his *Battalion of Police braves*, with his hat a little on one side, a big quid in his jaws, "eyes right;" thunder, was n't he the beau ideal of bravery. Then to make the thing more imposing, each officer was furnished with a mariner's cutlass, and after we had taken a march through Pemberton Square, and a dog trot three times around the Court House, our discipline was considered perfect, and we were ready for the fray.

At length all necessary arrangements were complete, and on the twelfth day of April, about four o'clock in the morning, Semmes, in the centre of a hollow square of armed Police, hailed by shouts from numerous boys, and groans from various other sources, was marched unmolested down State Street to the foot of Long Wharf, where he embarked on board of the Schooner Acron, Captain Coombs, for his native home in Savannah.

The Police, like true citizen soldiers, surrendered up the sword — for the *rattan*, and quietly returned to duty on their beats, wondering, in the innocence of their hearts, *how one man could own another*.

A KID GAME.

Those who made a practice of visiting our criminal courts for several years previous to the year 1857, will well recollect a slender-formed, thin-faced, gray-haired man who was in almost daily attendance about the prisoners' dock, apparently quite busy in endeavoring to aid and assist some poor unfortunate man, or woman whose misfortunes or mistakes had led them into the meshes of the law.

Indeed, so common were this gentleman's visits in the courts, that he came to be considered almost one of the fixtures; and as the *higher law* had set the example of providing a scapegoat for a certain class of offenders, our courts were sometimes thought inclined to imitate that *precedent* by admitting criminals to bail, occasionally taking this gentleman as surety for their reappearance. It was sometimes called straw bail.

This course was pursued by our friend, till at length he became universally known as a philanthropist, and generous individuals frequently furnished him with means wherewith to aid the erring and unfortunate, and also placed at his disposal a fine horse and chaise for his accommodation on numerous errands about the city and vicinity. Who that does not remember to have seen his sleek bay horse and silver-mounted chaise and harness, standing by the curbstone in front of the dwelling of some unfortunate brother or sister, while he was inside on some errand of business or mercy?

Some evil-disposed persons might have said that his visits were sometimes prolonged to an unnecessary length, and others that he bailed out the victims of dissipation and licentiousness, for a consideration; but what man ever lived whose good acts and kind motives were not misconstrued or misrepresented? However, it was all the same to him, and, happen what would, he still pursued the even tenor of his way.

Our friend must have seen much of the *shady side* of life, and he was a pretty close observer of human nature. He also had a little brass in his composition, and was one of the coolest men under adverse circumstances in court or out of it, that I ever saw.

I recollect a circumstance that seemed to me a test of this characteristic of the man.

I was one day called, in my official capacity, to go into a house not particularly noted for respectability, where I found my friend the worthy philanthropist, most patiently submitting to the most interminable kissing by one of the frail sisters, that my eyes ever beheld; and that, too, with the fortitude of a martyr. I remained silent till the scene was ended, and then ventured to inquire of him if he was aware how disgracefully he had been insulted. He looked up very calmly, it being the first he was aware of my presence, and meekly replied, " Certainly I am; but it did not hurt me." And, upon my soul, I could not see that it did. It was his way; and although he might sometimes have been imprudent in view of jealous eyes, yet I really think he did some good, and I never knew of his doing any hurt. He has gone to his long home some years since, and I really wish there were no worse men than he.

When he was alive, he used to tell me some queer stories of what he had seen and heard, and the following is one which I shall denominate a " kid game," for the reason that a certain class of *professional* gentlemen call a babe *a kid*. The transaction, so far as he was concerned, took place but a short time before his death.

It so happened that a man and wife who were residing in Boston, and who at the time were in comfortable circumstances, were childless. This, to them, was a matter of much regret, especially on the part of the husband; and in course of time his dissatisfaction became so great, that the spouse was constrained to put her woman's wits to work to remedy the evil; and in her extremity she decided to call in the aid of our philanthropist, whose ingenuity and shrewdness was a match for almost any emergency.

Accordingly plans were concocted, and in the course of a few months preparations were made in the aforesaid family for a *coming event*. At length the plan was fully matured, and one day when the husband chanced to be absent, the lady was taken *conveniently* ill; a physician (in the secret) was sent for, but before he arrived a covered carriage drove up to the door of the sick lady, and a person closely enveloped in a cloak alighted and entered the house, but immediately returned, reëntered the carriage, and hurried away. The physician soon came, apparently attended to his professional duties, and all things progressed favorably.

When the husband came home at night, he found himself not only a husband, but the father (as he believed) of a most beautiful little cherub, "*the very picture of its papa,*" as all the attendants said.

Of course the event was not altogether unexpected, and the father was one of the happiest of men; and if to lend a hand in making a fellow-mortal most innocently happy is worthy of praise, no doubt in this case our philanthropist is entitled to his full share. Nor was this all; a certain unmarried, unfortunate young lady of highly respectable connections, and heretofore unblemished character, was relieved of a serious responsibility not conveniently accounted or provided for, and our friend had added new laurels to his already deeply bedecked brow.

The only difficulty that seemed to arise in the whole transaction, was the want of the *fount of life* for the little stranger; but as that deficiency was nothing uncommon, and was readily provided for by artificial means, no serious difficulty ensued.

This was the happy terminus in the matter, so far as our friend was concerned; he did not live to witness the sequel, and little did he then know of the true character of the party he had so ingeniously befriended.

The lady whom he had so successfully aided might have had quite a reasonable excuse for the *little* deception practised upon her liege lord; but if so, this transgression only paved the way for a higher and a bolder stroke.

It seems that the would-be mother, whose moral principles proved not to be of the highest order, when the child, which was a boy, was but a few weeks old, concocted a plan for a further family benefit. Accordingly a secret message was transmitted to a certain *professional* gentleman in a neighboring town, requesting an interview without delay. That gentleman, as it proved, being rather an intimate acquaintance, immediately obeyed the summons; but the result of the interview is not on the records; but rumor had it that a plea of poverty, and an additional responsibility to provide for, together with a threat of exposure, brought out a handsome accommodation of about fifteen hundred dollars, which made matters satisfactory.

As time rolled on, the babe became a sprightly child; but the wife, who had taken so exclusive a part in the increase of the family, eventually took to her cups, to which the husband also was somewhat addicted, which did not add to the prosperity or the peace of the family.

One day as she was attempting to correct the child, who was now large enough to wear pantalets, the husband interfered; in the *mêlée* the wife became highly exasperated, and in her passion she boldly declared to the husband that in this child, the idol of his heart, not one drop of blood circulating in its veins ever belonged to him. Murder will out, although the whole truth was not out yet. The husband was thunderstruck; yet little did he then think, that the wife was no nearer akin than himself.

As may be readily supposed, from this day henceforth, the prospects of the family did not improve, the wife persistingly declaring to the husband that the professional gentleman was the real father of the boy.

The subsequent condition of the family, and the ill-usage of the child, coming to the knowledge of a person who knew the real mother, was the cause of an afterpiece in the drama.

It appears that the mother of the child, who, as has before been stated, was of highly respectable family, and without a blemish of character herself except this unfortunate affair, had emigrated to the far West, and there became acquainted with and married a wealthy young farmer, after having informed him of the true state of the case in relation to this child, as far as she knew; and the marriage, so far as is known, was a happy one.

But a message from a lady of intimate acquaintance in Boston, setting forth the condition of the child, and that there was a probability that it must be sent to the almshouse, set the mother's heart on fire: and, as she was otherwise childless, with the consent of her husband she was soon on her way to Boston.

On arriving in the city, with the aid of her friend, the mother sought out the parents by adoption; but on learning her errand, they thought they saw another opening to make money, and laid their plans accordingly. Although they had threatened the friend of the mother to turn the child over to the overseer of the poor, if the real mother did not come and take him away, now they could not think of parting with the little fellow without the payment of a large sum. The mother had not come prepared for this, but she was willing to part with anything, yes, everything she had. An agreement was finally made that the child should be given up to the mother, and she in return was to pay all the money she could raise, together with all of her jewelry, a gold watch, and some other articles of wearing apparel, everything that she could possibly spare. She was to be at the house where the child was, at an early hour in the evening, the woman pretending that her husband was not at home, and that the bargain must not be known to him till after it was completed and the exchange made.

At the time appointed the mother repaired to the house, with all the valuables she could here command, to give in exchange for her child. The woman received the consideration, and stooped to kiss her little *protégé* as he was about to depart, when she gave a loud shriek. The husband immediately rushed into the room, seized both the child and the property, and thrust the frightened mother into the street.

In her distress she came to the police. An investigation led to the arrest and detention of the guilty parties, and a subsequent examination before a legal tribunal. After a careful examination, the mother was awarded the custody of her child, and with apparently a light heart departed with him for her home in the West.

NEW CITY HALL.

NEW CITY HALL. — A DREAM.

For the last half century the government of the *town* and *city* of Boston have made an occasional effort to build a City Hall, for the want of which officials have been accommodated first at Faneuil Hall, next at the old *Town House*, and then at the Old Court House, and various hired offices in the neighborhood of Court Square.

At length, in the summer of 1862, the Hon. Joseph M. Wightman being Mayor, with his accustomed energy took the matter in hand, and the subject-matter of building a new Hall was fully investigated. It was said a New Hall, of sufficient magnitude to accommodate all the city officials, could be built for one hundred and sixty thousand dollars, the interest of which would amount to a less sum than that now paid for outside office hire, and a vote passed both branches of the City Government *to build*. Under the direction of an appropriate committee, plans and specifications were drawn, contracts entered into, and on the morning of the twenty-ninth of September, ground was broken directly under the office window of the writer.

The New Hall is rectangular in form, one hundred and thirty-eight feet long on the south and north façades, and ninety feet wide on the east and west façades respectively, having a central projection on the south fifty-one and one half feet in length, and fourteen and one half feet from the wings on a line of the façades; this brings the front up to within seven feet of the pedestal on which stands the life-size bronze figure of the venerated Franklin.

The Hall is four stories high on School Street, and five on Court Square, with a French roof, or Mansard story, the height of the stories being from eleven to fourteen and one half feet high, the ceiling to the common council chamber carried up in the centre to the height of twenty-three and one fourth feet. An attic story of square form covers the centre projection, forty-three feet square and fourteen and one half feet high, and on this attic rises a dome thirty-eight feet from the top of the mosaic cornice of the building.

The exterior walls are of granite, and lined up with brick work, and the dome iron work throughout. (Such was the plan of the building, and it was said it would be completed during the year 1863; but men are mortal, and 'tis human to err.)

At one time a religious society in a country village desired to build a new meeting-house, the old one having become dilapidated. After mature deliberation, the society, at a meeting called for the purpose, adopted the following resolutions : —

"*First. Resolved*, That we will build a new house.

"*Second. Resolved*, That we will build the new house on the site of the old one.

"*Third. Resolved*, That we will use the material of the old house in building the new one.

"*Fourth. Resolved*, That we will occupy the old house till the new one is completed."

The City Hall Committee virtually followed the rules above in the first and second resolutions, and the third also, as far as the material would go. But they furnished most excellent quarters for the removed City Officials at Mechanics Hall, with few exceptions, and these might as well have remained under the Fourth Resolve of the meeting-house committee.

I have said that the workmen broke ground September 29. The genteel iron fence in front of the Old Hall, next School Street, and the flowers and shrubbery it inclosed, disappeared in a few hours, and the whole beautiful little square and garden plat were soon one heap of rocks, broken bricks, mud, and dirt.

During the progress of the excavation, many things to remind one of other days were brought to light; and as the laborers continued their work, old wells, water cisterns, cellar walls, chimney foundations, and other relics of antiquity came in view.

Just in front of the south entrance of the east wing of the Old Hall appeared a deep well, which was safely covered over, for the protection of the tens of thousands who yearly passed over it. When or by whom it was built, no one seems to know. At the southeast corner, near Niles' Block, was an old cistern some fourteen feet deep, apparently built of brick, the mason work of which crumbled to dust on being exposed to air. On the opposite corner was another, not so deep or old as the first. Here was the foundation of an old engine house, and there of what was once Barristers' Block. On the western side, in an embankment, was seen the projecting edges of an innumerable number of stones; they were the outside walls of the dwellings of the dead, who lived two hundred years ago.

A large sidewalk committee were present daily to offer their remarks and suggestions free of charge, and to see that all things were properly done. One day I noticed a venerable-looking old gentleman standing near my window, with his ardent gaze fixed intently on a point further towards School Street.

"There," said he, with an energy much beyond his years, "on that spot stood *my* old schoolhouse, and there I went to school, seventy-two years ago; and just over there, it is said, stood *the first Boston schoolhouse,* where Philemon Pormort taught the young Boston idea how to shoot, two hundred and twenty-eight years ago."

Up to Thanksgiving Day, which was on the 27th of November, the excavations were continued as far as practicable, and the foundation, preparatory to placing the corner-stone, which was to be laid on Forefathers' Day, had progressed without cessation or accident, and in a manner that seemed intended to bid defiance to the hand of Time.

On the afternoon of Thanksgiving Day, business was dull, and being alone in the office, I seated myself in a chair, and placing my feet on the window-sill, where I could have a good view of the spot which has so long been of so much interest to every Bostonian, I prepared myself to enjoy a little meditation.

"Mr. Officer," said a voice at my elbow.

Supposing I was alone, I turned suddenly in the direction from whence the voice came, and to my great astonishment beheld at my side the figure of a most venerable personage, with his deep, dark, sunken eyes fixed intently on me. He was of medium stature, and his snow-white beard fell gracefully on his breast. His dress was neat, but very ancient, such as I had never seen. His countenance was grave, and unearthly in expression, and although I sat paralyzed beneath his look, yet the sensation was not painful.

"Mr. Officer," said he, with a familiarity that puzzled me, "why sittest thou here, gazing out upon the ruins before thee, as though it were sacrilege to remove these beautiful handiworks of olden time? Knowest thou not that *change* is engraven on all the works of earth? Knowest thou not that these beautiful structures, about being removed, were built upon the ruins of other structures, perhaps as beautiful, ornamental, and useful as themselves, and that they in turn were reared upon the ruins of still others of an earlier date, each in turn being the pride and glory of their age? Seest thou not these new foundations springing up on these ruins of ruins, to make room for which even the venerated form of him who tamed the storm and made the lightning of heaven subservient to his will is set aside, and wise men of the age may yet wrangle where his pedestal shall rest? Hath it not been so in all ages? And is it not so in the moral, religious, and political, as well as the material world?

"Am I not the spirit of Philemon Pormort, the

first Boston schoolmaster, who dwelt and taught on this consecrated ground more than two hundred years ago, and have I not long witnessed the doings of men? Hast thou not read how that those who entrusted me with the instruction of their children *one day*, banished me from my home *the next*, because I claimed justice for my friend the good Mr. Wheelwright, who could not embrace all the superstitions of his townsmen?

"Hast thou not read how that the people of Boston, in my day, tied men and women to the cart-tail, and whipped them through the town on account of their belief? And how they hanged their fellow-men on the limbs of trees on Boston Common, and when dead cast their naked bodies into the *Frog Pond*, to become food for dogs and vultures, because they were Quakers? Such were the men who built themselves on the ruined hopes and fortunes of Philemon Pormort."

Seeing I was about to attempt a reply, he slowly raised his withered finger, and continued: —

"Mr. Officer, art not thou in thy profession a servant of servants, and is not thy head ever subject to the whim or caprice of a master? Then let energy with prudence guide thee in duty, — but let thy tongue be silent."

At this moment most unearthly sounds greeted my ear, and darkness seemed inclosing the land; cannon were booming, — drums beating, — bells tolling, — strange lights were flickering hither and thither, and the elements even seemed to join in one general commotion; but Philemon Pormort stood unmoved. At length in a calm, prophetic voice, he said: —

"Mr. Officer, hearest thou not this din of approaching contention? Knowest thou not that the hand of man is against his brother? *Sir*, a crisis is approaching, and fearful events are in the future, — but the home of Philemon Pormort is with the just;" and he vanished from my sight.

In my eagerness to catch his last words, I sprang from my chair but to realize that I had been dreaming.

LITTLE RAGGED NELL.

LITTLE RAGGED NELL.

When on duty at the North End, I knew a bright-eyed, barefooted, ragged little orphan girl, who lived with some people in an alley-way near the Old Cockerel Church, whom we used to call Little Ragged Nell. Her pitiable story is told in the following lines; would to Heaven it was a solitary case.

  Adown the narrow alley-way,
   Where sun doth never shine;
  Where poverty is doomed to dwell,
   And babes grow up in crime;
  Where drunken mothers, wantons, thieves,
   These dens of darkness swell;
  And where, in sorrow and in tears,
   Lives little ragged Nell.

  No father, mother, kin, or friend;
   Not one that Nellie knows,
  Will speak a word, or lend a hand,
   To stay the outcast's blows.
  The homeless children, weak and lone,
   To shame and crime they sell;
  When buds the flower, the buyers come
   For little ragged Nell.

Fair jewels, soon, and gaudy silk,
 Will deck fair Nellie's form;
In gilded halls and mazy dance,
 She mingles with the throng.
Where vice, enshrined in mellow light,
 Tempting the young and fair,
Bewitching cheat — heartless deceit,
 Wooing but to ensnare.

Near by this narrow alley-way,
 Where little Nell was born,
A church-spire rears in proud display;
 And on each Sabbath morn,
The rich meet here to worship God,
 Who " doeth all things well;"
But no one feels, or cares, to pray
 For little ragged Nell.

Oh, would that Christians could but learn
 To labor, well as pray,
That kindness teaches to return
 Back from the sinful way.
Oh, if our preachers all would teach
 The people how to live;
And to the vile and suffering preach,
 And words of comfort give,

Then might the earth see less of strife;
 And dens, where sorrow dwells,
Be filled with joy, and hope, and life,
 And happy little Nells.

MY FATHER'S LIKENESS.

Oh, that those lips had language;
　　Then would my longing ear
The soothing tones of purest love
　　And fond affection hear.
Then would a whispered blessing
　　Rest on my soul like dew;
And tender words of sympathy
　　Breathe low, and soft, and true.

In vain; those lips are silent:
　　But in those thoughtful eyes,
So meekly on me beaming,
　　What hidden treasure lies.
Father, these looks are bringing
　　Visions of days long past;
And sad, yet pleasing memories
　　About my soul are cast.

Thoughts of my own beloved home,
　　Of friends that dwelt with thee,
Those dear familiar faces,
　　With smiles to welcome me;

Though years of care and sorrow,
　　Have vanished in the past, —
Yet still, methinks I see them now,
　　As when I saw them last.

Dear father, thou art now at rest;
　　Thy spirit wanders free;
Thy memory be a living light,
　　A guiding star to me.

THAT LITTLE CURL.

I KISSED that lovely brow in death,
   Cold as the winter's clay,
Ere the murmur of the parting breath
   Passed from the lips away;
And that bright, golden curl I shred
From the bright tresses of the dead.

That little curl! my hand had brushed
   Its ruffled gloss full oft,
As the sweet prattler's cries I hushed,
   With carol low and soft;
And, as he sank to silent rest,
That curl lay gleaming on my breast.

Dear child, it was no lightsome thing
   To watch thy spirit's flight,
To mark its struggling ushering
   To heaven's own world of light.
We bowed our weary heads to pray,
And angels bore our babe away.

I could not leave that lock to mould
   Within the lonely tomb;
That quenchless spark of living gold,
   To light so drear a gloom;
And now with mournful hearts we kiss
That Little Curl, that once was his.

MY MOTHER'S GRAVE.

I AM standing by thy grave, mother,
   And an autumn's sun has set,
But its purple rays, its golden light,
   Is lingering o'er me yet.
No murmur stirreth in the trees,
   No whisper on the hill;
The very air grows like my heart,
   So heavy, and so chill.

I am standing by thy grave, mother,
   But memory wanders free;
Fond recollections! happy hours,
   My childhood knew with thee.
But she who watched my youthful steps,
   Who shared each smile, each tear,
Lies cold and lifeless in the tomb,
   Mother, so loved, so dear!

I am standing by thy grave, mother,
   'Neath the cold, unfeeling sod,
And can I wish to call thee back?
   Thy dwelling is with God;
And when is past this wearied life,
   This pilgrimage of mine,
May I sleep then by thy side, mother,
   And my spirit blend with thine!

www.ingramcontent.com/pod-product-compliance
Lightning Source LLC
Chambersburg PA
CBHW051737300426
44115CB00007B/601